D0684330

Floating *through* France

Life between Locks on the Canal du Midi

Edited by Barbara J. Euser

TRAVELERS' TALES
PALO ALTO

Travelers' Tales and *Travelers' Tales Guides* are trademarks of Traveler's Tales, Inc., 853 Alma Street, Palo Alto, California 94301.

For permission to print essays in this volume, grateful acknowledgment is made to the holders of copyright named on pages 197-204.

Grateful acknowledgment is made to SportsFan Magazine (www.sportsfanmagazine.com) for permission to reprint "A Sports Fan in Spite of Herself: Or How Le Tour de France Came to Me" by Joanna Biggar.

Front and back cover photographs and interior illustrations copyright by April Orcutt.
All the photographs were taken during the first writers' workshop, July 2-9, 2005.
Front cover: *A farmhouse lies near the Canal du Midi, near Castelnaudary.*
Back cover left: *Locks open on the Canal du Midi between Toulouse and Montgiscard.*
Back cover right: *The Canal du Midi meanders beneath three-hundred-year-old plane trees and through the countryside of Southern France.*

Cover and interior design by Melanie Haage using the fonts Centaur and Californian.

Distributed by: Publishers Group West, 1700 Fourth Street, Berkeley, California 94710.

CATALOGUING DATA
Floating through France: Life Between Locks on the Canal du Midi/
    edited by Barbara J. Euser

    ISBN-10: 1-932361-38-3
    ISBN-13: 978-1-932361-38-4

    1. France – Description and travel. 2. France – Social life and customs. 3. Canal du Midi – Description and travel. 4. Canal du Midi – Social life and customs. I. Title. II. Euser, Barbara J.

First Edition
Printed in the United States of America
10 9 8 7 6 5 4 3 2 1

To my mother
Jeannette Virginia Flautz Euser

Contents

Contents

ix

Preface

Floating through France: Life Between Locks on the Canal du Midi is a collection of essays written during the summer of 2005 on the Canal du Midi. As you will discover, I plied the waters of the Canal in two different boats: *Lurley*, which my husband and I own, and *Royal Destiny*, which I rented to accommodate more writers. My desire was to share the peace and serenity of the Canal du Midi with writers who might use that space to focus on their creative energies.

During the month of July, I spent one week on *Royal Destiny* with Linda Watanabe McFerrin, instructor, and five writers: Connie Burke, Cristie Marcus, April Orcutt, Mary Jean Pramik and Ann Kathleen Ure. An accomplished poet, travel writer, novelist and teacher, Linda was instrumental in inviting writers to join the first, largest group, and worked tirelessly to ensure quality instruction for all. Between daily workshops and individual consultations, she still managed to help handle the lines, set a fine table, and keep the group in great spirits.

My friend Joanna Biggar joined me on *Lurley* for two weeks of cruising. A fellow Francophile, veteran traveler, writer and teacher, together we pushed past Castelnaudary to Carcassonne to view Bastille Day fireworks on the ramparts there.

The last week in July, Larry Habegger, instructor, and writers Lynn Branecky, Ethel F. Mussen and Stacie Williams, joined me on *Lurley*. Larry is a writer, editor and publisher who teaches personal travel writing at workshops and conferences. On *Lurley*, he shared his insights on effective writing and energetically participated in moving *Lurley* through the locks.

The essays and poetry selected for this volume reflect the experiences and impressions of the writers as they discovered life between the locks on the Canal du Midi.

— Barbara J. Euser

Illustrations

Page 28, opposite sonnet "Toulouse"
A flower vendor sells daisies, dahlias, camellias, azaleas and petunias at the Saint Aubin Sunday market in Toulouse.

Page 62, opposite sonnet "Canal du Midi"
A yacht glides beneath the 300-year-old plane trees that line the canal.

Page 88, opposite sonnet "The Lock Keeper of Renneville"
The Royal Destiny enters the Ecluse de la Méditerranée — the Lock of the Mediterranean.

Page 112, opposite sonnet "La Recette du Cassoulet"
The region's famous cassoulet is served at a restaurant in Villefranche de Lauragais.

Page 122, opposite sonnet "Bellevue La Foret"
Sunflowers fill many fields along the canal between Montgiscard and Gardouch.

Page 152, opposite "Alone, But Not Alone"
Bicyclists, rollerbladers and hikers enjoy the path that runs beside the canal between Montgiscard and Gardouch.

Page 174, opposite sonnet "Le Relais de Riquet"
Shallots are among the many vegetables, fruits, herbs, and flowers for sale in the Saint Aubin Sunday market in Toulouse.

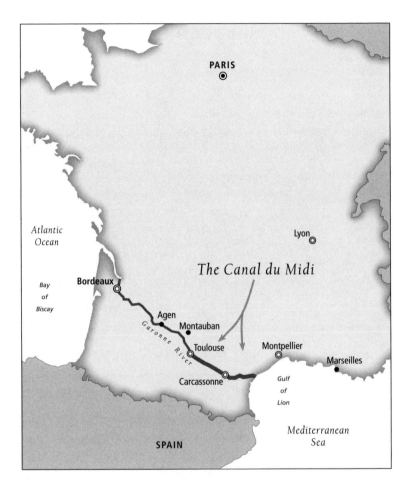

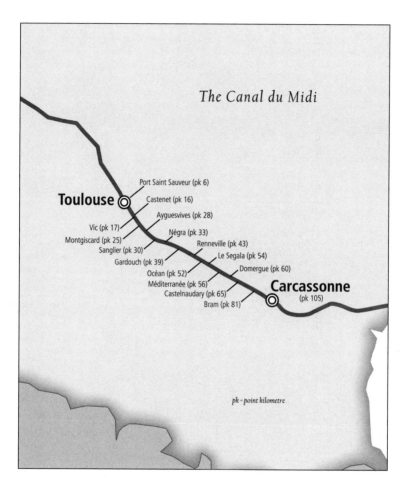

The Canal du Midi

Port Saint Sauveur (pk 6)

Toulouse

Castenet (pk 16)

Ayguesvives (pk 28)

Vic (pk 17)

Montgiscard (pk 25)

Négra (pk 33)

Sanglier (pk 30)

Renneville (pk 43)

Gardouch (pk 39)

Le Segala (pk 54)

Océan (pk 52)

Domergue (pk 60)

Méditerranée (pk 56)

Carcassonne
(pk 105)

Castelnaudary (pk 65)

Bram (pk 81)

pk = point kilometre

Lurley

BARBARA J. EUSER

I was scheduled to sail the Singlehanded TransPac, a solo race
from San Francisco to Hawaii, when I first saw *Lurley* and fell
in love with her.

Getting ready for the Singlehanded TransPac was a matter of
life and death. Sponsored by the Singlehanded Sailing Society,
monthly seminars for those planning to sail the 2004 race began in
December 2003. At the first seminar I was awed by sailors planning
to sail their second or third solo race. I was one of a handful of
neophytes, the only woman. I needed to absorb as much information as I could from every seminar. I needed every bit of help I
could get.

In the midst of these early preparations for the race, in early January 2004, I traveled to Europe on business. While in Paris, I surfed my favorite topic on the web – Canal Boats Europe. One site that came up was comprised of yachts for sale by British owners. Scrolling through, I found two boats that greatly appealed to me. One was in Britain, as were most all the boats on that site. The other was in France – Southern France, Le Segala on the Canal du Midi.

She was described as a gentleman's motor yacht, steel hull, graceful lines, place for seven to sleep. The photo looked like the boat I had been dreaming of for years. I e-mailed the yacht company asking for contact with the owner. The next day I received a reply, including a phone number. I called. The British owners were selling their beloved *Lurley* because Peter had grown too old to take care of her anymore. He and Caroline wanted to buy a house of their own in southern France and selling *Lurley* offered the way.

I needed to go see this boat. There are thousands of boats for sale at any given moment. But boats are not fungible. Each has her own characteristics and personality. I had looked at hundreds of boats on websites over the past seven years and had never fallen in love before.

From Paris it is a five-hour ride on the fast train to Toulouse. Then there is a short train ride to Castelnaudary. I had asked Caroline how I would recognize her and Peter. She said to look for a woman with bright red hair and a man with a full white beard. I saw them immediately.

Caroline drove us to Le Segala where *Lurley* was docked in front of their house. They shared the house with another couple, Caroline and Peter splitting their own time between the house and summers on the Canal du Midi on *Lurley*. They showed me through the boat and Peter gave me a thorough introduction to the two engines. Then we went inside the house for lunch. After lunch, Caroline drove me to Toulouse to catch the train back to Paris. I spent the entire ride back trying to figure out how to buy *Lurley*. I thought that if I could find another couple to join as partners in buying *Lurley*, it might be possible. When I got back to Paris, I e-mailed Caroline and Peter, told them how much I hoped I would be able to find a way to buy *Lurley*. It wasn't clear.

But I had other things on my mind. The Singlehanded TransPac was coming up at the end of June. Even though I had paid my entry fee, I couldn't start the race until I had completed my qualifying sail – a four-hundred-mile-long solo sail at least one hundred miles offshore. And before I could do that, I had a lot of preparation to do. I began by taking *Islander* out for short sails alone on San Francisco Bay. I would go out for a couple of hours. Just leaving the dock alone, motoring out to where I could raise the main sail and sailing the boat all by myself required new skills. I learned a lot, quickly. Then I had to venture out the Gate, that is, sail under the Golden Gate Bridge into the Pacific Ocean. I love to sail under that massive bridge and feel the heartbeat of the ocean, the ocean swell. Sailing under it alone was another matter.

One day, I sailed out to the Lightship, more accurately known as the San Francisco Buoy, about fourteen miles offshore. At Easter, I entered the Singlehanded Farallones Race, a race around a group of islands twenty-eight miles out. The Bay was shrouded in dense fog as I crossed the start line and sailed under the Gate. Halfway to the Lightship, the wind died. One by one, racers abandoned the race. Finally, I radioed the Race Committee, turned on my engine and motored home.

I needed to get closer to the Farallones. After all, if I couldn't get to the Farallones, how could I sail over two thousand miles to Hawaii? One week later, I had my chance. In clear weather, I made the sail.

Then I needed to spend one night at sea on my own. So I planned an overnight sail. I started in the afternoon and only went as far as the area south of the Farallones, between the southbound and westbound shipping lanes. During the night, the wind died. I floated uncomfortably, my sails hanging, rigging clanging. Every ten minutes I got up to check all around for boat traffic, then dropped back to sleep. By the time morning came, I was an exhausted wreck. But I had spent my first night alone at sea.

The final hurdle to entering the race was my qualifying sail. I couldn't wait until the last minute to do it. The weather could deteriorate. I might not make it on my first attempt. I wanted to minimize the pressure as much as I could. I prepared the boat, bought provisions — then waited for a window of good weather. Finally at the end of May, I had it: the five-day forecast was for moderate winds and moderate seas. The first night was horrible. Getting up every ten minutes was a rhythm I could not sustain — even for four nights. The next night I was past my required limit of one hundred miles offshore. I turned and sailed north. I got up every twenty minutes and felt marginally better the next morning. I spent four nights at sea. When

I returned to Richmond Yacht Club, completing my qualifying sail, I understood why it was a requirement. I had demonstrated to myself that I could sail all the way to Hawaii.

In the midst of my preparations for the Singlehanded TransPac, I was pursuing different alternatives for financing the purchase of *Lurley*. There were not many people I would feel comfortable sharing my boat with. Then a friend who is also a financial expert came up with a creative solution.

Excitedly, I e-mailed Caroline and Peter. I was worried *Lurley* might have already been sold. She had not. In a flurry of transatlantic e-mails and a wire transfer, the deed was done. *Lurley* belonged to my husband and me. I flew to Paris, took the train to Toulouse. This time I was not just checking on a boat, I was taking possession of *Lurley*.

Caroline and Peter had taken a last cruise from Le Segala to Toulouse and installed her at her new home in the Toulouse marina, Port Saint Sauveur. Caroline and Peter met me at the station and drove me to the marina. They had *Lurley* in sparkling condition. Midday in June, the port was hot. We boarded *Lurley* and, with Peter at the helm, motored up the canal to a shady spot. Caroline stepped onto the grassy bank and expertly drove in two stakes and we tied up. We ate lunch aboard on the calm canal in the shade of venerable plane trees and talked about *Lurley*. Then Peter asked me to take the helm. I drove us to the first lock, then handed the controls to Peter. He and Caroline showed me how it is done.

We dropped Caroline at the small wooden fishing pier before the lock. She walked to the lock keeper's, carrying a ball of blue cord with a large stainless steel hook on the end. Peter drove us through the narrow lock entrance and we pulled over to the left side where Caroline had dropped the hook for us, fishing for the two mooring lines with loops tied at their ends. I placed the loops on the hook and she pulled it up. No tossing of lines, no fuss. Like artists, they made a difficult maneuver look easy.

Caroline ran the stern line around one of the mushroom-shaped bollards on the quay and dropped the line down to me. Then she walked with the bow line to another bollard, ran it around the bollard and pulled the line taut.

The lock keeper opened the gate and water rushed into the lock, floating us up to the next level of the canal. When the water inside the lock was level with the water outside the lock, the lock keeper opened the lock gates, Caroline stabilized the boat while I pulled the lines in. Then with a small shove, she pushed the boat away from the side of the lock and stepped aboard. Peter maneuvered *Lurley* smoothly out of the lock into the canal.

Just above the lock, Peter pulled over. This time I jumped out and pounded in the stakes and tied *Lurley* to the bank. They spent another hour explaining *Lurley* and recounting their exploits in her over the years. After an interval they judged sufficient to keep the lock keeper from getting angry with us for wasting his time, I pulled up the stakes and Peter turned the boat around. It was my turn to take *Lurley* through a lock.

Very slowly and carefully, I lined *Lurley* up with the lock entrance. Slowly she moved into the lock. When we were alongside the quay, Caroline stepped onto the quay, ran the lines around the bollards and calmly stepped back aboard. She and Peter each took a line, while I stayed at the helm, tightly gripping the wheel.

At the bottom of the lock, I steered through the narrow opening into the seemingly broad canal. The longer I steered the boat, the less tightly I gripped the wheel. I had insisted on standing behind the wheel. After going under a couple of bridges, I relaxed enough to take my seat in the elevated captain's chair. I owned *Lurley* on paper, but it would take time and work and experience handling her to own her on the Canal.

When I got back to California, there were only two weeks to go until the race.

On June 26, the morning of the race, I printed out the weather map and forecast for San Francisco Bay to one hundred miles offshore. The word GALE featured prominently. Along the dock, racers joked, "Turn right at the A in GALE!" Dressed in full foul-weather gear, sails reefed, twenty-four sailors started. Within three days, three had dropped out due to problems with either health or equipment. For me, the first three days passed in a blur of sailing through heavy weather coupled with seasickness. At the first roll call, I discovered that, although I could hear the broadcast, my radio would not transmit. Using my handheld e-mail device, I communicated the difficulty to my husband Dean and the Race Committee. For the duration of the race, I e-mailed my position to my racing colleagues, but I did not speak with anyone.

By the fourth day, the weather improved. My stomach became accustomed to the motion of the waves. Days assumed a rhythm as I trimmed sails, adjusted the self-steering mechanism, charted my position, kept the log. I was free to enjoy the open expanse of the ocean.

I love sailing offshore. Out of sight of land, there are no pathways restricting movement. Surrounded completely by water, the choice is one's own. The race prescribed a destination, but each day offered a multitude of choices, dependent only on the direction of the wind.

In the middle of the ocean, my thoughts returned to *Lurley* and the Canal du Midi. Perhaps it is this contrast that gives *Lurley* most appeal. Compared to the open expanses of the ocean, the canal is at the opposite extreme. The canal is a narrow, man-made channel: no deviations allowed. A small boat in the wide ocean is essentially insecure; a boat in the canal is contained, enfolded within secure tree-lined banks. The ocean offers me the world. In *Islander*, I could sail anywhere. Ironically, that is also the appeal of the canals.

France boasts seven thousand kilometers of navigable waterways. Not all are as benign as the Canal du Midi. The Rhone, the main artery of France, is a forceful river, despite the gigantic locks that regulate its flow. The cities and countries of Europe are connected by waterways as well as by roads. I could take *Lurley* from Toulouse north to St. Petersburg or down the Danube to the Black Sea. Despite the contrast in watery milieu, *Islander* and *Lurley* are connected by the opportunities they afford for adventure and exploration.

Alone on *Islander*, it took me twenty days to reach Kauai. I was content in my solitude, but happy to reach the Islands and finish the race. Dean was there to meet me.

But that was only half the distance. Sailing to Hawaii is essentially a down-wind sail. Sailing back to San Francisco is harder and takes longer. I sailed back with a young woman named Mariah. Having just sailed to Hawaii by myself, I felt confident about my sailing abilities. But Mariah had a lot to teach me, and she did. The return sail took twenty-eight days. When we finally made it into *Islander's* slip at Richmond Yacht Club, I was ready for a rest. Spending time on *Lurley* on the Canal du Midi never sounded more appealing.

≻ ≻ ≻

In December, following a reading to celebrate publication of a new anthology, a group of writers retired to a nearby bar. The conversation turned to Europe, then France, then the South of France. I told about acquiring *Lurley*, berthed on the Canal du Midi.

"What a perfect place to write!" someone offered. I thought of the shady, tree-lined canal and violet-shuttered stucco houses, the fields of sunflowers. Looking around at the casually assembled writers, engaged in conversation, I felt a wave of affection.

"It would be fun to get a group of writers together," I said automatically. There were expressions of agreement, nodding of heads. "It could be workshop," someone offered. "We could publish a book," added a third. "It does sound like fun," I replied, and the conversation moved on.

The idea of a workshop took on a life of its own. How many people could *Lurley* hold? That would dictate how large the workshop could be. Who would the instructor be? Would there be one or several? If one were to publish an anthology, how many essays would be required? Who would the writers be? I had done some of these things before. In 2002, I had published an anthology of garden essays called *Bay Area Gardening*. The book included sixty-four short essays. A book of travel essays would contain longer essays, but the concept was the same. In 2002, I had been working as the director of a non-profit writers organization and organized writing seminars and hired writing instructors. The more I thought about it, the more feasible it seemed. I contacted a friend and fellow-writer with experience in publicity. She thought the idea sounded good – in fact, she would like to go on a seminar herself – and agreed to do it. But publicity for what exactly? The idea was still forming. A series of one-week workshops, with different instructors, sounded like a good way to organize the writing sessions. I contacted several friends who were writing instructors to test the idea. Each one I spoke to agreed to teach. Finding teachers was obviously not the challenge. Finding writers was. With a scant six months before the workshops would take place, we began to spread the word.

Writers, friends of mine, were all pressed for time. Pushed by deadlines and the constant press of the details of life, we all lead harried lives. On the Canal du Midi, I had discovered the antidote and I wanted to share it. We would slow down, enjoy the serenity of the canal, have time to reflect and write about whatever we encountered along our way. A select group of writers decided to take the voyage.

Land of the Troubadours

LINDA WATANABE MCFERRIN

⤳

Rose-colored Toulouse, often called the capital of old Provence, has a southern grandeur. Sensual and sensible, generous and austere, it rises from the banks of the River Garonne in the basin just north of the French Pyrenees. Once known as Tolosa, it was the Visigoth capital from AD 419 - 507 and its fortuitous setting both on Rome's ancient trade route, the Via Aquitaine, and, later, on the pilgrimage trail, engendered a popularity that guaranteed prosperity. In the twelfth and thirteenth centuries its rulers were among the most cultured and enlightened in the world. Urban, literate, tolerant and independent, the counts of Toulouse were wealthy and powerful – more powerful, in fact, than France's Capetian kings.

For me, Toulouse is the gateway to the legendary Languedoc, home of the troubadours whose poetry gave birth to modern romance and the novel. And though it was excluded from Languedoc-Rousillon when boundaries were redrawn in the 1960s, it is forever the historical heart of that region. In 1208, the Albigensian Crusade broke that heart in a bloodbath that put an end to the courts of the puissant southern aristocracy and ushered in the Inquisition. Called by Pope Innocent III ostensibly to root out the Cathar heresy (worldly and skeptical, the Cathars treated women with respect, believed in celibacy and pacifism and denied the miracle of Mass and the power of saints), the true purpose of the crusade was to subdue the far too independent and "free-thinking" south and to strip its landed intellectual elite of all their wealth. I remember reading about the troubadours, the Cathars, the Knights Templar and the brilliant courts of the southern nobles. I was incensed by the greed and duplicity that destroyed what I believed to be the very cradle of chivalry. Raymond-Roger Trenceval, patron of troubadours, the son of Raymond Trenceval and Adelaïde de Burlats, daughter of the count of Toulouse, was captured under a false flag of truce, imprisoned and murdered. The count of Toulouse met a similar fate. Properties were confiscated and gifted to the northern victors and to the Church as spoils. And though the light was extinguished, I like to think that the true song of the Langue d'Oc, a fiercely independent song that draws inspiration from the natural world and eschews hypocrisy with a passion, was not silenced. And later, in college, when I pored over the works of the Provençal poets, I saw how intensely a spirit can live on in a lyric line. But it took many years and an invitation to teach travel writing on the Canal du Midi to get me to Toulouse.

The Canal du Midi begins in Toulouse. Completed in 1681, it links the city of rose-colored brick to the Mediterranean Sea. It was Monsignor Bourlemont, the archbishop of Toulouse, who convinced his friend, Béziers native Pierre Paul Riquet, to propose a plan for what was then called the Canal Royal du Languedoc to Louis XIV's minister of building works. Construction of the canal began in 1667 and Riquet, who died in 1680, did not witness its completion. It's said that its olive-shaped locks were based on a Roman design. The first cargoes transported on the waterway were oil, wine, leather and Toulouse textiles. Lock keepers cottages were added in the eighteenth century. At its peak, in 1856, just before the railway took over, the Canal du Midi carried over one hundred million tons of freight. But rail transportation doomed it, and the last commercial freight boat motored the canal in 1979. In 1996 it was recognized as a UNESCO World Heritage Site.

I have always been crazy about canals. I first became acquainted with them at the age of seven when, returning to the United States from a childhood spent in England, I was delighted to sing about a mule by the name of Sal, a good ol' worker and a good ol' pal that worked for fifteen years on the Erie Canal. Later, other canals like the Panama and Suez would charge my studies in history and economics with a strange energy, and the canals of cities like Venice, Brugge and Amsterdam would color my travels.

My favorite canal experience was in Sweden, in Söderköping, a town of medieval origin situated south of Stockholm on the famed

Göta Canal, the fifty-two-lock engineering feat that joins the North and Baltic Seas. Count Baltazar Von Platen started the canal in 1800. Thirty-two years and two hundred million cubic feet of earth later, King Karl XIV Johan inaugurated it. I arrived in Söderköping on the Monday before midsummer. Midsummer is a joyous time in Sweden. I was staying at Söderköping Bruns, a historic two-hundred-year-old spa-turned-hotel. I loved the time I spent on the Göta Canal. Stig Eckblad, owner of Söderköping Bruns, took me to the park-like island of Ecknön on his yacht the Lindön, a vessel once owned by Czar Nicholas and his Czarina Alexandra. I cycled along the towpath that parallels the canal and once ran all the way to Mem and back in the pouring rain, past two locks, to the mouth of the Baltic Sea, looking for white-tailed eagles. And while the dark skies opened and closed with regularity, I saw jackdaws and mallards and fat-cheeked eider ducks. There were blue herons crisscrossing the skies and arctic terns – the kind that commute yearly from pole to pole – successfully fishing the waters. Battalions of mute swans zigzagged from bank to bank. It was breathtakingly wild and beautiful and, at a time when I felt pressured by work and life and my own expectations, I was blessedly alone.

This time I would not be alone. I had signed on to lead a writing workshop on a Dutch motor cruiser that would motor from Toulouse to Castelnaudary and back. The writers were all friends, women I'd known and worked with and with whom I wanted to travel: My dear friend Connie from Greece; Ann with whom I'd traveled before on assignment through the rainforests of Costa Rica; April, a very pretty and intrepid traveler; Mary Jean who was reinventing her life; Barbara, our skipper and the genius behind the adventure; and Cristie, a vivacious real estate agent with a talent for storytelling whom I'd met through my sister. At Ann's suggestion, I had rented an apartment in Paris. Of course I invited everyone to join me, and I was a little surprised when four out of six – Barbara was already on Lurley and Cristie was entertaining her niece somewhere else in the city – took me up on the offer. Situated on rue Lamarck in picturesque Montmartre, not far from Montmartre Cemetery where Stendahl, Berlioz, Alexander Dumas the younger, Degas and Nijinksy were buried, it was conveniently located across the street from the Lamarck-Caulaincourt metro stop, so we could catch the train from Charles de Gaulle airport to the Gare de l'Est and then take the metro to our very doorstep. The apartment was on the ground or garden level of an attractive building at the foot of the Montmartre stairs. To my mind, it was perfect. It had a fireplace, a tiny kitchen and bath and one bedroom. It was, in short, just the kind of bohemian hangout in which I imagined Picasso, Braque, Jan Gris, Toulouse-Lautrec or any of the other painters, poets and writers who dwelled in this part of the city might have lived.

"It reminds me of college," said April who immediately camped out in the living room and hung a big Paris map on the wall. Mary Jean staked a claim on the couch cushions, Ann opted for an air mattress in the dining area and Connie and I shared a double bed in the apartment's only bedroom. The apartment, which was small, was filled with sounds. Nights there were a virtual symphony of snores and the snuffling of my slumbering companions. Days were filled with the horse-like clip-clop of heels ascending the nearby stairs, the laughter and chatter of passersby and what April called "the sandworm-like rumble" of the metro almost directly below us. We roamed Paris by day, often together, though we clearly had very different interests, sightseeing, eating, drinking, shopping and writing poetry around our dining room table at night. We explored the Right Bank, the Left Bank, the Latin Quarter, the Marais and the colorful Place Pigalle. One morning I walked up the hill to Sacre Coeur just in time to catch the nuns singing matins beneath the cathedral's flashy neo-Byzantine mosaic. Sweet as it was, it could not go on forever, and all too soon we were racing to Gare Montparnasse to catch the high-speed train to Gare Matabiau and Toulouse.

Sun-drenched Toulouse seemed so quiet after Paris. *Lurley* was berthed in the unruffled waters of Port Saint Sauveur. Trim and squeaky-clean, she was beautiful but a little . . . small. Our close quarters in Paris had prepared us for intimacy but not quite for this. But Barbara very quickly advised that we would not be traveling on *Lurley*. She felt our group was a little large for *Lurley*, so she'd rented a roomier yacht, the *Royal Destiny*, for our journey. She plied us with olives and cheese and delicious wines, helped us settle in, then threw us into the arms of Toulouse and the charms of a restaurant she'd discovered called Chez Fazoul where we indulged in the first of a series of banquet-style dinners featuring delicacies like pate, roast duck, cassis sorbet and the region's famous cassoulet.

The next morning I got up early to go for a run along the Canal du Midi. Scooting out of the gated dock through the rough edge of the fence, I set out on a path umbrellaed by the wide limbs of gigantic plane trees that lined the canal. Mallards paddled peacefully in the leaf-green waters. Dragonflies skittered back and forth from canal to shore. The air was crisp and clean as newly picked fruit. By the time I returned a rooster was crowing, and I could hear the bells of nearby Saint Aubin. I returned to the smell of coffee and plans to visit the farmer's market before we set out for the *Ecluse de Castanet*, the first of three locks that we would traverse that day.

The market at Saint Aubin is a Sunday affair. By nine a.m. it was bustling, its stalls filled with vegetables and fruit and textiles and shoes giving it an almost medieval feel. The scent of flowers and herbs and chickens roasting filled the air. Paella simmered in huge cast iron pots. We filled our bags with fresh produce, with sandals, with straw bags and hats and headed back to *Royal Destiny*. April was the last to return proudly brandishing a bouquet of roses given to her by a new-found friend. By mid morning we had rather clumsily cast off and our skipper, Barbara, and her landlubberly crew of pen-wielding women were headed southeast on the canal.

"Sweat-passay," spelled *"souhaite passer,"* is the open sesame of locks. And Cristophe, the round-faced, apple-cheeked owner of the *Royal Destiny* met up with us and acquainted us with this and other significant bits of canal etiquette before we entered the first lock. He accompanied Connie to the lock keeper's cottage where they were informed that the lock was closed till half past one. So we tied up right where we stopped and broke for lunch. Connie is mercurial. She is charismatic. Put her around people and she is like a magnet, people fly toward her like iron shavings. *"Agape-mou.*

Darling," she drawls as she jumps into action when time comes to approach the *écluse*.

The lock gates opened like gigantic castle doors, our large boat maneuvered in between them. We were at the bottom of the olive-shaped enclosure. We cast the lines up fore and aft and Connie, waiting on the lock's edge, wrapped them around the bollards. As the water rushed in, we held the ropes, tightening them as we rose with the level of the water. Once the chamber was full, the gates on the other side of the lock were opened, and we were on our way.

Vic, Montgiscard, Ayguesvives, *Deux écluses du Sanglier*, Négra, *Deux écluses de Laval*, Gardouch — in the days that followed, we made slow progress through twenty-three locks and back. Barbara, the only able-bodied sea-person among us, quite literally showed us the ropes until we were casting off and heaving lines with the best of them. Days took on a gentle rhythm, the slow pace of canal life where the maximum speed is eight kilometers an hour.

There is a Provençal poetic form called the Alba. It is a kind of hymn to dawn, a farewell to night, and for me it has always represented the most graceful of transitions. Most mornings I woke early and set out for a walk or run. Sometimes Mary Jean would join me, but often we would keep to ourselves. Meanwhile I was studying maps and reading about the towns adjacent, following Barbara's patient instructions, lecturing on writing and constantly working with these writers on their stories. The ensuing days became a twist of lines and knots, of hasty canal-side excursions, of leads and closes and transitions. There was always the writing — snatches of poetry and prose lighting up the terrain that we traversed. Each of the participants began to weave a tale from the threads that surrounded us – the sunflowers, the people, the food, the gentle rocking of the boat, the space between things. And there was music, the music that we made when Connie and I gathered the group in our cabin at night, to drink and sing and talk about love and life. I was sailing through troubadour country on a boat full of writers, writers who laughed easily, worked hard and struggled to capture the essence of their inner and outer worlds in a graceful torrent of words. Every day I listened to them, the songs that were taking shape around me, and I watched them, dear women, full of poetry and promise. We proceeded from lock to lock, each person learning to manage some part of the boat. There was a quiet energy to this, to the exhilaration of learning and, always, there was the writing: snatches of poetry and prose lighting up the landscape. I'm not quite sure when it was that I realized that I was falling in love with them all. It was the kind of love I feel for many of my woman friends, a profound mixture of respect and tenderness, a heart-and-holding kind of fondness that makes me smile when I see them reaching beyond themselves and makes me grateful when they support me in the same way – and they do. I'm sure it had something to do with the magic of Languedoc, the mystery of canals and the way in this region, beloved of the troubadours, dawn always seems to break like a song.

The Gift

CRISTIE MARCUS

The French can look at you and through you. Their expression doesn't change. Their focus doesn't either, not really. I first became aware of this trait when I visited Paris years ago as a college student and later as a casual traveler. Trying to emulate their mannerisms, to blend in, to be French, I copied the lack of acknowledgment, how their eyes glaze over when passing a stranger on the street.

I began my recent visit to Paris with the same attitude. I made sure to pack my more sophisticated clothes and accessories, leaving the jogging shoes and sweat-shirts behind. French women wouldn't be caught dead in that attire, even at a gym. But come to think of it, I have never seen a gym in the City of Light.

The trip was instigated when I received a flyer in the mail inviting me to attend a week-long workshop, sharing a boat with six other writers while navigating from Toulouse along the Canal du Midi in Southern France. It was a no-brainer. I e-mailed my definite yes that afternoon and sent my check the next day.

Of course, spending an extra week in Paris was a must. I quickly reserved my seat on the Air France non-stop San Francisco to Charles de Gaulle. While making hotel arrangements, I had an *a-ha* moment. I had been struggling with what to give Emily, my sister's firstborn, to commemorate passage from high school to her upcoming freshman year at one of the prestigious Claremont Colleges in Southern California.

"I'm stumped, too," my sister had said. "I don't know what to tell you. We'll probably just go with a new computer. At least it's something useful."

"Oh great, there goes my best idea," I grumbled, but that was actually fine by me. With rapid technology, I figured my gift would be obsolete, needing replacement long before Emily completed her sophomore year.

A savings bond seemed way too impersonal and for what amount? Stock certificates ridiculous — with my luck in the market, the value would surely plummet. I wanted to give Emily something more meaningful, something that would last a lifetime. When her parents gave me their nod of approval, I knew I'd selected the perfect gift.

"Hey, Emily," I said when I called her on the phone. "I have a surprise for you."

"Hi, Auntie. You do? What?" I could hear the volume of her stereo in the background go quiet. "What surprise?"

"Well, Sweetie, for your graduation present." I paused. "How would you like to go with me to Paris for a week?"

She shrieked into the receiver. Then kept repeating, "Oh my God!"

"I'll take that as a yes."

"Paris? I get to go to Paris with you? Oh my God!"

I never had a burning desire to be a mother; never really missed having kids and being a mom. Divorced for over a decade, my responsibilities to others were few. Travel had become a priority and now I had the opportunity to share my passion. If I could impart to my niece just a small taste of my lust for travel, her life would forever be altered in a curious and expanded way.

Emily and I rarely got the opportunity to spend any one-on-one time, although we'd always been close. At the airport, going through the series of lines to board the plane, I sensed a different type of closeness.

"I'll wait for you right here," I said at the doorway to the ladies room.

"You don't have to," Emily protested. "I'll find you, Auntie."

"I know, Sweetie, but I want to. Go on. I'll be here."

I had the best of all circumstances – feeling the authority and protectiveness of a parent and the casualness of a confidante and a pal. My love for Emily deepened, I felt a twinge of what I may have missed and as my maternal instincts blossomed, I began to understand my sister a little better.

Monday morning, having given ourselves a decent eighteen hours to overcome Pacific-daylight-time jet lag, Emily and I left our Latin Quarter hotel and trotted off to destination number one: the Louvre. I had visited Paris four times in the past few years, but it had been nearly three decades since I last ventured into the Louvre. Too many tourists, and besides "been there, done that" I'd ridiculously convinced myself, when drawn toward the boutiques of the Left Bank or the Marais. I whiled away many an hour in the picturesque cafes and brasseries sipping wine or *café au lait*, people watching rather than viewing the world's greatest collection of art. Now Emily gave me a reason to go back.

So off we went, wallets full of euros, digital cameras void of old photos and batteries charged, wearing our most comfortable yet stylish shoes – Emily donning argyle-print canvas slip-ons and I happy in mid-heeled strappy sandals.

Giddy with excitement, we meandered from our hotel on Rue Jacob, making our way to the Louvre. I guided us down Rue Bonaparte towards the Seine and my favorite bridge, the Pont des Arts. We stopped in the middle of this wooden walking-bridge and I turned Emily by her shoulders to face the Eiffel Tower.

"Oh my God! Auntie! It's so big. It's so," she hesitated, "real." Her eyes wide, Emily repeatedly looked from the tower to me and back again. "It's amazing." She put her arm through mine and leaned into my side. "Now I really feel like we're in Paris." Her reaction was worth the entire trip. I felt like I was seeing Paris for the first time myself.

The days whizzed by as we walked and walked and walked

throughout the city. We toured and viewed the requisite, as well as the lesser-known sights. We forged our own paths and languished in gardens and at fountains. We sipped cold Orangina and refreshing Crème-de-Menthe with soda over ice at delightful sidewalk cafés. We tasted varieties of renowned Berthillon ice cream served from an open window to those waiting in the long line on Rue St. Louis-en-l'Ile. All of France was enduring a heat wave and we suffered right along, but were never deterred – this was Paris!

"Auntie," Emily pointed out on day two, "nobody yields."

"What?" I said over my shoulder as we marched single file down a narrow sidewalk on a narrow street. When we got to the entrance of a cobblestone courtyard, I pulled over out of the stream of foot-traffic. "What, Sweetie? What'd you say?"

"I said nobody yields. They'd just as soon knock us off the sidewalk into cars than change their path."

She was absolutely correct. Many times we had pressed our backs to plaster, stone or brick buildings giving way to oncoming pedestrians. I let them pass without looking at them – I did the French thing – averted my eyes. Frequently we had hopped off an inadequate sidewalk to let faster paced walkers overtake and pass when the klop-klop of their heels on pavement proved too rapid for us not to relent.

"You're right, Honey. It's something they do; it's the way they are. Like a game of Chicken or Dare. It's French."

We laughed and shrugged and after Emily declared, "They don't even see us, it's like we're invisible," we eased into the pedestrian flow and plodded off to the next attraction.

That's when I realized my attempt to mimic the aloof, typically French trait of ignoring others did not serve me well. It had a technique to it, one that I had always tried to copy, but who was I kidding? It was a game of Chicken and I always lost. Besides, I don't have the lithe, pale arms so many French women are blessed with. I couldn't fit one thigh (let alone a cheek) into the slacks or jeans that hug the tiny butts of young femmes. I was obviously a foreigner, why was I trying to hide the fact? Being unique and outstanding should be celebrated. Why was I so willing to fade and conform, to blend in? This was not behavior I wanted to teach Emily. I wanted her to go off to college confidant and completely comfortable with herself — as the marvelous young woman she had become.

We forged our way down Rue St. Honoré towards the Place Vendôme. The first gentleman we passed, I didn't glaze my gaze. I caught and held his eyes with mine and nodded a hello. He nodded back acknowledging me, even altered his course to let Emily and me pass — side by side. We continued walking, and a few paces ahead a pair of businessmen approached wearing similar navy-blue sport coats, crisp white shirts and dark ties — one patterned with a sapphire print and the other with crimson. They were engrossed in conversation, one raising his arm, pounding the air for emphasis. As they got closer, I smiled and said hello. Not in a *"Hey, I'm hitting on you, get it?"* way, but in a *"Bonjour, ça va?"* friendly American way. They stopped talking, gave cheerful grins and as we passed, said hello back. I continued this sociable practice. The response, without exception, was positive. It seemed the French were shaken from their norm by something different, a refreshing greeting – a Californian with a smile.

Rather than being cool and looking like a local, I had probably appeared dour and maybe even pissed off. Or just plain silly. Emily's simple observation became my lesson. She taught me not to acquiesce, not to submit. I would stay true to myself, be real, be *me*.

As we walked towards the end of a block, an elderly woman rounded the corner, two heavy grocery bags pulling her shoulders downward. She looked up from the sidewalk and caught Emily and me smiling at her. Her eyes brightened. *"Bonjour,"* she sang out. We harmonized, *"Bonjour, Madame,"* and all of our smiles broadened.

Then I really got it. My gift to Emily was Emily's gift to me. I put my arm around her shoulder and pulled her close. I kissed the top of her shiny dark hair and Emily slipped her arm around my waist.

"Hey, Auntie," she said halting in the middle of the sidewalk. "I just love Paris. And you know, I think for lunch I'm ready to give that steak tartare a try." We continued walking. "And after we eat, could we go back to see the rest of the Louvre?"

"Sure, Honey," I said. "We can do that."

Toulouse

City celebrated in song and verse,
Hallmarked by lavish stonework and rose brick,
Medieval merchants who padded their purse,
Adorning walls from the finest of picks.

Capital of the Midi-Pyrénées,
Of plane and maple, of nettle and lime,
Walking round Renaissance fountains of clay,
Composed and cloistered in Jacobin time.

Sunday market surrounding Saint Aubin
Housewives haggle for cheeses plump and round,
Stalls of foods and flowers and fresh-baked *pain*
Bargains and treasures waiting to be found.

With gargoyles protecting *la cité,*
Your troubadours singing *la verité.*

– CONNIE BURKE

Good Roots

Stacie M. Williams

Ͽ

"No garden is without weeds."
— Thomas Fuller

The first thing I did after I arrived at Dune Capitainerie, 7 Port Saint Sauveur in Toulouse, was pull weeds. Barbara, our group's fearless leader, said she had something to do before the others arrived, "A silly little project." I was welcome to join her. I asked if it was something fun as I stood up to go along. No, no, we were going to start a garden.

Our target plot of ground? The side of the marina where the fuel dock is located. While it already boasted a lush, albeit prickly bush in one corner, the rest of it was in sore need of sprucing up: a clearing out of weeds and garbage. I could instantly see it needed something, particularly in comparison to another square earthy patch in which varied shrubs eked out an apparently happy existence. Barbara, a Master Gardener, had selected something specific to place into the sparse, dry ground. At the local market she had purchased her choice, rosemary. While we twisted roots out of the ground, I listened to Barbara's hope for these small shoots: they would grow tall and thick, spreading out nicely across the small barren plot. I learned that rosemary is perfect for this Mediterranean climate where it originated. The prickly, threatening bush in the corner? Barberry, with a medicinal purpose.

As we worked, the searing sun baking our faces and hands, I recalled weeding as a child. I was on the cusp of adolescence, at a time when chores and punishments in our house combined as modes of discipline. Weeding was not only expected as a chore, but utilized as punishment. The severity of the crime was indicated by the number of brown paper grocery bags assigned to be amassed with weeds, culled from a hill in our backyard. Mouth off, one bag of weeds. Get home after curfew, two bags of weeds. And if there weren't enough because you'd had a bad month? Well, too bad, work harder, find them. Needless to say, I detested weeding.

Hatred, however, led to development of a skill. If there is one thing I excel at, it is weeding. The identification of weeds takes practice, as there is such a variety of plants that can fall under this classification. A weed is essentially something that chokes out new life, something that does not belong in a certain garden's theme.

Even daisies can be weeds if you are trying to nurture a plot of rosebushes. Beyond that basic rule, it can get tricky. I like to think of weeds as people. Lovers, for example, can be the deceiving sort of weeds that have brightly colored petals or fringes to mislead you from the thorny, invasive nature at their cores. Weeds can be anything intrusive, not originally planted by you – like pushy, clingy acquaintances who insist on becoming your new best friends. Some weeds are clearly just that, a breed that quickly spreads its evil and poison. We all know these people. They are also the most contentious ones – thorny, sharp and eager to cause pain; once they root in it may be easy to break off their stalks but it is nearly impossible to wrench out the feeding tendrils that give them life. This eye for identifying weeds is now second nature to me – weeding out clingy friends, bad boyfriends, the bullshit people are so wont to fling at others. I can spot these out-of-place greens, I know how to dig my fingers into the soil, twist and yank out those encroachers.

Ironically, though I may be adept at pulling out the bad and invasive around me, when it comes to gardening, I have a black thumb. I cannot nurture new greenery, flowers or foliage of any kind. It isn't as though I have not attempted to do so. I have a history of purchasing hanging plants for my apartments and potted sprouts for my house. But I kill them all. I have even killed a cactus. I'd had it for several years and, presumably, did not give it enough water. I think I assumed it was fine, being a cactus and all. What sort of person kills a cactus? Am I so thorough in weeding, pulling out the roots of things that don't belong that I have been completely lax in learning how to nurture new growth? My lack

33

of many close, long-term friendships attests to that void in my garden.

Yet plants call my name. Colorful flowers, expansive hedges and tall, elegant trees invigorate me. What a grand thing it would be to plant an oleander and watch it bloom.

As we motor lazily down the Canal du Midi, we come upon the occasional *écluse* (lock), which boasts a garden fully cultivated or a simple array of rainbow-hued flowers. Back at the *Ecluse La Domergue* there are gardens on both sides of the *bassin* in which boats are raised and lowered to different water levels. A sweet lock keeper named Raymond is the proud gardener. He is subtle in his manners, speaking with the rhythmic style of the Occitan or Catalan, taking cue from Spain just over the Pyrenees. In his garden, Raymond has a hibiscus tree. Usually a bush, he has trained this purple-sparked beauty to be something different, and more glorious, than expected. One large stalk is its trunk, its branches rising skyward with leaves and flowers perched triumphantly at the top.

One of my next-door neighbors back home has a similar garden. A variety of hanging baskets, small pots of flowers, climbing vines and tomatoes — all in her suburban, postage-stamp sized backyard. Considering the size of her workspace, it is quite exceptional. Of course, Jean has time to keep such a delightfully attractive collection of plants in a climate that wilts them with summer's heat and freezes them with winter's frosts and snow. She has time for this because she is retired. At least, that is what I tell myself.

Jean has offered to teach me how to establish and sustain some verdant greenery and color around my house. She has even extended several invitations to join her at our nearby farmer's market to find the appropriate flowering shrubs for my taste and our weather. She has been this generous to me in numerous ways since I moved in with my husband four years past. Until two months ago, I always found a way to politely decline while maintaining a "later, soon" attitude.

Then, Jean brought us some hostas that had overgrown their welcome in her yard. She offered, again, to help with the planting, in this case transplanting. We worked for nearly two hours. We picked out spots the correct distance apart. We dug small holes, then filled the emptiness with water before adding a section of hosta. Finally we returned the vacated dirt to its home. The finished look was a line of wimpy plants, some with slightly browned leaves and others half-wilted, that protruded from the ground in front of the house and along the walk. But it was a wonderful experience: cool mud and soil caking my fingers, sweat on my forehead from the hot summer sun and a satisfying ache in my muscles from crouching for such a lengthy period. The result was promising. However meager, I finally had some greens in my yard.

Two months later, how do these sturdy, fast-growing, un-killable hostas look? You could not see most of them. My dear, sweet better half got the grass trimmer too close, chopping them to bits. The others have dried to a light brown in our summer drought. But I keep watering the ground. Why do I do this? Because the roots are good; they are well planted and healthy. If the roots stay that way, the leaves will return from their "whacked" state, broad and vibrantly green and white. I have faith in my new roots, in the advice of my neighbor friend. I simply must be patient.

From the dry heat of California to the sticky humidity of Wisconsin, and on to the breezy, sunny, Mediterranean climate of the Canal du Midi, I attempt to garden, to nurture new life, to weed efficiently without over-doing it: this lesson of balance follows me.

At the last stop of our week-long journey, we have dinner at a small patio restaurant overlooking the last lock before Toulouse. As I laugh with my new friends, I glance out across the basin of the lock, filled with life-giving water. I survey the plants along the edge and one particular hedge of shrubs catches my eye. They look awfully familiar in their shade of green, their multi-pronged needlelike leaves. I turn to Barbara and ask, pointing, "Isn't that rosemary?" It is.

And at 7 Port Saint Sauveur in Toulouse? There is a small brown plot of dirt that has three tiny shoots trying to begin a new life. I helped with that meager garden, with my own talent for weeding. I can only hope to take what I have learned when I leave the canal and continue to nurture the roots of my transplanted green friends at home. After departing *Lurley*, my home for the last week, before continuing on my way, I will be sure to stop and check on our little dockside rosemary, seeking assurance that their roots are good.

Matters of Trust

ETHEL F. MUSSEN

҂

He was tall and thin, his dark hair topped by a puffy round cap whose visor tamed dark curls. A shallow curly beard framed his chin and his tanned skin suggested a North African origin. Between swigs of juice, he surveyed me and my map with dancing dark eyes. *"Puis-je vous aider?* (Can I help?)" he asked.

"Je suis perdue! (I am lost!)" I lamented, aware that my helplessness at being lost could only make me fair game for skullduggery.

"Where do you want to go?" I decided to opt for the train station instead of my hotel, to return my rental car before noon and avoid an extra day's charge.

"I will show you," he volunteered, and I expected him to lead the way out of the maze. Instead he came to the car with me and, as soon as I unlocked it, got into the passenger side, juice carton in hand.

"Where are you from?" I asked, and I was not surprised when he replied, "*Tunisie.*" His eyebrows rose when he learned I was from California and I tried to guess his intentions as he gazed at me for a while, smiling and twinkling. I couldn't decide whether he was considering me old and helpless or a daft adventurer.

In that noonday heat I felt truly daft and misdirected. After two weeks in a familiar village in Provence, I had scurried in my compact Opel amidst the truckers crisscrossing the European union on the autoroutes of Southern France on my way to an unfamiliar city, Toulouse. For one week I was to join a small group of strangers on the Canal du Midi that connects the Atlantic with the Mediterranean. I knew only the publisher-teacher I had written with during the past year and I hoped to review with him the material I'd gathered in Moustiers, a village of ceramicists. The other writers in the small group were unknown women of unknown ages, skills and temperaments. I feared the boat-owner and captain of our motley group must be half-mad herself to plump us together and expect us to crew the boat as we chugged slowly or moored at locks along the green canal and simultaneously produce wise, sensitive observations of life on the waterway.

On the day before the canal trip, I had made it to Toulouse and was attempting to drop my bags at my hotel, but I'd turned onto a network of small one-way streets as the noon car rental return time was approaching. Hot, apprehensive, and lost, I surrendered to the possibly dangerous offer of assistance.

He gestured for me to start the car, and I turned the key. I questioned my judgment at leaving him beside me as we moved out and he pointed the way, left, then right and right again until we were on a major road facing the train station. Roads intersected and traffic passed in all directions but this was indeed the Rue P. Semard I sought. On the other side, an Avis sign hung at the base of a three-story parking structure connected to the entrance of Toulouse's grand old Gare Matabiau. We crossed the intersection and a uniformed attendant urged us to enter the garage and proceed to the third level. We circled to the top, cars close behind me, only to discover that the gate at the top was not for sissies or tourists. My companion jumped out and got assistance and we finally swung into an open Hertz space. I was grateful for his direction and help. It was twelve minutes to noon.

Abruptly I realized that the trunk was still filled with bags, large and small, and I looked for a trolley that could be loaded and taken down to the office while I completed the paperwork of the car return. The smile on his slender face faded when he saw the array, but he repeated, "*Je vous aide.*" I clutched my large soft bag that held my purse, my money belt and passport and the contract documents I would need. I slung the camera and computer bags over my shoulders, while he rolled the two suitcases toward the elevator. The Hertz counter was just to our left on the ground floor and I gave them my name and the key. I had no problems to report and they didn't ask to check the car. Relieved, the two of us carted the bags outside and I looked for a taxi.

"*Vous cherchez un hotel?* (You are searching for a hotel?)" he asked, "*Quel prix?* (What price?)" He was clearly ready to lead me on.

"*Non, non!*" I protested, "I have a reservation! *Un taxi, s'il vous plait.*" I stood ready to guard the luggage while he found a cab.

I got out my hotel reservation to check the number on Allée Jean Jaures. He looked at it and announced, "*Ce n'est pas loin!* (It's not far!) *Je vous aide.*" I hoisted the cameras in my backpack and was reaching for the soft bag when he shoved the juice in my right hand, suggesting that I drink. He gathered together the computer, the large and small rolling stock and my essential soft bag and began leading the way. Across major crosswalks and between traffic signals he headed to Jean Jaures, at first just a few steps ahead of me, then increasingly distant as his long legs covered the streets leading to the Allée. We were a peculiar pair, he always ahead, stopping at times to readjust the weight, and I lagging behind, always trying to catch up, insisting I should carry the soft bag he had slung over his right shoulder. I knew he could turn off at any of the side streets, leaving me with nothing but cameras and juice, and I fought to keep him in sight.

Jean Jaures proved to be dusty, with frequently blocked access and few shade trees, as the city constructed its Metro line directly beneath the street. The noon sun beat down on us. Each time he stopped, I gestured that he should take his juice and I would take the soft bag. He stayed ahead, barely turning to see that I was still coming. The address was in the low numbers, very close to the Place Wilson and the Place du Capitole. A cab could have made it in ten minutes, but I decided that he really needed the extra money or had gotten in over his head. If he had found me his hotel where would he have led me? What would he hold onto now when we found mine?

How much should I give him? Twenty euros? Buy him lunch? Would he hold out for more? What was appropriate and what was an insult? Would we ever reach the Hotel du Capitole? What madness pursued me into braving scorching Toulouse in the first place, when I could have stayed safely in my friendly village of Moustiers?

Suddenly he paused and waited for me to catch up. Beyond a plane tree, a vertical sign spelled out "du Capitole" and a neat, recessed entryway led to glass doors that opened magically before us as we trundled all the bags to the reception desk. Feeling mixed exhaustion and relief, secure at last, I lifted my soft bag from the floor where my volunteer porter had placed it and drew out the voucher for the receptionist. The young lady verified the voucher and busied herself with making up a magnetic key to my room. The Tunisian hovered next to my right elbow the whole time, attentive to every detail, until I pulled my purse from the soft bag and tentatively offered him twenty euros, wondering if this was enough, even as I murmured, *"Merci."*

"Non, Madame, non!" he declared vehemently, and grabbing the juice carton, he darted quickly away, through the magical doors.

A number of agents had tried to help me arrange this trip. Every one had either cost me more or served me less well than this frightening young man, whose name I never asked, who selflessly offered me juice and guidance and a strong back. In an unexpected and alarming encounter, fraught with suspicion, I could as easily have been victimized or conned and totally impoverished in a strange city if he had acted as I feared. In fact, he smiled and asked if he could aid me, and I trusted him.

Relating all this to my shipmates on the Canal helped me share the fear and the peril of my adventurous entry into Toulouse. It was our experienced and wise Captain who explained that for a young Muslim a deed of helpfulness offers the possibility of pleasing Allah and rising that much closer to Paradise.

Following my week's adventure on the Canal du Midi, I decompressed at the Hotel de Brienne. It is nestled in the heart of the neighborhood of the famed University of Toulouse. On Sunday, with many of the local residents, I wandered in the nearby public gardens, meditated in a classic Zen garden from Japan, set above a teahouse and a green moss-covered lake filled with gigantic hungry koi fed by little boys standing on an arching red bridge. I had a beer in a pub whose buxom Madame owned three dogs like my own, who noisily greeted all patrons. I dined in a bistro favored by families and groups who kissed each other and the chef before they sat down for a true Tolosaine dinner at moderate prices. I discovered that the first lock on the Canal de Brienne as it leads from the Garonne River actually has its name spray-painted on the river side. Hopefully the anonymous young man from the Arab quarter blocks away will find it someday: it proclaims *"Paradise."*

Sunday Market Largesse

APRIL ORCUTT

꙳

"You take the photo because the vegetables are too heavy to carry?" said a deep, accented voice while I focused the macro lens of my camera on shallots at one of the numerous stands of tomatoes, beets, olives, apricots, jams, daisies, shoes, shirts, toys, and a thousand other assorted items at the Sunday market by the Saint Aubin church in Toulouse in Southern France.

I clicked the shutter, then turned to see a rotund man with a drooping gray moustache, mirrored sunglasses, shorts, and a broad straw hat smiling at me. He looked remarkably relaxed among the scores of intense shoppers searching for soft rosy peaches, aromatic melons, juicy plums, and a bargain on sandals.

"My name is Robert," he said.

"I'm April," I replied. "I'm leaving for a week-long yacht trip on the Canal du Midi so you're almost right: it's not the weight of the shallots that's the issue but the space. I'm sorry I can't take the vegetables."

"Too bad," he said. "This man has the best garlic and leeks."

For me it seemed hard to pick out the best. Organic strawberries, plump ripe tomatoes, firm purple eggplants, vivid yellow and green beans, bushels of garlic, and baskets of sweet-smelling herbs lined table after table, three rows deep along the side of the church. Perhaps other French shoppers had their favorite stands, too — at every table hip twenty-somethings, middle-aged couples with wallets open, and well-fed gray-haired women in flower-print dresses and heavy shoes eagerly filled square canvas tote bags with succulent apricots, velvety peaches, and crisp florina and St. Jean apples.

"This is the best market in Southern France," Robert added. "It is the most typical of Toulouse — the most traditional." I did feel like I had gone back a hundred years to the time before supermarkets and fast food.

Still empty-handed, I bade *"Au revoir"* to Robert and returned to wandering among the stalls.

A pungent scent lured me to rectangular white bins full of whole spices. Yellow-beige cumin seeds and golden fenugreek released the aroma of curry. White cardamom pods added sweetness. Dark gray "smoked cardamom" paraded next to curled red-orange blades of mace. Black "hot peppercorns" from Mexico posed for my camera near deep red peppercorns from the Sichuan province of China. Here was the world in a stall.

Fresh spices and vegetables only entered my own world in college — after I left my mother's home. Before that, I thought that herbs and spices only came powdered in small red-and-white metal boxes marked McCormick and that a vegetable was a half-inch cube, sphere, or tube of mushy, slightly gray cellulose.

My mom, a post-World War II bride who didn't learn to cook until she was married at twenty-five, always resisted the culinary arts. After the war, when the canning companies that had provided packaged food for troops needed new markets, they pushed their products on American housewives, and my mother shamelessly collaborated.

I hardly knew a piece of chicken that wasn't covered in canned cream of chicken soup, but casseroles were her mainstay. She layered tuna or ground round with cans of mushrooms or Mexicorn in a baking dish, covered the concoction with condensed cream of celery soup or tomato sauce, sprinkled chopped nuts or bread crumbs on top, put the casserole in the oven, and ignored it for an hour. Her tuna, mixed vegetable, and mushroom soup combo was my favorite — what made it good was its thick topping of crushed potato chips.

Side dishes were canned green beans or frozen broccoli. When relatives visited, she dressed up frozen French-cut green beans with mushroom soup, canned almond slivers, and crushed packaged onion rings.

Her spice rack contained only powdered nutmeg, ground cinnamon, dried basil, and garlic salt.

For hors d'oeuvres she served canned black olives or maybe green ones stuffed with pimentos, from a jar.

Fresh vegetables meant salads: pale iceberg lettuce with chunks of carrots and celery. That was my entire growing-up experience with non-canned or non-frozen vegetables.

Arrayed before me now was more fresh food than my entire family had eaten — or even seen — in all the years of my childhood and adolescence. I slowly circled all the stalls twice and then strolled around one more time to savor the experience.

Beneath a black-and-white awning, I watched a shopkeeper dip a six-inch-wide wire ladle into five-gallon buckets of preserved black olives from Portugal, yellow-green lemon-herb Provençal olives, dark Greek-style olives with garlic, and a Tahitian-style mix of green and black olives with hot red peppers. Not a jar in sight.

A couple in their twenties sold organic goat cheese and local honeys, and next to them a woman offered baguettes. I could almost taste slices of baguette spread with honey, topped with goat cheese — broiled until the warm white cheese melted slightly — and placed on a deep green salad.

Suddenly I could smell steaming seafood cooking with saffron, a scent I associated with Spain, which was sixty miles away. The alluring aroma enticed me to a just-unveiled, four-foot-wide pan of paella filled with six-inch golden whole langoustines, pink shrimp, dark mussels, and red and green peppers so thick that I couldn't see even one grain of the golden rice that must have been below the oceanic sampler. A crowd began to gather.

I wondered: Do the mothers in the South of France routinely

fix paella for their families' dinners? Were the fathers buying white beans and sausage to make the region's famous cassoulet for their children? Were the grandmothers stuffing their tote bags with heavy tomatoes, eggplants, garlic, and fresh basil so they could go home and make ratatouille for their extended families? I doubted that Campbell's makes sauce Provençal.

I pulled myself away from the massive pan of paella and joined another crowd of a dozen people engrossed in watching a salesman demonstrate a small Vegematic-type gadget that turned cucumbers into long scalloped garlands and apples into peony-like "flowers."

Real flowers — yellow gerbera daisies, pale pink roses, and white baby's breath — filled buckets under a yellow and green market umbrella, and there Robert gossiped with another vendor-friend. When he saw me, he said, "Hello, again!"

"*Bonjour*," I replied. It was like meeting an old friend.

"Here is another excellent man," he said, waving his arm toward the grinning white-haired vendor with bushy salt-and-pepper eyebrows and an apricot-colored T-shirt. Then he pointed to red, pink, peach, white, and yellow roses. "Which bouquet do you like?"

Startled, I wasn't sure what to say.

"Pick one from my friend here," he said.

I looked over the bouquets and pointed to one that held mostly yellow roses with two pink, one peach, and one red one. The vendor wrapped the long stems of the flowers in a white paper cone and handed them to me while Robert gave him two euros.

I snapped a photograph of Robert and his jovial friend since I couldn't otherwise take their big smiles with me.

The sweet scent of the roses perfumed the air, and I again said, *"Au revoir"* to Robert, reluctantly left the market, and walked along the path beside the Canal du Midi back to the yacht. I looked forward to the boat journey, to eating French food, to being outside in sunshine and nature, and to journeying along the Canal du Midi with new friends.

As I walked, I kept raising the roses to my nose, breathing their fresh fragrance. Those roses were all I carried back from the market. They were not too heavy at all.

Navigating Sleep

CRISTIE MARCUS

⠀

꙳

I am a lousy sleeper. Always have been. I'm no sleepwalker waking up in the cookie aisle of 7-11 at four a.m. wearing my Nick & Nora pjs and fuzzy slippers, and I don't suffer from a clinical sleep disorder like restless leg syndrome or apnea, but I do have a close relationship with late night TV and shows like *Insomniac Theatre* and *Movies 'Til Dawn.*

Over the years I have resorted to a variety of available remedies promising relief from insomnia. I graduated from natural cures like melatonin and valerian root to the more serious over-the-counter sleep aids, such as Tylenol or Excedrin-PM, which left my brain foggy until midday. I gave Unisom a two-month stint, to no avail. My sister once slipped me some of her prescription Ambien.

"Get it?" she gleefully pointed out, sans the usual dark circles under her eyes. "A.M.-Bien; Bien-A.M. Good Morning!" She took a slug of her third cup of coffee. "Works great."

"Yeah, great. Great for you," I said, disappointed. "Up all night and I'm groggy for days. You know, Deb, this could kill me. Sleep deprivation has been used as a torture technique on prisoners of war. I could die."

Because of my dreadful sleep patterns, it was with great trepidation that I considered joining a group of six fellow writers, whom I had never met, on a boat climbing and descending the series of locks, marvelously engineered by Pierre Paul Riquet in 1667, on the Canal du Midi in Southern France. The idea of spending a week writing, exploring the Languedoc region, eating and drinking local offerings, was one I couldn't pass up. But having to share a cabin, or worse a bed, was a likely possibility and one that I dreaded. Pity the poor shipmate stuck with splitting her space with me. I anticipated tight quarters, and psyched myself to face the challenge.

Falling asleep is no problem. It's staying asleep that plagues me. Getting up to pee, I check the bedside clock, thinking it a bit of numerological good luck if the digits glow 2:22 or 3:33. A bowl of Cheerios, shared with Cosmo, my pup, me doling out one tiny milk-soaked O at a time, sometimes helps put me back into slumber. My very expensive Chatham & Wells extra-firm with plush pillow-top mattress has fallen far short of the salesman's promise of, "You'll get your best night's sleep — ever."

What kind of mattress could there be on a boat? I wondered. What if the beds are hammocks? Should I pack a zip-lock bag of Cheerios?

I occasionally pass a night pacing the house, mentally creating to-do lists and schedules. I'm sure my shipmates would be horrified to learn that I've been known to run the vacuum at three a.m., Cosmo looking at me like I've gone mad then scurrying behind the couch to hide from the machine's wicked whirr. Back in bed I toss and shift, punch and plump the pillows, curl up and straighten out under the fluffy cloud of down covers. Eventually I fall back to sleep. I must. I'm not dead.

The night before flying from Paris to Toulouse to join the other writers, I stayed at l'Hotel d'Angleterre on Rue Jacob, my favorite Latin Quarter inn, enduring one of my worst sleepless nights. Brain on overdrive, I worried – what if I disturb everyone on the boat? What if there's a vacuum cleaner on board? I contemplated canceling. I could send an e-mail with my regrets. Better yet, I could send a telegram to the dock at Port Saint Sauveur in Toulouse, a Western Union telegram, like in the old black and white movies I've watched on TV until dawn. I was obsessing, but that's what one tends to do between the hours of two and four a.m. I waited and watched as dawn broke the night, Paris brightened and I headed to Toulouse.

Lucky for me, I was the first passenger to arrive at the Saint Sauveur dock to find Barbara, our skipper, enjoying a leisurely lunch of ripe tomatoes, sliced soft cheese and chunks of crusty country bread. She had arrived in Toulouse four days earlier and clearly adjusted to the relaxed pace of boating life.

Barbara wisely determined that her own yacht, *Lurley*, was too small to accommodate seven females toting backpacks, laptop computers and suitcases on wheels. Nor could *Lurley* have contained the variety of personalities, styles and moods. She had commandeered a thirty-eight-foot three stateroom, two bath aptly described pleasure cruiser, the *Royal Destiny*, from Sunshine Cruise Line. At Barbara's encouragement, I explored the *Royal Destiny* then, as she suggested, selected my bunk.

The mini-kitchen equipped with a three-burner stove and oven, double stainless sink and refrigerator / freezer had a large formica dining table that easily converted to become Barbara's bunk each night. Guess I won't be munching Cheerios in the middle of the night here, I resigned.

The head with toilet, sink and shower all in one tiny room, was tricky at first, until "turn switch to left – pump four to six times to let canal water in – switch to right – repeat until all is pumped out" instructions became an easy procedure. The shower, also initially a little daunting, proved to be no big deal, either. "Leave dry towel outside – close door – room becomes shower" with plenty of hot water and great pressure.

Staterooms were compact, each with bunks for two people. They were all made up with crisp white sheets and fuzzy blankets the color of sunflowers, neatly folded at the foot of each bed. The forward cabin, though not the largest, had the biggest single bunk that narrowed at the foot, conforming to the shape of the hull. Separated by a narrow, one-person-only strip and elevated above a storage cabinet was another bunk, slightly wider than a mummy sleeping bag.

Naturally, I chose the bigger one and as a gesture intended to at least eliminate guilt as a source of my insomnia, I forfeited use of the closet. I could pile my gear around the edges of my bed and still have more room to lie down than anyone else. The walls, covered in midnight-blue carpeting trimmed with dark mahogany wood, and the low ceiling with hatch for light and fresh air, made the cabin delightfully cozy. Hopefully I'll be able to get some sleep here. At least I don't have to share a bed, just a cabin, though my poor roomie will be relegated to a much smaller, upper bunk.

When the others arrived on foot, dragging their bulging suitcases and gear, hot and parched by the unexpectedly long walk from the train depot to the dock, Barbara quickly popped two bottles of rosé.

Which one, I fretted, as I surveyed the group. Which poor soul will be stuck sharing her space with me? Our instructor, Linda, had already volunteered to share a room with Connie, a close friend who joined us from her home in Greece.

"Connie," Linda said, "we never get to spend any time together. You only visit every few years, so it's only fitting that you and I bunk together. Besides, no one else could. Between your jokes and your snoring..." Linda's bright humor and easygoing personality were evident.

"My snoring? I only snore when I've been drinking."

"Uh, yeah," Linda chided, holding up her filled wine glass. We all laughed and raised our glasses to toast Connie.

I sensed that Ann and April knew each other from back home and were an obvious roommate match: both laid-back and definitely more subdued than the jolly Connie and Linda. That left Mary Jean, a very pretty, petite woman who did not hesitate to voice her discomfort. Oh, God, please let her be a narcoleptic, I prayed.

"About the wine," Barbara continued, refilling our glasses. "I chose these from the Fronton and Gaillac appellations, the two appellations closest to Toulouse."

"What's an appellation?"

Over an array of anchovy stuffed olives, roasted nuts and Roquefort cheese, Barbara shared information about the grape-growing regions of France; we shared more introductions and relaxed on the deck.

"Tomorrow," Barbara informed us, "Christophe from Sunshine will come to instruct how we work the boat through the locks of the canal. Hope you're all up for crewing. Then we'll hit the farmer's market, before we set off."

"Crew? We're the crew?" someone blurted. "Good God."

"Well, yes," Barbara looked us over dismissing the question with, "It's no biggie. Two people hop off the boat. I'll try to get it as close to the banks as possible to make it easy."

"While it's moving? We just *hop off* the boat while it's *moving*? That's a three or four-foot drop!"

"Yes, but don't worry, I'll go real slow." She dragged out slow. "Then you hustle and run up to the lock keeper to let him know we're coming. I'll ease *Royal Destiny* into the lock then cut the motor to neutral as two of you on deck toss the lines up to the two on ground who quickly wrap them once around the bollards and toss them back onboard. If the line gets wet, which it usually does, it can be pretty heavy and the end can really whip you, so watch out."

"Ew! That water's dirty. A soggy rope? And we have to throw it? How far?"

"Actually, it's a line, not a rope. We might as well use proper nautical terms. You know like port and starboard, fore and aft. Like that. Anyway, it's maybe ten, twelve feet. May take a few tries, but be very careful – get the line out of the water immediately – do not let it get pulled into the propeller. It could get wrapped around and we'd be in real trouble. Stuck."

"Aw, jeeze."

Barbara nodded. "So, then the two of you on deck grab the line and pull-pull-pull tight as we rise with the water; got to keep the boat from moving around in the lock while it fills. You all look fairly strong. You can do it."

We all laughed nervously, looking for crew-mate reaction and went to unpack.

"What the hell's a bollard?" someone whispered as we filed below deck.

"I have no idea."

"Good God."

I sensed more discord and heard grumblings over my jump-start to stake claim of the premier bunk.

"Shouldn't we draw straws, or something?"

"My suitcase won't fit in here! This room is so small," I heard April's voice. "And what? That's it? That's the bathroom?"

"It's a head," Barbara corrected, her voice bordering on stern. "And your room is called a cabin or if you like, a stateroom. And I'm sleeping up here, in the galley."

Thank God Connie and Linda took the double bed. "Well, we've known each other for decades," Connie said. "Our friendship survived this long, sharing a bed won't kill us."

"Yeah, but your snoring might," Ann joked from across the hall. More laughter from everyone. The tension in the air eventually dissipated as we settled in.

What nobody realized was that I was really doing them a favor. No one should have to share the one double-sized bed with me, me tossing and flopping all night, just as no one should have to suffer in a cabin with me if I were trapped in a bunk so narrow it guaranteed my sleeplessness. I was really sparing my crew-mates misery, I reasoned, banishing any pangs of guilt once and for all.

Sylvianne, the harbor master, generously allowed us after-hour's use of the Port Saint Sauveur facilities to freshen up. A quick reviving shower, the last on dry land for a few days, and we were ready for dinner at the superb bistro, Chez Fazoul.

From the dock, we walked a block then edged the Grand Rond, a lovely park with a spouting, spraying fountain in the center and paths and lawns encircling it. We continued down the tree-covered promenade, Allée François Verdier, in the direction of the Toulouse cathedral.

"The cathedral is even prettier after dark when the ground lights shine up on it," Barbara pointed out. "You can really see the details better then. Maybe we'll stop back later."

"Later, maybe later. I'm starving. Let's get to the restaurant. How much farther is it?"

Uh-oh, I thought. Was that my roommate? Is she difficult or is she just speaking for everyone's hunger? Will she be tough to live with? What if I wake her up? Will she be upset? Maybe I should offer her my spare pair of earplugs. Yeah, and my Air France freebie eye patches, just in case.

We turned left on to a series of narrow residence-lined streets that wound towards the nearly hidden entry to tiny Chez Fazoul at #2 rue Tolosane.

Vincent, the maitre d', who hails from the Bretagne department of France, greeted Barbara with a warm and familiar hello, then escorted the seven of us through the vestibule into the dining area. The atmosphere was charming, with a fireplace on one wall and windowed doors open to a lovely patio on the other, letting in the evening breeze. We were the first party seated in the small room, having promptly arrived for our eight p.m. reservation. Before we finished perusing our menus, drilling Barbara for translations, every remaining table in the room and the patio was filled with what seemed to be locals, all definitely French.

The menu offered a variety of regional specialties including duck confit and cassoulet.

"*J'ai* this and this," someone said pointing to two choices on the *prix fixe* menu, as Vincent leaned over her shoulder, scribbling something illegible on a note pad.

"*Moi, aussi,*" another chimed, "the same, please."

All orders discussed and placed, we settled into the surprisingly comfortable wooden-backed chairs and sipped glasses of chilled house rosé poured from ceramic carafes. Dinner conversation was friendly and fun, filled with excitement and anticipation.

I avoided the light fare like cold tomato bisque and the variety of fish dishes, and chose more heavy, sleep inducing foods. It was sometime between my *salade de foie gras* and *canard au poivre* that I realized night was falling. I began to worry. What if I really can't sleep or wake up and stay awake? Would I bother anyone?

We all topped off the excellent dinner with cassis sorbet the color of light pinot noir. Vincent set seven tiny, stemmed glasses on our table and poured us each a chilled after dinner wine. "This should complement your meal."

"I don't drink," whispered April on my left as we passed the filled glasses around the table.

"No worries," I said. "I'll help you out." I picked up her serving and quickly downed the flowery-honey liquid in two sips. Anything in any size wine glass could only help sedate me, I rationalized.

"So far, so great, Barbara," I said and we all toasted. "Thank you. You planned a perfect start."

We meandered back to *Royal Destiny* through the surprisingly quiet streets, trying to keep our voices hushed. Our bursts of tipsy laughter over Linda's witty play on words or Connie's funny bits about Greece or Ann's clever double-entendres interrupted the peacefulness, our jovial sounds echoing between the buildings. Individual personalities were beginning to emerge. The sky was nearly dark, save the last bit of light reflecting off the tiled roofs of the ancient brick and plaster structures that still felt warm to the touch from the extreme heat of the afternoon sun. It had been a long day of travel and hitting the bunks was on everyone's mind.

"How am I supposed to climb up there?" I heard someone in the aft cabin complain.

"Wanna trade?" came a reply, "I can't even sit up without cracking my head."

I finished washing my face and brushing my teeth, a challenging feat in the miniscule sink of the compact head. Completing my usual series of sleep-inducing rituals, I pulled my hair into a tight ponytail, keeping it from annoying and waking me. Donning my most-appropriate-for-a-trip-with-six-other-women nightie, I slid into bed.

Mary Jean stepped onto the foot of my bunk and hoisted herself up and across to her bunk in a horizontal dive, landing with an "Ugh."

"Mind if I read for a little while?" she asked squirming awkwardly to get under the covers. "The light won't bother you?"

Trying to be accommodating and polite and dreading that I could potentially be disturbing her sleep later on, I said, "Of course not, read. I'm fine." I tucked Barbara's book on nautical knot tying under my pillow, should I need reading material later on.

"Okay. *Bonne nuit.* Sleep well."

"*Bonne nuit,*" I sang back. "You, too."

I closed my eyes and felt the *Royal Destiny* slightly rock and sway in the gentle flow of the canal. In the quiet, I could faintly hear water lapping against the hull.

Coffee? The delicious fragrance of coffee wafted into my cabin. I rolled onto my back and felt the refreshing breeze on my face.

Soft light filtered through the open hatch making a sunny stripe across my blanket, its path climbed up the wall and to the other side of the cabin. At first I thought my roommate was snuggled under her fuzzy blanket but, no, she was gone. How did she do that – up and out without me hearing a thing? Impossible. I checked my watch and was astonished: nine thirty-five. I hadn't slept that late or soundly in decades. How could it be? Feeling amazingly relaxed, I lay in my bunk for a while longer. I had no schedules to attend to, no reason to fling my blankets off to make a dash to the shower, no computer to turn on with e-mails requiring replies, no phone calls to make, messages to return. I felt no stress, no pressure. I could just be.

I slowly wiggled upright and propped against the pillows breathing in the morning air. I sat there, savoring the quiet. When finally feeling ready, I crept from the warmth of my bed, out of the cabin to find Barbara in the galley placing flakey, shiny-with-butter croissants and soft centered baguettes on a platter. Espresso ready to be topped with hot milk she had frothed with her nifty Aero-latté tool and breakfast was served.

"Go on up top. Take it easy." Barbara smiled. "I'll pass the fresh fruit and yoghurt up to you. Who takes sugar in their cappuccino?"

Still in my nightgown, I climbed to the aft deck. The sun warmed my bare arms. The clouds were a brilliant white with lacey petticoat edges against a sky of rich blue, more beautiful than I ever remembered seeing. Relieved and rested, I laughed to myself – all that worry and fretting for nothing. I don't need Ambien or any other PM drug. I need calm, I need tranquility. And with that peaceful notion I was ready for what lay ahead, ready for the challenge, ready to learn the difference between a rope and a line, port and starboard and how to navigate the locks of the delightful Canal du Midi. That kind of pressure, I can sleep with. That kind of pressure I can *live* with.

Canal du Midi

Leaving behind vines and flow'rs of Laval
Past the warming rooftops of Montgiscard
We journey east, upon this old canal,
To find a story, challenging the Bard.

Hanging branches curtain this play we write
Under barren bridges and double locks,
Through galleries of trees and tinseled light,
Sipping from vineyards of the Languedoc.

And through the locks, those stepping stones to town,
We pattern our approach by pulling lines,
A couplet rhymed by weathered rope and sound,
In search of words that take us back in time.

Les Muses of the Midi beyond the helm,
The Canal conducting us to higher realms.

– CONNIE BURKE

Images du Canal

JOANNA BIGGAR

ᕗ

Canals, like bridges, are first feats of engineering, marvels of construction. They traverse, connect, give passage to people or goods where they could not pass before. Then they surpass the pragmatic boundaries of their conception to become something more: a thing of beauty, a work of art, a metaphor. A canal, which may cross a large area, also reflects the character of the region, its landscape, its crops, its history. Certainly this is true for the Canal du Midi, which twists sinuously through Languedoc from Toulouse to Sete on the sea, a land of sunflowers, wheat fields, vineyards, ancient cities with red-tiled roofs, crumbling ruins wrapped in mystery.

The canal mirrors the land as it appears today, but beneath the quiet of its gentle surface, the eternal contradictions of its tortured past still echo: the songs of troubadours and the *joie de vivre* that played out in sumptuous courtly life strained against the counterpoint of deep religious fervor, then the cries of horror from relentless warfare, torture, bloodshed, Crusade, and Inquisition. To travel the canal now is to enter into a different time and space, one that alters previous assumptions as effortlessly as the opening and closing of locks. In the end, one question surely arises for any thoughtful traveler of the twenty-first century: Which of this land's many pasts prevails?

REALITES

The idea of building a Canal du Midi had existed from the time of Charlemagne. In the seventeenth century, it was taken up by Beziers native and salt-tax collector Pierre Paul Riquet, and put to Louis XIV's powerful minister, Jean-Baptiste Colbert. It was a bold and muscular proposal, one to link the Mediterranean from Beziers to the Atlantic via the Garonne River through Bordeaux. The canal would increase commerce, travel, and wealth, to say nothing of strengthening the royal hold on the ever-rebellious South. Colbert liked the idea, and the main part of the canal, from Beziers to Toulouse, begun in 1667, was completed in 1681.

Marvelous as it was, Riquet's project was hardly the first of its kind in the region. The Romans, geniuses of engineering, had created a Mediterranean seaport at the landlocked city of Narbonne in part by constructing a canal. A later version of that canal on the Aude River, named the Robine, is one of many branches built after 1681 as part of the extended Canal du Midi system.

A century later, when a young America began finding its way as a political and economic entity, the idea of canal building, particularly for a project called the Potowmack Canal sponsored by George Washington, became popular again. Washington was sent detailed notes and a map about the Canal du Midi from his enthusiastic compatriot, Thomas Jefferson, then Minister to France. During his three-month tour in the South of France in 1787, Jefferson followed the Canal du Midi from Beziers to Toulouse.

His diary notes the rich soil, the vines, the overhanging willows, the delicious local wine (especially the Muscat de Frontignan), and the abundance of fish in the canal. He remarks on "the great good number of chateaux and good houses in the neighborhood," and the slightly shocking fact that women worked as lock keepers and did other "manly" jobs, while men did "women's" work. Despite some changes – the canal is now for pleasure boats and families of ducks who dart everywhere, enjoying free rides through the locks; and the maize, mulberries and beans he noted have given way to broad brown wheat fields, alternating with swaths of shimmering *tournesols* or sunflowers, turning their million faces to the sun – there is much that Jefferson would recognize. Willows still drape their long arms over calm waters and colonnades of plane trees still give needed shade; vineyards and great houses still line the banks; fishermen still troll for crawfish, catfish, eels and other fish; and those shocking women still operate locks and perform other "manly" tasks.

In particular, the pace at which boats pass through the canal would be very familiar to Jefferson. The thirty-five-foot long, horse-drawn "bark" in which he started out, followed by a private boat that he hired to haul his carriage while he walked much of the way alongside, traveled only about three to four miles an hour. He also noted that a round trip from Toulouse to Beziers would take about fourteen days if one really pushed – about the same amount of time it would take today. Because of the hours the locks are open – nine a.m. to seven p.m. in summer, with an hour out for lunch – and the speed limit of eight kilometers per hour for boats, the canal imposes its own slow and timeless reality on the modern visitor.

Indeed, the modern world speeds past on parallel tracks. A national highway runs close to the canal, and the high-speed train announces itself as it streaks past the nearby fields several times a day. Even the tow path where a horse pulled Jefferson's bark now serves bikers, runners, inline skaters, some of them pushing prams, who all, save the walkers, go faster than the boats.

Time then becomes one measure of the alternate reality that is travel on the Canal du Midi.

LE PASSE

First there is the slowness of passage through Languedoc by canal boat, then there are the inevitable reflections from the past which seem to float on the languid current. The words *passage* and *passé* – passage and the past – are cousins. This kinship is keenly felt on the canal, which winds like a slow green ribbon through a minefield of history, so much of it bloody that it seems natural that its earth is red.

It is seeped in war: Celt, Roman, Visigoth, Viking, Christian and Moor; Hundred Years Wars, Wars of Religion and Revolution; World Wars I and II, racist purges and Nazi occupation. Above all, however, the region identifies with the Christian religious sect that flourished in the twelfth and thirteenth centuries, the Cathars. The Cathars were brutally crushed by Pope and King in what became known as the Albigensian Crusade (after the Cathar stronghold of Albi, a town north of Toulouse), and the century and a-half of Inquisition that followed. Although the Cathars were supposed to have been finally vanquished after that horrendous onslaught, and the Midi is said to have never recovered, Carcassonne, whose "heretics" were all massacred, is especially proud now to declare itself "Cathar Country."

It is claimed that the *meridonial*, or southern, atmosphere of tolerance and anti-authoritarianism gave rise to this movement of Christians who rejected church authority (including the mystery of the mass and the pope), who believed in an individual's direct relationship to God, and who in some cases lived a life of extreme asceticism, turning from this world to prepare for the next.

That same tolerance also gave rise to another, and seemingly opposite, movement, which sprang up at the same time under the *meridonial* sun. The Midi — broadly the South of France — was the territory of song and poetry, the land of the troubadours. Alongside them and their travels from castle to castle, a culture of civility and the art of living well grew up. Eating and drinking for pleasure, manners and beautiful clothes, lavish banquets and "Courts of Love," where love poetry was sung and judged, all flowered with the arts of the wandering troubadours. This "renaissance," as it was sometimes called, and which predated the Florentine Renaissance by two hundred years, also fell victim to the cruelty of crusade and inquisition. Its spirit and traditions spread to Italy, to the north of France and beyond, but the country of light, joy, and tolerance in which it had flourished was no more.

Guidebooks, pamphlets and even billboards in Languedoc constantly remind the modern visitor of this past with its tangled contradictions. But they seem to be embedded in the landscape, too. The lyrical beauty, the warmth of the sun, the soft air, the imposing church towers, the fortified wall, the crumbling towers, the underground dungeons.

And for the traveler on the canal, even the locks themselves offer stark and distilled images from the past. Entering the bottom of a deep lock intimates trappings of terror — the steep walls, covered with the slime of centuries, resemble nothing so much as the dungeons where thousands of miserable souls met their ends; and the huge iron gates clanging noisily shut resemble nothing so much as the closing, against all hope, of the iron maw of a prison gate. But if this is a prison, it is one unenclosed, its roof the bright blue or cloud-strewn sky of Midi. That is the same sky the Cathars sought in order to find their heaven and their salvation. And even on the forbidding iron gates, poised to hold back or release water, there is often a flowerpot, a touch of poetry, put there by the caring hands of the lock keeper. The lock keepers' houses, too, in the colors of the earth of Midi, with light green or blue shutters and covered with vines, with gardens in full bloom, tables on shaded terraces set with checkered cloths, a carafe of wine and glasses ready, are their own testimony to beauty and living well. That refrain was ever the song, sometimes tinged with longing, of the troubadours.

ILLUSIONS ET BONHEUR

If for the modern traveler it is difficult to sort out the contradictions of Languedoc through the dappled reflections on the canal, it is worth noting that official history is equally shaded. It seems at every turn there is a legend, a good story, or a plain whopper to explain important events.

Take, for example, the famous regional dish, cassoulet, made of white beans, broth, garlic, sage, sausage, duck and pork. Legend has it that it was first created in Castelnaudary during the mid-fourteenth century when Black Prince Henry besieged the town during the Hundred Years War. Hungry defenders collected all their remaining scraps including some meat and beans, and, according to regional historian Brian Catlos, "concocted not just a culinary triumph, but a meal so hardy they were able to defeat the English whose inferior syrupy brown-baked bean dish could not compete." And to safeguard the original prized recipe, there is actually a Confraternity of the Grand Cassoulet, a group of local chefs who sometimes dress up in medieval garb to attend culinary fairs featuring cassoulet.

Another great whopper also connects food and military victory, as well as explaining how Europe's largest walled city, Carcassonne, got its name. It goes like this: During the terrible dark years when Muslims held the city, Charlemagne came to the rescue and laid siege, knowing that the inhabitants would run out of food. But Madame Carcas, the Muslim ruler's wife, had an inspiration. Gathering scraps of food from starving citizens, she fed them to a pig, then threw the pig over the wall. The pig split open on the ground to reveal how well-fed it was. Upon seeing that, Charlemagne deduced there was still an abundance of food in the city and, dispirited, left. Delighted, Madame Carcas rang the bells in victory, hence "Carcas – sonne," French for "Carcas rings." Never mind that she never existed, Charlemagne never came, and in the early ninth century, they spoke some version of Latin, not French.

But Carcassonne itself, in the very imposing silhouette of its architecture, represents a fable of another order. The crumbling and ruined remains of the ancient Carcassonne, as distinct from the "new town" across the Aude River, which dates from the fourteenth century and is the inhabited part of Carcassonne today, became part of the massive nineteenth century medieval restoration project of Viollet-le-Duc. In Carcassonne as elsewhere across France, rather than adhering to historical accuracy, Viollet-le-Duc imposed his own vision, colored by nineteenth century romanticism, on Carcassonne. His restored city included a bridge, slits in walls, crenellations, and pointed Gothic-style towers, all of which had never been there in the first place, as opposed to the flat-topped, tiled-roof round towers typical of Midi which had. In a word, he created a fantasy, a fairy-tale version of a medieval city, much like a Disneyland castle, to rise on the foundations of an ancient reality. But his illusion is breath-taking, glorious — and seductive. The French public embraced it, and it became to the French imagination the physical embodiment as well as the symbol of their own medieval past.

If there is a common thread to these stories, and perhaps a key to the puzzle of which reality prevails, it is that they all have a happy ending. To see the celebration of Bastille Day in the dazzling display of fireworks spilling above, through the crenellations and down the walls of medieval Carcassonne, is to see the triumph of illusion over the brutal reality that lies beneath. And to join in the happy, relaxed multitudes of French people who gather to watch this wonderful summer fantasy is to also embrace their *bonheur.*

For in the end, it is my conclusion that *bonheur,* or happiness, prevails. Of course, the religious reforms, and the severe asceticism, of the ancient Cathars morphed into the practices of very like-minded Protestants soon after the Cathars were finally vanquished. Languedoc, particularly in the country traced by the Canal du Midi, became the most Protestant of France. Surely this Protestantism has left its stamp on the region, although to the casual passerby, it is hard to see. On the other hand, the formidable and ancient presence of the Catholic Church is very easy to see as cathedrals, basilicas, and church spires dominate the landscape, while monuments and plaques everywhere tell the stories of relics, saints, martyrs, and the thousands of pilgrims who crossed it. Still, for all that, Languedoc appears to be very secular country with a very Catholic history, and in that regard much like the rest of France. As for the torture, brutality, and cruelty, they, too are there, a constant presence like a layer in each stone or brick wall, a foundation upon which all subsequent layers are built. But perhaps, like the walls of Carcassonne, or the ruined castles and fortifications dotting the land, with the distorting angle of time and a conscious dose of illusion, they become objects of beauty, and the blood-soaked land merely rich red soil for producing wine, sunflowers, life.

Indeed to be in a crowded market square, a café on a shaded ancient street, beside a serene flower-encircled fountain in Toulouse, or charming restaurant beside the canal, to smell the air after summer rain, drink the local rosé, and feel the welcoming breeze is to know that it is *bonheur* — or the Troubadour's sense of *joie de vivre* — which still dominates here. And to attend an open-air concert, where people of all ages sing and sway far into the late summer night, is to also know that despite everything, song never left the heart of Midi. It is as if all the riddles of the past were submitted to a "Court of Love" and judged by the ultimate jury, present-day citizens of Languedoc, whose judgment comes down in the still-spoken Occitan language: *The spirit of the troubadours lives, and has outlasted all the rest.*

Searching for Bread
in Montgiscard

APRIL ORCUTT

୬

We were in France, and we had no bread. (And certainly no cake.) Bread is an integral part of France, so clearly this problem needed to be solved.

Late in the afternoon of the previous day the captain had docked our thirty-eight-foot yacht near the village of Montgiscard along the Canal du Midi in Southern France. The seven of us – all women – walked across the narrow lane running parallel to the canal to a bar and a pizza parlor, which – in a break from cassoulet and *coquilles Saint-Jacques* – provided dinner: a large pizza with pepperoni and olives and another large with grilled vegetables. But by morning, the pizza place was closed, the gray sky drizzling, and we were seven active women who would soon want breakfast.

While the captain worked on charts and maps, one woman had gone running, one poked around the galley, and three still slept. The bread problem needed to be addressed before the women returned or awakened. The captain sent me on the mission.

"The bakery's up the street," she said. "Go to the main road and turn left. Then take the road on the right that goes up the hill. You'll find it. It's called a *boulangerie*."

"*Boulangerie*." I repeated the word. The language tip was good – I speak no French and didn't even know the word for "bread." "*Boulangerie*" seemed like the more important word – you could get croissants and pastries layered with almonds or strawberries or whipped cream in a bakery, but if I just asked for bread I might sound like a panhandler requesting a handout. In my tired blue rain jacket and beat-up "boat pants," I could forgive someone for coming to that conclusion, but I wouldn't be able to explain to them that they had the wrong idea.

My crew-mate gave up searching the galley and decided to help me on the quest. She spoke a few words of French. I was glad.

I put on the rain jacket, pulled the hood tightly around my head, and picked up my yellow umbrella with the duck on the handle, in case the increasing wind blew rain into my face. My crew-mate donned her clear plastic rain jacket. Suitably attired, the two of us headed up the hill.

With rain pelting our tightened hoods, we walked up the empty single lane street lined with two-story red-brick buildings built with common walls.

Most of the brick buildings had wooden window frames and shutters, either of dark natural wood or painted a deep warm brown. Pots of red geraniums and white begonias sat in front of some houses. One home made of new bright red bricks had Greek columns with Corinthian capitals built into the second floor.

The residents – if there were residents in this silent village – seemed to live indoors and play in unseen gardens hidden on the opposite side of the buildings.

A foot-high iron horseshoe with its opening at the bottom adorned the front of a home built of narrow red used bricks and wide bands of yellow mortar. For centuries some Europeans have believed that used horseshoes, which may represent the crescent moon and symbolize protection from the moon goddess Artemis/ Diana (or, specifically, her "sacred vulva") would bring good luck. I thought we should get a horseshoe for the *Royal Destiny* and her seven-woman crew.

Americans would say the big horseshoe was "upside down" and its "luck would run out," but for the French this position means its "luck will pour out onto you." By facing the opening downward, according to superstition, residents keep evil spirits out.

Radiating outward from the big horseshoe like rays of the sun were eight normal-size horseshoes, each attached to the big one by six-inch iron bars. Their openings faced away from the big horseshoe: Perhaps the homeowners wanted to spread the "luck" out to all their neighbors, like luck spewing from a garden sprinkler. I hoped some would fall on us, and we would find the bakery.

And perhaps the luck did reach us. Sort of. We discovered the *boulangerie* – with its tiny sign – on the left near the top of the hill. The bakery was the only shop in this residential area – but it was closed. I couldn't hear or see anyone inside preparing for a later opening. And there was no one on the lane to ask.

Although it was seven a.m. on a non-holiday Monday and we had walked for fifteen minutes, we had seen no one. No people, no cars, no cats, and none of the ubiquitous French dogs. Montgiscard appeared to be a ghost town.

We climbed to the top of the hill to an informal grass-and-dirt square to continue the search. There my crew-mate announced, "I'm going to look for the statue of Joan of Arc," and took off. It was a statue of some note, but it was not at the top of my agenda.

Finding bread *was* at the top of my agenda, and the bread quest now belonged to me alone.

I wanted to find the business district. I headed north along the widest lane I saw but found no businesses, only homes. Through the downpour I thought I saw a child, but when closer I discovered instead a metal sign cut along the outline of a life-size photograph of the back of a grade-school-age boy with dark hair wearing black pants and, appropriately, a yellow slicker (sans hood) and a huge red backpack emblazoned with the word "PRUDENCE."

One off-white stucco house sported a life-size white clay beagle on a stucco pillar in the front yard and a similar bulldog guarding the garden shed. Now I'm a cat-person so I might not have the breeds right, but I can accurately report that there was no one on this lane either – only two dog statues.

Past a Chinese-style house guarded by statues of two lions — representing good luck — I ran into the Joan of Arc statue but not my crew-mate. She, like everyone else, had quietly disappeared.

Joan of Arc carried a flag and stepped resolutely to fulfill her task — as I myself needed to do.

I returned to the top of the hill and the rustic square. The rain had stopped. Along the edge of the square I found a small, nearly hidden grocery store with an older man behind the counter inside and another gray-haired man in a maroon sweater approaching the door. At last! Human contact!

I approached the man in the sweater, intent on putting together my few words of French to accomplish the task of finding another bakery.

"*Pardon,*" I said. "*Où est la boulangerie?* (Where is the bakery?)"

He smiled and said a few sentences that I, of course, couldn't understand, but he motioned with his hand to go around the corner of the square to the street we first walked up — where the closed bakery was. I did know "closed" in French.

"*Fermée,*" I said.

"Fermée?" he asked. By now the store owner came outside to join the conversation. The two of them conferred in low and serious tones, and I heard "*boulangerie*" and "*fermée*" and gasps of astonishment.

I wished I had asked our captain the word for "bread."

"*Avoir vous . . .* " (Do you have . . .) — I *really* wished I knew the word for "bread."

But it was obvious by now what I wanted. "*Non,*" the shopkeeper said. He offered advice (I assumed) in French and pointed with full arm extension toward a road leaving the village on the opposite side of the square. All I could understand was *"trois kilomètres."*

Three kilometers would be too far for me to walk on this rainy morning – the other women on the boat were probably already wondering what happened to the bread and me.

I pointed to my feet and did a moonwalk.

They laughed, and the man in the sweater said, *"A pied."*

By foot. I understood it. *"Oui! Oui!"* Yes! Communication! Then I shook my head to say I couldn't walk there.

They shrugged their shoulders and looked sad so I realized the village had no other bakery.

"How sweet," I thought. These kind gentlemen spent their precious time trying to help me, a monolingual American, and they're sad they couldn't help me. I appreciated their efforts and their warmth. Maybe the town wasn't so odd after all. Maybe the evil spirit that the village talismans had banished was the Wicked Witch of the Alarm Clock. Maybe everyone here could sleep late and start their days relaxed and calm. What a marvelous idea. What a delightful village.

I thanked the gentlemen, bade them adieu and walked toward the lane that would lead me, breadless, back to the yacht. As I neared the corner, I saw a restaurant – no, a cafe – no, it was a bar. "They might serve food," I thought. It would be my one last chance to fulfill my mission – to return to the boat with armloads of bread. If only I knew the word for it.

The door being closed, I peered into a window and saw a

burly, middle-aged man sweeping the floor behind the bar. He had straight dark hair past his shoulders and a beard that touched his collarbone. His black T-shirt was emblazoned with red and orange flames and some stylized lettering I couldn't read.

I walked around the corner to find a better window to catch his attention, but he headed toward the door so I walked back. A beefy man with long, black curly hair and a bushy beard wearing a black leather jacket, pants, and boots approached the door, which the barman opened. They spoke the delicate language of French in deep tones.

I took a breath and walked toward them. This was my last chance to accomplish the mission. I had to do it. And so I approached the husky duo.

"*Pardon,*" I said. "*Avoir vous* . . . (Do you have) — I took a breath to formulate the only bread-word I knew — "*croissants?*"

"*Non!*" They spit out the word in unison. I didn't mean to offend. I just had to ask.

"*Merci!*" I said as I dashed around the corner and back to the *Royal Destiny.*

My crew-mate had arrived before me and informed the captain about the closed bakery so the captain thought of another place to try. She told me "bread" is "*pain.*" Not pronounced "pain" like "That was painful — some American chick just asked us tough biker-dude types if we have wimpy croissants" but "pahn" like a burst of warmth coming from opening a hot bread-oven.

My bread-quest was a failure, but my cultural-quest was fun. I would like to return to Montgiscard some day — to arrive midday in the sunshine on a weekend and meet the kind people, the children playing, and the living dogs and cats. Maybe I'll take my husband to the biker bar.

Chez Paul

BARBARA J. EUSER

꒜

W e were having our breakfast coffee and croissants under the red and white-striped awning of Chez Paul, a small rural bar on the Canal du Midi. Madame, the proprietor's wife, arrived with a piece of fabric, actually two pieces of fabric, one red and one black, sewn together. She stood at the pool table in the center of the room and carefully cut the fabric in strips, creating half-red, half-black ribbons. Then she began festooning the bar. We asked why.

Madame looked amazed. "*Vous ne savez pas?* (You don't know?)" That afternoon, she explained, the World Cup Rugby Championship game would be played in Scotland. The teams vying for World Champion were the local Stade Toulousain and Stade France, the Paris team.

She pointed to an old photograph on the wall. *"Ça c'est un stade rugby. C'est mon mari."* She pointed first to the fit, handsome young man in the photo, then to Paul, her husband, still trim and relatively fit but with a shock of white hair, behind the bar. Full-color posters of the Stade Toulousain lineup covered the pool table. When we left, Madame offered us one.

Dean and I took our boat *Lurley* for an excursion further along the canal. At the lock called Negra, we stopped for lunch and walked up the hill to Montesquieu-Lauragais. After coffee at the only restaurant in town, we worked our way back through the locks to our comfortable mooring of the night before.

As we approached Chez Paul, shouts rang out. *"Merde!* Goal Stade France!"* The wrong team had just scored a goal. The atmosphere in the bar was tense. Eyes riveted to the television set hanging from the ceiling in the corner took no notice as Dean and I squeezed our way inside.

Trying our best to be invisible – to avoid blocking anyone's view – we maneuvered ourselves to the bar. Only the bartender stood behind us, and he had space enough for a clear view of the game. Just one barstool was available. The only other seat not occupied was covered by a coat, abandoned by its owner, who was engrossed in the game. The bartender, Paul himself, saw our dilemma, reached for the coat, stuffed it behind the counter and took our order. Without taking his eyes off the game, he poured our drinks and pushed them our way.

We were trying to figure out how this all-engrossing game of rugby might be scored, when a wave of expressions of disgust rolled through the crowd. A player from Stade Toulousain had blown a chance to score.

Chez Paul had been empty at breakfast. That afternoon, it was packed. The pool table had been moved into the corner. Seven of the bar's ten tables had been stacked on top of it. Only one group sat at a table – the remaining three tables pushed into one. The rest of the room was standing room only.

A full commentary blared from the television. An even fuller commentary was conducted by rugby pundits in the bar, first from one side of the room, then another.

We reached for a half-empty plate of peanuts.

Only one man in the room wore a suit and tie. He pushed back from the table where he held the patriarchal position and worked his way to the bar. Another round of drinks for his table, he ordered. He examined us intently, then asked which team we were for. "Toulouse!" Dean and I exclaimed. "Where are you from?" he demanded. I told him we were Americans, but we kept our boat in Toulouse, so we were partly from Toulouse. That was the right answer. He motioned to Paul to fill up our glasses.

Then he explained the reason this rugby match was so important: Stade Toulousain was playing against Stade France. Toulouse was not a part of France, he said. Toulouse had never really been a part of France. After the Albigensian Crusade [i.e., in the early 1200s], the French kings from the north had claimed Toulouse, but Toulouse was still not part of France. Today's match would show the victor.

There was more riding on this match than we had supposed.

The ball moved up and down the field. First one team formed a scrum, then the other. The first half was almost over. Stade France was up one goal. Then Stade Toulousain seized an opportunity and scored. We all cheered loudly. At the half, the score was tied.

Halftime offered an opportunity for everyone to order another drink. Once again our glasses were refilled. This time it was a man of Middle Eastern demeanor who welcomed us to root for Stade Toulousain. And we truly did. A huge mound of peanuts appeared on our plate.

It crossed my mind briefly that, not far away, Toulon and several other cities had elected mayors from the Front National, the party of Jean-Marie Le Pen, which opposes any immigration, especially from Islamist countries, into France. But that didn't mar this patron's enthusiasm — or ours.

Stade Toulousain was playing as though their lives depended on the outcome of this match, as though it actually was part of the centuries' old division between north and south. And Stade Toulousain scored again! The bar erupted in shouts and clapping. We were up one goal.

The game was clearly not over yet. Stade France fought back. Every time they approached the goal, the bar quieted and people pulled in their breath. Waves of emotion surged across the room as the two teams waged battle on TV. Dean and I were hoarse from shouting.

But this was Stade Toulousain's match. With one final goal, Stade Toulousain secured the World Cup and victory — for Toulouse, and, at least in Chez Paul, for the South of France.

Ship Shape

LYNN BRANECKY

A square-shaped woman in her fifties sways side-to-side on the deck of her cruiser, gripping a mop that rests on her shoulders. The woman's black swimsuit is covered by a red tank top that proudly proclaims: *Je veux du soleil!* (I want the sun!) She stands opposite a tall, large man — too large for his boxers covered with pandas. He balances a push pole over his shoulders like a sturdy fulcrum. His tanned head with short black hair juts forward. Together, they sway in rhythmic calisthenics, exercising their way down the canal. As their cruiser approaches a lock, the man grabs the tow lines and hops off. The woman flips her wide-frame sunglasses up on her messy blond head, rushes over in her brown wedges and puts her mop to use, pushing the boat away from the lock's wall.

The Lock Keeper of Renneville

You, Guardian of Water, inviting
Us into your proud and oval basin,
Bollarding our lines to keep from drifting
When upstream doors lock and sluices open.

Your gentle face within this reservoir
Assisting those who seek out belfry walls,
Or half-timber'd houses as in the Loire,
Your voice, an echo through these stone slabb'd halls.

A wooden plaque upon your stucco'd home,
Naming lock and distance from here to there,
Guiding Midi-an boaters as they roam,
From lock to lock, past sunflowers in prayer.

Souhaite passer, s'il vous plait, we proclaim
Souhaite passer, never knowing your name.

— CONNIE BURKE

A SPORTS FAN
IN SPITE OF HERSELF:
Or How Le Tour de France
Came to Me

By Joanna Biggar

҂

There are times in a woman's life when the sports gods come down from their Olympian heights to intervene, as if to say, "Repent. See the light before it's too late." I can now comment on just such a miraculous visitation. I was living in darkness before Le Tour de France ran me down.

I do admit the sports gods had a case of obdurate cluelessness on their hands. During my one semester at UC Berkeley, on the Big Game Day with Stanford, I unknowingly wore Stanford Red, usually a hanging offense in Blue and Gold Berkeley. Now living in Oakland, California, "Raider Nation," I have blurted out that my favorite football team is the Redskins, and I inevitably schedule family excursions during Superbowls and World Series. I would watch Wimbledon, as tennis is a sport I really get, but it always comes during summer break and would require getting up for breakfast.

This year, however, I did know that my trip to France coincided exactly with the Tour (my sons, all major sports fans, hammered me with this fact), and I did concede it would be "cool," to say nothing of patriotic, to catch this particular race – Lance Armstrong's seventh and last. I even went so far as to study French newspapers showing the route – inscrutable yellow squiggles each representing a particular stage of the race all over the French map. No way, I concluded. I was going to be in deep Languedoc on a boat on the Canal du Midi, a notoriously unpredictable and s-l-o-w means of transportation that has changed little since the seventeenth century when the canal was built. Threading the needle of precision required to meet the Tour was out of the question.

Instead I flew to Toulouse to join my friend and expert pilot, Barbara Euser, on her boat *Lurley* to explore a section of the canal. By July 20, having spent ten days pulling the lines to haul us through the interminable locks, doing my own version of a "Spaghetti Western," and having further distinguished myself by falling in the canal two days previously, I found I was relishing an unexpected respite. It seemed we were stuck at a small lock named Gardouch.

The lock, we had been forewarned, was having a "crisis." Nobody knew how long it would take to fix, so in effect we were locked out. Therefore we had tied up and settled down for a long stretch of reading and writing. We had barely gotten into our books when Madame the Lock keeper approached us and called out to ask if we wanted to pass.

Startled, we asked if it was fixed already. She replied no, probably not, but the gate was open for the moment. In minutes we pulled into the lock's basin, and because we were descending, began at the top of the lock, ready to float down as the water went out. It was there, holding the lines before getting back on the boat, that I noticed an ancient bridge immediately past the lock's gate — and a huge amount of commotion. *"Madame,"* I yelled over to the lock keeper in French, "what's going on here?" *"Le Tour de France,"* she yelled back.

Barbara and I exchanged thunderstruck looks as we passed under that bridge the great event would soon pass over. We tied up on the other side of the bridge, and realized that our streak of dumb luck had also given us a prime viewing spot of the gathering crowd. Along the towpath beside the canal, the usual strollers, runners, bikers, inline skaters had multiplied. Entire families, camp kids and their counselors joined them along with an ancient man with deep blue eyes in boxer shorts, and a fit young couple on roller blades clad in scanty shorts, he shirtless, she in a sports bra, pushing a baby carriage. We jumped off the boat to join the masses and met first a young man in biking gear lounging on the bank in some needed shade. He called out to us in an English accent, and said how he had himself biked for a few hours to get there. "Wouldn't want to miss Lance on his last tour, would we?" he asked rhetorically.

"Wouldn't miss it for the world," I answered.

We also learned that nothing would actually happen for at least an hour and a half. The heat was intense, so we decided to keep our cool awhile longer in the cover of the boat. It was then that I remembered Barbara had talked of having a camera on board that she would have to get out at the appropriate moment. I asked her if this was it. She said it was, and pulled out a new digital camera, one she had never used. Happily it came with instructions, which she proceeded to read with intermittent mutters for the next half hour. It seemed that step one, turning the thing on, was just not happening. We reasoned the battery might be dead. It seemed a cruel turn of fate, right at the moment of glory when we had prime seats at Le Tour de France, that it would go unrecorded for posterity. But ever the resourceful captain, Barbara had a plan. "Maybe Madame (the lock keeper) would plug it in for me," she said, and off she ran. Within a half-hour the camera light was on, and our place in sports fan history was looking more assured.

Meanwhile from the vantage point of the boat, I was taking in the prelude to the great event, a parade crossing the bridge: platoons of water trucks carrying "official" Tour de France water; yellow cars zipping past with music and ads; crazy vehicles sporting huge talking teddy bears or Donald Duck heads; a "supermarket" featuring fruits and vegetables; a huge picture of the smiling cow, *la vache qui rit*, reminding all to buy that smiling cow cheese. Then, finally, a man with a fire hose came by, spraying some welcome relief onto the crowd.

It seemed the opportune time to abandon our spot of shade to find our place in the sun — on the bridge. The crowds had thickened and stretched down the country road as far as I could see in either direction. The few cops around seemed inadequate to the task of keeping everybody in line (the French being notorious free-thinkers) should they not feel inclined to. But the mood was of great good fun, especially as kids armed with long plastic blue Tour de France "clappers" banged on them with abandon, adding a huge smacking sound to the general din. People everywhere reported home on their cell phones. Two young brothers opposite me stood on the narrow cement ledge of the bridge, shoving each other, oblivious to the murky water, or worse, the scary lock gate below. Next to me, a pot-bellied dad in a "muscle" shirt and his two teenage sons, all sporting diamond stud earrings and backwards baseball caps, could have stepped out of downtown Oakland; the old guy in boxer shorts wandered by, determinedly staring into some other world. I spotted the English biker with some newly arrived friends. He waved. I was beginning to feel like an old-timer.

It was then that I noticed a couple of signature yellow "official" cars stopping at the other end of the bridge, and people suddenly sprouting "official" stuff: hats, tee-shirts, canvas bags. "Are they giving away souvenirs?" I asked some happily laden kid. "No," he replied. "You have to buy them." Right. In my swift exit from the boat all I had managed to bring was my water bottle. I loped off the bridge, down the path, and back to the boat only to return triumphantly with a pocket stuffed with euros. The yellow cars had, of course, by then vanished and were barely visible at a far bend in the road.

By now, the heat was having a dizzying effect on everyone, and in the persistently shimmering sun, the scene took on a surreal cast. Were there really cyclists on the Tour de France, or was it just a parade with Donald Duck, jingles, laughing cow cheese, and official water? Suddenly, as if in response, helicopters appeared overhead. A cry went out from the crowd: "in three minutes." Twenty minutes later, brigades of motorcycles plunged down the road and over the narrow bridge. As they whizzed past, I caught their curious dual purpose. Some of them said Security; others said Press. The latter included the cameras that so vividly recorded the oncoming race. But security took care of itself. With the roar of those cycles so close, people instinctively drew back and out of the way. I personally inhaled and sucked it up, retracting my toes at the same time, which seemed mere inches from pulverization.

After the rush and roar, everyone was more than ready to see some real riders. But there was another wait, filled by cries of "in three minutes," followed by another fifteen minutes, more cries of "in three minutes" and another roar and whoosh of motorcycles. This time, however, in their wake the riders came, a jubilee of colored jerseys and flashing wheels that passed so fast it was hard to know what we had seen. Barbara's camera whirred, and in what seemed an instant, we were looking at the back of them.

Could that be it? A blur that passed in a minute and disappeared in a cloud of dust? More importantly, who had we seen?

Without programs or guides of any kind, we had no clue. Was it possible Lance had come our way and we had actually missed it? Luckily, just then I spotted my English friend, who seemed to know every number and jersey and score. He filled me in. The first riders had all been independents. Lance and his Discovery Team were still to come.

And so we waited. The heat only intensified and it staggered me to think of men cycling that far and fast in such weather. There were more helos, more cries of "in three minutes," punctuated by waits of five, ten, fifteen minutes and then, finally more motorcycles. "Lance has more security than the President of the United States," the Englishman had told me, and I was prepared to believe him. In the roar and excitement, the crowd seemed to come to attention, straining in earnest to see what I, too, was looking for — the signature yellow shirt. The Discovery Team arrived in a pack, amazingly close together for such a narrow bridge, and I instinctively drew myself back even more.

Then there they were, two or three riders in the lead, followed by Lance himself. The yellow shirt, the helmet, the determined jaw set, the eyes focused on some distant place, the body and the bike in motion as if one inseparable and amazing creature. Lance Armstrong passed no more than four feet away from me on his last triumphal return to Paris. The crowd was more hushed than cheering, and I felt a palpable respect. I also felt an unexpected thrill, and sent up a little word of thanks to the sports gods.

As the Tour disappeared around the bend and out of sight, the crowd slowly began to break up and as Barbara and I made our way back to the boat, we noted that although this was a moment of glory for American sport, there were no Americans to be seen anywhere. It was a phenomenon we had noticed on the canal, too. Amongst the flags flying the courtesy flag of France and then their national colors on the boats, we had seen flags from England, Germany, the Netherlands, Scandinavian countries, Austria and even Australia, but not one Stars and Stripes. Barbara had in fact been asked along the way, with an edge of sadness, "Where are the Americans?"

It was no use to answer, really, given the huge disarray over the Iraq War, Freedom Fries, and related miseries. It was also no use to respond that the two of us were unabashed Francophiles who were following in the footsteps of Thomas Jefferson when he remarked that "Every man has two homes, and one of those is France." Despite everything, we were there, and would return. Meanwhile, Lance had just passed by on his way to a final phenomenal victory, capping an almost superhuman career, and in his passage it seemed a spirit of America had gone by, too. It was something to be proud of.

When we returned to *Lurley* , I noted again that she was sadly lacking any flag. When Barbara had purchased her the year before from an English couple, she simply hadn't had one. But now she vowed, when she went home, she would remember to buy one. So next year, when *Lurley* plies the canal, the Stars and Stripes and the Tricolore will fly behind her, and the spirit that passed by with Lance will still be in the wind.

Personal Soundtrack

ANN KATHLEEN URE

Music is like alcohol for me. As is true for many introverts, alcohol strips off my inhibitions. It's the spark to my flame. Music does more. It not only strips off the inhibitions, it releases my "inner-exhibitionist" whose secret ambition is to sing and dance. Usually, I am my own audience. Stone cold sober, the music frees me to try out the moves I see on *Soul Train* or MTV videos. That's also when I make up harmonies in an attempt to entwine my voice with the singers' melodies. I am the third Everly Brother. From trio to quartet, it's now Peter, Paul, Mary & Ann. Musically, nothing tastes sweeter than harmony. And now, with the help of an apple green mini iPod that I bought for my travels, I can take my drink with me anywhere.

On this adventure I'm cruising on a pleasure craft from Toulouse towards Castelnaudary on the Canal du Midi in Southern France. I'm traveling with six Californians, all women, and, with the exception of our experienced captain, we have more in common with the cast of the S.S. Minnow than a seasoned crew. Despite our lack of boating experience, we are an extraordinarily outgoing group: lots of extroverts, more talkers than listeners, more divas than chorus members. As one of the introverts, I'm more comfortable as follower than leader. My energy and enthusiasm come from introspection, nature, animals, art, and music. And I live alone. With a thirty-five-pound spaniel mix named Sandy as daily companion, outside of work I'm often a solo act. Music finds its way into much of my home life too. When I'm alone I'll blast Joe Cocker's "Feelin' Alright" at extreme Dolby sound levels, ignore the phone, and keep humanity at a comfortable distance.

Regarding the vacation, I knew what I was getting into. I signed on to a seven-day trip on a thirty-eight-foot boat with accommodations for seven. Friends pointed out what they perceived to be a cavernous gap between my personal lifestyle and my plans: *"Are you crazy?"* Additionally, I'd opted to share a petite one-bedroom apartment in Paris with four other trip-mates during the week preceding the canal adventure: *"Have you lost your mind?"*

"It's a two week slumber party, not a luxury retreat," I responded. Describing the junket as a party was as much for my benefit as anyone else's. It was one of the ways I psyched myself into following through once my check had been cashed. I then exerted what little control I had over the events to come, as inoffensively as possible.

"I'll take the air mattress," was my subtle way of saying, "Please don't make me share the Paris sofa bed with another menopausal woman. I'll die. I'll just die." I also went out and bought my iPod, thinking it could insulate me from the group – like the force field around the Enterprise that kept the Klingons at bay. Both acts were examples of how a shy person, like me, will do her utmost to stake out even a modicum of territory.

There isn't much time for music when the canal journey begins. This new crew must literally learn the ropes. My first assignment is to help tether the bow of our boat, the *Royal Destiny*, in the Castanet lock (*écluse*, in French), approximately ten kilometers outside of Toulouse. I take the job very seriously. To do this effectively, I must first drape the line, anchored at the cleat, over the pulpit (we are mastering a new vocabulary here); gather the free end into three-foot-long loops to be cast to the crew member astride the lock (two loops are too few, four too many); hurl the line to the crew-member above so it may be looped around the bollard; catch the line which comes right back to me, and pull it taut to keep the bow from drifting. This routine, which is also carried out at the ship's stern, is how we secure the *Royal Destiny* to prevent it from bouncing off the walls of the lock when it's flooded with canal water from above. Lock after lock – we motor thorough approximately six per day – we collectively improve our techniques. There is harmony to this, too.

On day two, I seize the opportunity to disembark when it's offered. Now, for the first time, I can tune into the music I brought with me. A wide-brimmed hat and the iPod are my sole accessories on a three and a half kilometer walk from *Ecluse Négra* to our first double lock, *Deux écluses de Laval*. I slip into a terra firma trot and it's off to the races with the Beatles' "I Feel Fine." And I do.

My view of the canal is immediately enhanced. Lined by deep-green, large-canopy plane trees, it stretches gracefully from bend to bend and I have a clear view of the countryside it divides. Pacing myself with the beat, my perspective broadens. Brilliant sunflowers on my left — each as strong and clear as an individual note. Collectively, they make up an "Ode to Joy" chorus. On my right are the canal and a family of wading mallards that glide in time. A forgettable bird at home, when accompanied by music they form a graceful unit. I follow them with my eyes until they disappear behind the gnarled roots of the plane trees that grip the bank of the canal.

My iPod shuffles to the Byrds' "Turn, Turn, Turn." The lyrics suggest that everything is just as it should be. The musical prompt helps me see the negative space between the distant buildings which is filled with clouds. It converts the branches of the trees to window frames through which I watch the slow-motion waterway ease right, then left.

They say people with iPods are prone to bursting into song and dance. I thought they were wrong; apparently they're not. With an unrestrained enthusiasm that surprises even me, I begin to belt out lyric after lyric and my pace accelerates. Some other force has control of my hips when Trini Lopez launches into "La Bamba." And I don't care. An elderly man wearing a beret cycles toward me. We acknowledge this shared moment of rhythm and time with *"Bonjours"* and smiles. The music is making France more French today.

I glance over at the *Royal Destiny* and my six companions. They're jostling each other while swapping space and tasks that must be performed. Their dance is choreographed by our captain and the requirements of crewing a boat. In fact, a lot of our experience is being driven by the boat's operation and size. Thus, music has played a shipboard role too. My shared cabin has maneuvering room of four feet by three and a half feet. The horizontal space is cozy too. There are nine inches from the tip of my nose to the base of the bunk above. This is not a place for relaxation without Xanex or music, or both. Gregorian chants, wafting from my iPod like a sedative, have made it possible for me to adapt to this floating casket, or the "space beneath the torpedo" as one travel-mate, a *Das Boot* enthusiast, has named it.

Back on the path paralleling the canal, I enjoy an easy-listening portion of the play list featuring Joni Mitchell, Stevie Wonder, the Eagles, Elton John. My companions on deck look to the shore and witness a different me. Light on her feet, her arms pump and her fingers snap to a melody they cannot hear. She twirls like Ginger Rogers. She waltzes with an unseen Fred Astaire. She is oblivious to passers-by. Who is this woman? I hardly recognize her myself. Middle-aged, I'm feeling ten years younger, twenty pounds lighter, and not at all concerned with anything beyond this place and moment in time.

I watch the languid canal stretch before me, seemingly infinite. And the music moves on from one cut to the next. One speaks to an eternity, the other – for the most part – to the hits of the '70s and '80s. I revel in this unique marriage of music to the three hundred-year-old waterway and its locks, the most graphic examples of the canal's legacy. It is a literal rush to be encapsulated by the locks and spirited by the flow of water that lifts us up (heading east) or down (heading west). The stone walls that encase us fill my senses with smells and sounds. When water surges in to support the boat's ascent, it's got the force and feel of Beethoven's *Ninth Symphony*. When the water subsides, it's like his *Fifth*, providing tranquility and time for me to examine the tiny, vulnerable vines growing out of cracks in the stone as we descend.

Experiencing the canal and the music together is the tonic I need. I go public on the second evening when we gather on deck, under the stars, to cap off a full day with a bottle of the region's crisp rosé.

"Let's sing!" I announce.

Getting the group into the mood is relatively simple due to the fact that we've completed several other bottles of the region's wine with dinner only moments earlier – and just fifteen yards away. One of my companions suggests show tunes. I suggest rounds due to my harmony fixation. Despite the fact that we're all game to sing, there is a dearth of memory for lyrics. Only our captain can recall the lyrics for her favorites and she suggests an intellectual round that renounces war and celebrates plowshares in a vaguely medieval way. (There will be no "Row, Row, Row Your Boat" upon the Canal du Midi tonight.) We eventually nail its simple melody but struggle mightily to master its words. After fifteen minutes we succumb to laughter and switch to "White Choral Bells" which resonates with at least two of us. We master it after a few false starts, though we are never really sure as to whether lilies of the valley "deck my garden walk" or "climb my garden wall."

Our foray into show tunes is much briefer. Andrew Lloyd Weber's songs prove too difficult for inebriated women with untrained voices. And, with apologies to Lerner, Loewe, Rodgers, and Hammerstein, we are only slightly more successful with standards. For example, none of us can remember exactly how to navigate Eliza Doolittle's "street where you live." Similarly, in our *Sound of Music*, Maria's "few of my favorite things" are downgraded to one or two at best.

As the evening wanes, we opt to move down below. This spares the passengers of the boats docked alongside us who may run out of wine or patience before we run out of breath. Once sprawled on Linda and Connie's double bed, we begin to scrounge around our memories looking for lines that follow the opening lines of our favorite folk songs. I have a slight advantage in that I recently made a generous pledge to national public radio in exchange for a five-CD compilation of American folk music. Realizing that I have an entire folk play list on my mini iPod I flee the group with a Pink-like promise to "come back and get this party started." Taking just enough time to slip on my nightgown and strap on my music, I jet back to the group, ready to rock and roll. Picture the introvert in her Eileen West nightie, who sings "Me and Bobbi McGee" to music that no one else can hear, then speaks the next lyric so that they can join in. I'm guessing it isn't pretty to watch or to listen to since the one with the iPod has a tendency to sing VERY LOUDLY. I'm also guessing that it is damned funny for them to observe me dancing through the musical interludes that, again, they can't hear. Thankfully, my travel-mates cheer me on with laughter and applause. They are amazed by my transformation to Janis Joplin and to the other chanteuses I adopt. Then they adopt them too.

Tonight this new group of friends has become more than a crew. We are folk singers on the Canal du Midi. We are rock stars in a little town in Southern France. A group that sings together comes together, and so my iPod morphs from security blanket to a soundtrack for the unfolding week. Once more, we begin to sing rounds which double back on themselves, as we will when we make the turn at Castelnaudary and begin our journey back to Toulouse. We are laughing, and singing, and dancing, and the wine is flowing. But I don't really need it at all.

Fish out of Water

By Lynn Branecky

꩜

I boarded the canal boat looking for water. Not the olive-colored glaze that thirty-five-foot *Lurley* navigated. No, I wanted nostril-burning chlorinated blue water, preferably six feet deep. When I travel, the one thing I refuse to leave at home is my goggles. Swimming always grounds me. If I don't swim, I don't feel good. If I don't feel good, look out. I was hoping to find a swimming pool in one of the small towns along the Canal du Midi. Swimming pools, especially during the hottest days of summer, seemed to be secrets closely guarded by the locals.

I had started my search for the *piscine municipale* as soon as I arrived at my hotel in Toulouse. When I asked the desk clerk where I might find one, she looked at me as if I had asked for her secret cassoulet recipe. Then, warily, she nodded her head, unfolded a city map and tapped on the wooden reception desk, five inches off the city map. Obviously, the pool was a fair distance, so she phoned and then said "*Non.*" They were closed, even though it was a sweltering July day. I carried my swimsuit and goggles with me anyway, in case a pool appeared like an apparition behind the Cathédrale Saint Etienne.

When I boarded the canal boat the next day, my first question was *Will there be pools along the way?* My guidebook only listed general swimming in general areas under the heading of General Activities. But I refused to miss my daily swim.

A few years ago, I had raced a bike through Copenhagen to drop into a pool on the outskirts of town. I have breast-stroked my way through five of Sydney's pools, braved a pool in Mumbai while the other travelers in the rest of my group teased me about drinking the water. Ditto for one outside of Nairobi. I knew that if I could find a swimming pool below an office building in the middle of Manhattan where I live, I could find one alongside the Canal du Midi.

Puttering through the sluggish water in the heat only exacerbated my urge to swim. The buoyancy of the boat was like bobbing in the slow lane. I watched the ducks dip into the cool water as I tugged at the sweaty shirt sticking to my back. But the canal was not clean enough for swimming and the large rat I had seen nosing its way through the water would not make a good lane partner.

People in swimsuits are always a good sign of a pool nearby, even if the pool happens to be at a restaurant. One night, my boat-mates and I walked into a local eatery where swimsuited diners had that glowing "just swum" look on their faces. And there it was: a large pool on the restaurant patio. But I knew we were here to eat, not swim. I set down my forkful of Camembert salad to trail my fingers through the enticingly cool water.

The next day, I asked one of the French lock keepers about the local pools. I approached her because she looked like she may have just spent an afternoon sunning by one. She was petite and blond and talked about moving to San Diego as soon as she heard my American accent. She would have fit perfectly in San Diego, trading the yellow remote control box she used here to open locks for one that opened a two-car garage. In English, I told her I liked to be near the water, too — especially water I could swim in. Did she know where I could find a pool? She hesitated and then said maybe Villefranche, pointing far up the canal. I scribbled down this valuable information from Mademoiselle San Diego.

Gravel crunched under my bicycle tires after I hopped off the boat and pedaled towards Villefranche the next afternoon. The wind tapped at the bell on the handlebars, providing a hypnotic soundtrack for the journey. I scanned backyards along the tree-shaded path for pools. A stately house with a sculpture on its mani-cured grounds must certainly have a mosaic-tiled pool. The green towels waving on a line seemed to signal: "Swimming, over here!" Just to check my directions, I skidded down to the next lock keeper in Gardouch, and forgetting "*piscine*" made a diving motion with my arms blurting out "*Agua!*" "*Non*" this very French woman said, pointing to the thick canal water. No, not there. But just as I started hurling my arms into a swimming motion that must have looked more like digging, she pointed to a sign on her office wall: *Villefranche Piscine Municipale,* the address, the hours, the tariff. I couldn't have pedaled faster.

I paid two euros and entered a dressing room painted in bright yellow, blue and orange. I inhaled the chlorinated air like it was fresh *pain.* Averting my eyes, I slipped past the coed dressing area into a room marked "personal." But just as I slipped one leg in my suit, I noticed white shoes lined up in a row and purses hanging in wide-open lockers. I was in the "personnel" room. Clutching at my one piece to keep it from sliding down, I ran out and stowed my belongings in a locker. My twisted suit, shiny silver cap and goggles said only one thing to the locals: "Not from here." I ran to the pool where the rules were, fortunately, displayed as symbols with a cross through each: A baguette, a bottle of wine and a person standing knee deep in waves. I had no food, no wine and no plans to surf. I chose a lane.

One swimmer, a man whose bald head could have doubled as a swim cap, looked positioned for serious laps. But after diving in, he zigzagged across the lanes turning the pool into an autoroute. Meanwhile, three young girls dropped into the water like gumballs from a candy machine. When I tried to swim straight, a girl pirouetted wildly down into my lane. A whistle blew and the lifeguard shouted in French. She must have said "Adult Swim" because the kids scattered and clung to the edges like water bugs.

Eight locks later, an even larger pool awaited me in Castelnaudary: fifty meters long, six lanes wide and as barren as the sea. Here, the kids had their own small pool to splash in, their laughter and screams bouncing off the walls. Five teenage boys sunned on chairs pretending not to notice the girls lounging in front of them, and vice versa. I had the entire pool to myself. Black lines marked six wide lanes. Like a fish set free, I just swam. No direction necessary.

La Recette du Cassoulet
(Served with salad and a light dessert)

Soak dried *haricot blanc* beans through the night,
Casserole with pork rind first, then bacon,
Add peeled onions pricked with cloves to delight,
Remember crush'd garlic and simmer in.

Peeled, cut carrots and the bouquet garni,
Water and season with salt and pepper,
Simmer for two hours, fry thoroughly
Pork and lamb pieces, all in good temper.

Add peal'd minc'd onions, two cloves of garlic
Spread thyme and tomatoes, Midi-an lore,
Simmer again, delectably magic,
Remove garni, rind, onions, season once more.

Add cut rind, sausage and simmer in juice
In Castelnaudary, they add the goose!

— CONNIE BURKE

The Ultimate French Casserole:
Or Finding the Best Pork and Beans

ANN KATHLEEN URE

⟩⟨

When touring the South of France, sensual epicurean experiences surround you: fresh, butter-laden breads from the
local patisseries; foie gras that you've given yourself permission to
sample for the first and, perhaps, only time; cheeses that are softer,
runnier and more tantalizing than any you've ever tasted; and cassoulet – beans transformed into a casserole as sinful as it is filling. On
our trip we find ourselves indulging in the breads, cheeses, and even
foie gras with requisite abandon. After all, we're on vacation. But
ordering and consuming cassoulet with any frequency requires more
than an allegiance to regional culinary custom. It requires stamina.

One may argue that it *is* necessary to sample cassoulet repeatedly throughout a Canal du Midi journey, because every restaurant touts their recipe as the original and the best. Collectively, restaurants do agree on one thing: that the Languedoc region is *the* undisputed birthplace of cassoulet. And three principal Midi cities amicably share the spotlight based on French writer and critic Anatole France's pronouncement. He declared that together they form a holy cassoulet triumvirate with Castelnaudary as the father, Carcassonne, the son, and Toulouse, the holy ghost.

A traditional cassoulet combines *haricots blancs secs* (dry white beans) with delicious, albeit heart-stopping, meats: *canard, porc ou d'oie confites* (preserved duck, pork or goose), *saucisse de pur porc* (pure pork sausage), *viande de porc ou canard* (pork or duck meat) and *couenne de porc* (pork rind). These are not ingredients that come out of cans. Each fresh ingredient is individually prepared to play its role in the larger, savory union that sweeps in garlic, onion, broth and herbs. Additional ingredients are up for grabs, determined by which town you're in when you place your order. Regardless, when mingled and simmered, their marriage forms a meal that is seductive and satisfying – a gourmand's dream.

The alluring cassoulet also boasts a distinguished history, or two. One version traces it back to the seventh century when Arabs introduced the region to white beans that were in turn introduced to a mutton stew. A more popular legend suggests that the first cassoulet was a One Hundred Years War "stone soup." In the early 1400s, they say, Castelnaudary was surrounded by the British army and dependent upon the locals to stay the siege.

A fortifying last meal that combined everything available into a single pot – with beans in the greatest supply – gave the French the energy and courage they needed to charge and overwhelm the British. That original, much-heralded dish became the forerunner of cassoulet. And today, centuries later, the mystique of the meal is lauded by virtually every restaurant and dockside tavern from Toulouse to Carcassonne.

My own experience with this *legume mélange* began in San Francisco. Le Central is a popular French bistro that has been in operation since 1974. Diners are assured that cassoulet will always be on the menu. In fact, the restaurant boasts that they are serving from the original batch which began simmering almost thirty-one years ago when Le Central first opened its doors.

On our trip along the Canal du Midi in southern France in the summer of 2005, we did not encounter chefs or proprietors who made a similar claim. Their cassoulets were put together the day they were to be served or maybe the day before. This notion of the starter bean – or an eternal simmer, like the Olympic torch of stews – does not appear to be on the French radar screen. But cassoulet itself – in the menus and in the local literature – is omnipresent. And it is often recommended to visitors, like us, who are new to the region and looking for something uniquely-Languedoc for dinner.

The activities required to crew a boat correlate to healthy appetites. Our weather was blessedly mild and overcast, some days with thundershowers and light rain. Rather than the elements sapping our strength, we were invigorated. We ate like it, too. Each morning we consumed hot, steamy cappuccinos or herb teas, fresh breads, and yogurt. Midday we refueled on delicious breads, cheeses, olives, cornichons, salads, and wine. Before dinner we drank again, this time with a few mixed nuts. Then, at a civilized eight in the evening, we hiked to a local restaurant – once dockside, within yards of the boat, other times a twenty-minute walk away.

The days' exertions contributed to our nightly appetites for hearty French fare. They also granted permission to routinely consume three courses with wine, usually a main course plus a starter and dessert. In France, one feels obliged to sample and savor as many regional dishes as possible. When one's main dish is repeatedly cassoulet, this custom comes dangerously close to what my friends call "strapping on the feed bag."

As a group, we had varied tastes and opinions about which cassoulet was best. One crewmember preferred the Toulouse recipe prepared for us on our first evening at Chez Fazoul. It was delicious, and soupier than any we tasted as the journey progressed. Her preference for this cassoulet was based on a single principle: "The beans are all individuals. They retain their identities." Without endorsing her fondness for the soupy variety, we collectively agreed to her assessment, even though beans and identities are not often paired in the same breath. (Our conceding this point may be attributed to the bottomless carafe of rosé wine we were served throughout the three-hour dinner.)

Another popular cassoulet was served to us in Castelnaudary, our eastern-most destination before motoring back to Toulouse. Going in, it was deemed necessary that at least one of us would order the dish. Why? The restaurant itself. It was called La Maison du Cassoulet. La Maison not only dished up hundreds of servings a day, it featured the dish on its placemats. Its tables had large, glass-encased cutaways filled with *haricots blancs*. And, from the kitchen we could view a *haricot blanc* wall. La Maison du Cassoulet's cassoulet was hot, chunky, and satisfying, but it wasn't my personal favorite.

My favorite was the cassoulet served at the Hotel Restaurant du Lauragais. Their simmery stew was beautifully served in its own crock with a light, oven-browned bread crumb crust. The crispy-skinned duck leg protruded at a perfect, just so, angle. The sausage was delightfully seasoned and juicy. And the beans . . . well they were a wonderful blend of both puréed and individual legumes, the latter with their identities firmly intact. This cassoulet married all the best tastes and textures in a single, savory serving: beans that were both creamy and chewy, and meats that were succulent, tender, and crisp.

Back in the United States, I offer to make a cassoulet for the first "maidens of Midi" reunion. A web search produces many variations of the ancient dish: Creole, mushroom, chicken, vegetarian, not to mention slow cooker, quick-and-easy, and low fat recipes. As there are so many to choose from, and there is no single Languedoc recipe I can fall back on, I decide that my main course will derive from the bible: a 1961 edition of *Mastering the Art of French Cooking* by Simone Beck, Louisette Bertholle, and Julia Child.

Julia, et al., devote five pages to the recipe. It's introduced by a retelling of the dish's storied past. They suggest when it should be served ("noontime dinner") and with what accompaniments ("clear soup, jellied soup or oysters, then a green salad and fruits with a strong, dry rosé wine"). They provide a paragraph of instructions on selecting, soaking, cooking, and "standing" the beans. The recipe itself, which combines pork loin with white beans, water, pork rind, lean bacon, onions, an herb bouquet, mutton or lamb, garlic, tomato purée, thyme, bay leaves, dry white wine, brown stock or bouillon, salt and pepper, home made sausage (another eight ingredients), bread crumbs, parsley, and goose fat, is a little intimidating.

All-American gal that I am, I slide back into my all-American, easy-going frame of reference. I google cassoulet one more time and identify a relatively simple chicken cassoulet recipe that compromises around several fresh ingredients (chicken, soaked white beans, garlic, carrot, celery) and sausage off the refrigerated supermarket shelf. One of its selling features is that the simmered beans are divided into two portions, half puréed and half whole. This should satisfy all my trip-mates!

I make and serve the dumbed-down chicken cassoulet to our group. It is more than complemented by the wonderful foods the others have brought. Delicious baguettes, runny cheese, steamed artichokes, olives, cornichons, a green salad with goat cheese croutons, and several bottles of rosé wine all elicit memories of the meals we enjoyed together in Southern France. And, since no self-respecting French meal would conclude without something sweet, we indulge in two fantastic desserts: home made prune and Armagnac cake and cassis sorbet. (My travel mates suggest that cassis sorbet deserves a story of its own.) As centerpiece, my cassoulet gets some praise too, but it really isn't all that good.

And so, sitting at the table, surrounded by my friends, I wonder if I should have tried harder. I could have sought out duck over chicken. And I know now that Farmer John's sausage can't pass for *saucisse de pur porc* out of Toulouse. I'm beginning to second guess the decision to spend just one day at the stove instead of investing the time and energy it would have required to make Julia's classic recipe. And then there's the thirty-one-year-old Le Central cassoulet for me to consider. Talk about getting an early start. I pour myself a final glass of rosé to gain some distance, some perspective. And, taking a sip, I ponder. What is a cassoulet, really? I break it down. I face the facts. And I rationalize. Wouldn't those first French defenders of Castelnaudary, and even Julia herself, support me in the admission that, at its soul, cassoulet really *is* just a crock of pork and beans?

Bellevue La Fôret

Bellevue La Fôret, Côtes du Frontonnais
Imbibing this tabled moment, you stand
Robed and handsome beside your cassoulet
A welcomed guest, poured by Midi-an hand.

Brushed and boating from Négra to Renneville,
You, from forested field and vintaged vine,
Fully bodied, fermented, warm, and still,
Flirting with a ratatouille, most sublime.

Pouring forth your fair and French libation
A pleasant sacrifice fulfilling all,
Salute this succulent situation,
Brimming our Gardouch'd glasses glazed and tall.

Bellevue La Fôret, Côtes du Frontonnais
We toast to you, celebrating this day.

– CONNIE BURKE

A Trickle of Time and Water

Larry Habegger

The church steeple in the village of Montesquieu-Lauragais in the Haute Garonne of France's Midi-Pyrenees has stood for hundreds of years. From its perch above the gently recumbent wheat and sunflower fields caressing the Canal du Midi it has seen scourges, sieges, and the everyday life of countless generations. But tonight it looked as if it was finally coming down.

Smoke wafted out of the belfry. Fire within threw a red glow on the stone tower. Sparks spurted into the air and fell toward the crowd below. A series of explosions erupted in the sky to the oohs and oh la las of the throng. But no, the church wasn't burning down, these were *feu d'artifice* – fireworks. The fete was on.

Moments later, the lights came up in the plaza and a band began to play French popular standards from the '30s and '40s. The "dance floor" filled with couples in their 80s, 70s, 60s, while the young stood back in the comfort of their peers, and the younger still rode a mini-carousel of cars or "fished" for plastic ducks or lit up at the sight of cotton candy swirls larger than their heads.

"These are the men who fought my war," said eighty-four-year-old Ethel, one of my four companions, nodding toward the dancers. Her war, of course, was World War II, the war that Europeans hoped would be their last after centuries of conflict and bloodshed.

We'd stumbled upon the fete by chance, a festival like so many in rural France to celebrate saints, tradition, life. I had come hoping to sample some of this life, life described by one of the lock keepers on the canal as *"une vie à part."* This is the land of Airbus and the TGV in a time of globalization. Is life along the canal still *"une vie à part"*?

The Canal du Midi cuts a clean swath across Southern France, connecting the Mediterranean Sea to the River Garonne, and thus the Atlantic Ocean. It was built during the reign of Louis XIV and completed in 1681. The French-born engineer of Italian origin, Pierre Paul Riquet, was the driving force behind the project, convincing King Louis's *contrôleur général* (minister of finance), Jean Baptiste Colbert, that the project would be viable, generating vast revenues and developing the economy of the Languedoc. The canal took fifteen years and twelve thousand workers to build. It has sixty-four locks over its two hundred forty kilometer length (one hundred forty nine miles), and equally important to today's boaters, some twenty thousand plane trees that shade it with old-world glory.

For years I'd wanted to cruise the canal. Two decades ago a brochure of a barge on a canal raised the fantasy of a quiet, sun-dappled life on the water beneath sentinel plane trees. The air would be warm and moist against the skin, fragrant with lavender and rose; the birds would sing into the early afternoon, then give way to the cicadas and other insects to pick up the chorus. The pace would be as slow as the lazy canal waters that trickle downstream captured and released by the opening and closing of the locks. Yes, it would be a peaceful, quiet time. And it took twenty years to realize.

Barges and *peniches* lined the canal near Toulouse, gradually giving way to open banks as the canal flowed through the outlying areas of the city. Many of the *peniches* — barge-like boats with a slight upturn at the bow and stern — had delicate lace curtains in their windows convey-ing a grandmotherly essence. An hour and a half at the canal speed limit of eight kilometers per hour (five miles per hour) removed us from the urban remnants and into a quieter, dreamier place. We were motoring through an Impressionist painting, dappled light on the water, grasses and shrubs festooning the banks beneath plane trees with their high arching limbs, delicate green leaves, yellow, brown, and green patterned trunks where the bark had fallen away. The trees created a canopy to shade our cabin, their roots gnarled toes reaching for purchase along the banks where the soil had eroded. Sunflowers raised their yellow faces or turned down as one, penitents burdened by the heavy weight of their seeds.

From downstream an open lock, or *écluse*, is a thing of beauty. Water sprays feather-like from both sides toward the center, a fountain worthy of Louis XIV, with flat water in front to welcome you in. *Écluse Ayguesvives*, a lock we entered early in our journey, had jets shooting from below, from both sides, and a full falls over the top. It's a four and a half meter change in depth, or fourteen and a half feet, one of the deepest on this section of the canal. The stone-walled locks are ovals, but I imagined them to be fish, with the gates the heads and tails. None are watertight; all spray water when closed, but they dam enough of the canal to fill and empty fast enough. Going through a single lock takes about ten minutes.

I was expecting the lock keepers (*éclusiers*) to be gnarled veterans in their 60s or older. Perhaps I was looking for that timeless quality a tourist asks of a place, the romanticized view we bring with us when seduced by slick brochures, the promises of ideal photographs, the needs we have to connect with something we perceive to be authentic even if it's a figment of our imagination. I know I was looking for a link with a quieter era as solace for my harried modern soul. But many turned out to be kids on summer jobs, including one young blond woman who, upon hearing my blundering French, recognized me as an American and asked why we weren't flying the United States flag. "People will be happy to see it," she said, then went on to say that she planned to move to the United States as soon as she got the green card she'd been pursuing for months.

After a continental breakfast on the boat, I spent most mornings cycling along the canal to alert the *éclusiers* that we were coming, hoping that they'd open the locks before the boat arrived. The cycle path followed the old towpath used before the advent of engines. Now the path is paved and flat and provides a leisurely passage beneath the plane trees. It was so smooth that cycling was almost effortless, mirroring the gentle pace of the boat.

Passage through the locks took on a pattern, much as our days took on a pattern of ease and tranquility: enter the lock, loop the bow and stern lines to the hook dangled by a boat-mate from above. Pull the lines up, throw them around the bollards and pull the boat against the wall of the lock, hold on tight while the lock fills and fend off the boat from the walls as it rises. When the gates open fully, cast off, push off the bow, and climb aboard or cycle on to the next lock.

Except for the motors that drive the boats and the power that opens and closes the gates, this process hasn't changed in three hundred years. It was still the same old stone lock, still the same tossing and tugging of lines. And perhaps the tranquility we felt reflected what the freight haulers of old experienced as they made their way through the locks carrying their goods to market.

It must have been a thrill to them, perhaps even a marvel, to get over the hump and begin heading down toward an otherwise inaccessible sea. *Ecluse l'Océan* marks that spot where the canal begins to flow downstream in two directions, and it is also the rough portal between the modern world and the rural landscape. Going east from Toulouse, the canal follows the autoroute and the traffic of modern times is never far away. Beyond *Océan*, the freeway and canal separate and you drift into a different age, where few roads follow and the trees and crops are as old as the centuries.

It was near here that life on the canal began to converge with my romantic notions of the region. After passing through fifteen locks, at Domergue we finally found the veteran *éclusier* I was expecting. Raymond didn't look much older than fifty, but he'd been running the locks here for the past six years after manning other locks for shorter periods. Gray tresses streamed from beneath his baseball cap and his gap-toothed smile shone with the energy of a man pleased with his situation in life. His surroundings confirmed it. He had turned his domain into a peaceful garden with roses, geraniums, petunias, and hibiscus he'd pruned to grow tall. Like so many of the other *écluses*, Raymond's patch of France was a place to admire when passing through, and a welcoming place to reflect for those who moored to stay awhile.

Did Raymond care if the high-speed train could get him from Toulouse to Paris in five hours? That Airbus was working on the largest aircraft ever built? He opened the locks, tended his garden, and conversed with passing boat-hands as if this was the world that truly mattered.

And at that moment it mattered to me. The calm here allowed my mind to detach from everyday worries and wander. In the dreamy green light after we'd left Raymond's garden, ducks swam along the canal's edges, and I remembered other ducks, other times.

The ducks' eyes always looked so cold, glazed, dull. It was hard to imagine they were part of the same creature whose feathers were so vibrant — the iridescent green head, the brilliant blue bar on the wings, the dark brown tail that fanned like a broad hand when pulled apart. I held the ducks my father hunted, looking at those glistening patterns of color so bright in death. Only the eyes told the truth.

The ducks always turned up roasted in brown gravy, and my brothers and I bit carefully, if eagerly, waiting for the crunch of our teeth on shot — bee-bees — the steel pellets that brought down the birds. Then we pulled them out of our mouths and wiped them on our plates, shot mixed with duck flesh and saliva. Somehow none of us ever broke a tooth.

Now eighty years old, my father doesn't hunt anymore. I don't hunt, either. I never did. When I was young it was foreign to me, something adults did, when instead I played sports with my brothers. My father never asked me if I wanted to hunt, never encouraged me to fire a gun. Did he think it was an unnecessary pursuit, an anachronism in the modern age, a pleasure only for those who had done it out of necessity as youths? Or did he simply enjoy the solitude, the opportunity to tramp off on his own through the woods, open fields, and sloughs? Perhaps he simply didn't want the responsibility of teaching kids gun safety and skills.

To this day I've hunted only twice, and neither time would I consider it hunting. Once, in Montana, friends and I were looking for ducks but never got off a shot. I had one opportunity when we flushed three mallards from the rushes but as I raised the gun I felt they were already out of range. The other time was in Minnesota on a friend's farm, when among three of us we had one shotgun and another friend, discouraged by having found nothing to shoot at all day, obliterated a white-breasted nuthatch that had the misfortune to fly toward us from a tree not ten feet away. I was so revolted by this senseless killing that I've never intentionally seen that friend again.

My father didn't go to war. His war, of course, was also World War II. He was relieved of duty for medical reasons, reasons that were always ambiguous and never discussed. My war was Vietnam, and having devoured World War II books as a boy, I had learned that war wasn't glory and honor but death and maiming. I remember as a trembling ten-year-old asking my mother if I would have to go to war when I grew up.

"No, there won't be a war when you're older," she said, but from the tightness in her face I could tell she was trying to convince herself that this was true. Just a few years later, after a disturbing radio report, she confessed in anguish, "They say this war could go on for ten years – it could involve all of you boys."

My two older brothers and I, fighting and dying in a faraway land: I was too young to believe it, and so naïve as to think it couldn't be true.

One older brother failed the army medical exam for impaired hearing, of all things. Another died in a canoeing accident before the draft board called him in. I simply got lucky. By the time I'd reached draft age the Selective Service had implemented a lottery, and my number was a good one, well beyond the reach of the army's needs.

So my brothers and I didn't serve in the military, nor did we hunt ducks. We watched them fly south for the winter, and now here, in France, I observed them in the canal and marveled at how they marked my life.

In Castelnaudary, after we'd moored in the Grand Bassin, a lake designed to provide moorage for boats before moving on through the canal, the wind urged me uphill, pushing dust through the narrow streets keeping its constant hand on my back. Rue du Comédie led past a tiny cinema and topped out at the end of town, on a hill that gave way to wheat fields rolling across a broad valley. Nearby stood the old windmill, *moulin de Cugarel*, and as I shuffled through the heat I was aware of a young woman hurrying behind me. Above the whir of wind I heard the scuffle of gravel beneath her feet. Just as I approached the mill she cut in front of me, speaking in French I didn't understand. My blank expression and embarrassed "I don't speak French" shifted her to English as she unlocked the latch. "It is broken," she said.

She was the mill keeper, the tourist guide working a summer job, and she invited me in for a private tour. This was the last of the thirty-two mills that had made Castelnaudary a commerce center from the time of the canal's opening. Wheat from the surrounding fields came here to be ground into flour to be shipped east and west along the canal. With the wind whistling through the old door it was easy to imagine how it might have been: chaff whipping down the cobbled streets, clouds of flour whirling off in a constant storm of dust as the mill workers applied the brakes to the sails to slow the wheel down.

The mechanism was all there, wholly restored with parts from other mills now long gone. The gear system to change the mill's orientation, to transfer the wind power to the grinding stone, the levers that apply the pressure to press brake shoe against wheel – it was all simple but ingenious.

My private guide explained everything in fractured English and I thanked her in more heavily fractured French before heading back out into the wind to make my way to the boat. The wind whooshed through the plane trees, sent flags snapping, leaves swirling, scraps flying, dust whizzing, and bent people at the waist. It carried dust through the narrow streets like the flour from the mills of the past. Bicyclists zoomed with it, stopped dead against it, and a family of ducks, wings beating furiously, hung in the air going nowhere until they gave in and diverted in a dash to starboard. It was a Wicked Witch of the West sort of wind.

When it comes up like this, the *tramontana* sweeps through the wide plain between the Massif Central and the Pyrenees, scrubbing Castelnaudary clean of paint. The dun of sandblasted stone and low profile of the town on the slope above the Grand Bassin anchor it in the Middle Ages. From the canal the steeples of Saint Michel and Saint Francis mark the center of town. People squeezed their small Peugeots through the narrow lanes, met before doorways to chat, sat on benches in the shade along the Bassin with their friends. The pace was slow in this community that thrived when the mills turned and the canal was the principal channel of transport, before the trains came, and then the autoroute, and changed the way of life.

The thirteenth-century Church of Saint Michel was a sanctuary from the wind. The stone walls and vaulted ceiling created a peaceful space and muffled all sound from outside. An old man sat at a table in the back of the church, talking quietly with visitors, answering their questions about the place's history, perhaps sharing thoughts about the town and surrounding area. The church possessed a historic organ and religious paintings decorated the chorus, but a different display drew me to an alcove near the door. There on the wall were inscribed the names of local people who had died in war. It was not grand or ornate, just the names of townspeople who left to fight and never returned.

You see this sort of memorial all over France, and it's not dissimilar from simple memorials you find in small towns across the United States: names of native sons and daughters who never returned from the fighting in World War I and II. The carnage here was almost beyond comprehension, the victims from towns and villages scattered across the land. Today it's easy to forget, even when looking back over a long and bloody past, even when knowing the history. The landscape seems too benign, the people too engaged with concerns of everyday living. Maybe here, maybe now, such conflict is unimaginable.

The next day, Castelnaudary was a different place. It wasn't the morning light or the soft sky behind it or the perfect panoramic framing of the medieval town by the wide window of my cabin when I sat up. It was the wind. The gale was gone, replaced by a breeze that barely rippled the surface of the Grand Bassin.

We turned back and retraced our wake toward Toulouse. Everything seemed familiar now: the pace, the tranquility, the sound of birdsong, the fountain-like locks that bespoke the centuries-old French love of manipulating water. Wheat fields rolled up the surrounding hillsides while a distant whine rose above the silence. A train passed a stone farmhouse, sped through the fields, and was gone. That night, no doubt, another fete would animate another village somewhere in these hills, and partners would take each other in their arms for another dance, forgetting the wars of the past, hoping for a peaceful future. It may or may not be *une vie à part*, maybe no place can truly detach itself from the modern world, but by looking to the future while enjoying the present moment, these people keep step with the passage of time and hang on to traditions that have sustained them for generations. Maybe this time, at the dance, the young would join in.

Letter to My Father

MARY JEAN PRAMIK

꒰

July 2005, Canal du Midi

Dear Daddy,

The sunflowers smell like cantaloupe in the rain. Acres – no miles – of sunflower fields, all saluting east, line both banks of the Canal du Midi, the waterway built four centuries ago to connect the Atlantic Ocean and the Mediterranean Sea. They remind me of your full summer garden, with its border of these stalwart plants. Here I am in France and you, at eighty-eight, are recovering in

Ohio from three recent bouts of pneumonia, a collapsed lung, and the confusion that illness sometimes brings.

In so many ways, though, you are with me on this journey. Walking along the canal this morning, a deluge quickened my strides. At a run, the sunflowers on my right blended with the rain to fill the air with the essence of melon. The musky atmosphere also reminded me of how you courted the cantaloupes in your garden in May. You would gently lift their delicate tendrils from under the thicker vines, rearranging them for growth and ordered your five children not to traverse the melon section of the quarter-acre plot.

We usually obeyed this command, because in late July you would call us into the kitchen to share in an especially exquisite melon. You waited until it had fallen from the vine of its own accord. As if in a religious procession, you carried it to the kitchen counter. Next you sacrificed it with your sharpest knife, filling the air with a sweetness not often found in today's market fruits. You scooped the abundant wet seeds from the center, sliced thin slivers, and placed one each into our tiny upturned hands. The deep orange-pink of the flesh delighted your five small congregants. As in a ritual benediction, we would silently eat the melon to the rind. You would then collect the seeds from this one melon and dry and store them along with the memory and hope for more of the sweetest next year.

You would have meandered through the Saint Aubin's Sunday market all morning, past the vendors with your arms folded, head slightly cocked, judging growers by the fruits of their labors. Sunday in Toulouse, with its bright clear sunlight and crystal crisp air, found us, however, bareheaded, marching in disarray to the weekly farmer's market. We walked through the streets along the canal to Saint Aubin church with its beige towers and fortress-like straight walls. Encircling this imposing structure was stall after stall brimming with local fruits and vegetables. The aubergines had a high gloss sheen that reflected each other, as the middle-aged gentleman piled them gently in a high pyramid. We wandered through each row as it braided itself around the edge of the old church. Long loaves of fresh baked bread lined the tables on our right, while flower stalls punctuated our left. We admired the small fragrant strawberries in their wood-slat baskets.

Our mission was to gather vegetables for our week on the canal aboard the *Royal Destiny*, the thirty-eight-foot cruiser rented for our writers' journey down the waterway. We bought a head of cauliflower as wide as a dinner plate and pungent long white-tipped radishes. Heads of lettuce and cantaloupes seemed to climb into our sacks. We stopped at the dried herb and spice stand just to enjoy the earthy fragrance of anise and other weedy-looking bouquets. I bought a straw hat that would come into service later on the canal. But we had to return to the boat after an hour to meet our cast off schedule.

The Canal du Midi is about as wide as Wheeling Creek in some places as our creek winds through the valleys of Jug Run and Slag Hill and Blaine toward the Ohio River. The Canal winds past more poetic places like Montgiscard, Laval, Encassan, Laurens, and Domergue on its path to the Mediterranean Sea. Wheeling Creek had its peculiar orange and gray-brown murkiness depending on the seasonal runoff, but the Canal keeps its solid green color throughout the year.

As we motored quietly along after castoff, I wondered what we would have done had our Ohio creek been blocked up with locks, single, double, or even six at a time. So far south of the Erie Canal with its own lock system, we missed the seawardness of the waterway. Land-locked in Ohio, we had not much chance to develop boating skills for navigating the narrow streams as they did in France. Lock keepers live year-round in assigned cottages to maintain the locks and allow boats passage. Several of the lock keepers cultivate flowering gardens, some with exotic and some with native plantings. Each lock had its own personality, it seemed.

Our first evening found us moored at *Ecluse Montgiscard*. *Ecluse* is the French word for lock. As the boat rocked so gently I did not notice the motion, I sat on the deck and watched the swallows glide and swoop overhead. With their distinctive black-tipped tails held proudly aloft, the white birds dove toward the yellow-green canal waters, sliced the surface, then soared into the evening pink-tinged sky. They carried on an energetic banter among each other — a loud screaming "peep – peep – peep" that seemed to say "ready or not, here I come with reckless abandon, ha ha." Over and over and over again, it was a nonstop ballet for over an hour. This contrasted mightily to we humans on the boat who sat with our notebooks and pens, thinking about writing. We were motionless while the swallows performed a continuing aerial dance. Their enthusiasm moved me to want to join them, they were so enjoying their glides and pirouettes.

Glancing toward the destination of their dives, I saw a different dance. Stick-thin, almost imperceptible water striders zigzagged over the hazy green canal surface. They seemed to be holding a convention on this section of the Canal. Dressed in their yellow-backed bodies with black lines and legs, I observed some astride each other in homage to their short summer lifespan. They continued their mating ritual and hoped the swallows would miss them on the next dive.

The vegetation in France, where you never have visited, is very similar to that of Ohio, with the plane trees, locusts, maples and oaks. I pressed a representative leaf of each in my notebook, which brought back memories of elementary school when I would walk through the woods behind our home to collect samples to label and know. The plane trees are anything but plain. They bow towards each other from complementary shores to form a leafy archway under which we pass. Their roots stand exposed at the waterline, resembling the talons of birds holding their prey. I saw several families of ducks hiding this year's new hatchlings under rooty grids of the plane trees.

The locust trees responded to touch just as those trees did outside Grandma's summer kitchen. As my finger neared the oval leaves, an almost imperceptible pressure would raise the alarm along the thin branch. The leaves would recoil in mad succession, alerting their fellow foliage as if my finger were tinged with poison.

However, nowhere have I seen fields of cultivated sunflowers other than in Southern France. There was an aura of sheer joy in the miles and miles of ten and twelve-foot-high bobbing flowers.

You would plant two rows at the most of these starchy-stemmed plants at the bottom end of your garden. But here, the French seem to thrive on their yellow and brown blossoms. You could almost hear them laugh from the fields as we motored past.

The French cook much like your Polish family did. The food here is just what you would order, since you were the meat-and-potatoes member of the family. However, you and I share a love of seafood and I so wished you could have shared the *marée grille* with its scallops, fish, and shrimp in a butter sauce with Parmesan that I ordered last night at dinner. You would have polished the baking dish with the walnut bread that brought back the texture and aroma of Grandma's – your mother's – Sunday rolls. This loaf tasted like each ingredient was lovingly selected and added one at a time and kneaded into the dough with determination yet grace. You, the middle-most child of a dozen or more offspring, would have cracked those walnuts. Your mother would have just said, in her native Polish of course, walnuts we need. And you would have run off to the fruit cellar that burrowed into the hill behind your house and pulled out the sack of walnuts you had collected the previous August. Expert at whatever you do, you would have filled the Mason quart jar full of nuts in less than a quarter hour, returning to the kitchen with your contribution to the bread.

At the town of Montesquieu-Lauragais, above *Ecluse Négra* where we moored our boat *Royal Destiny*, I was stopped by two gardens after our mile climb up a country road. These two rectangular plots felt so much like home in the evening, so like your meditative space where we would watch you out of the corner of our eyes as you hoed rhythmically in darkening summer evening or directed the hose's heavy sprinkle onto the potato rows, then to the fledgling three-foot-high corn and next toward the tomatoes tied to sturdy stakes. We ate at a restaurant called The Old Oven. After dinner, the rain poured down and the kind cook drove us back to the boat.

I just want you to know that, though I am far away, you are with me. I think constantly about the someday of your death, and Mommy's, and about how I will feel when I become a midlife orphan in this world. Over the years I grew up, married and divorced, my children became adults themselves. But the Canal du Midi, *une vie à part*, seemed to stop time. To be here in the now and live each day was what you with your quiet ways seemed to teach us all the while we focused on growing up and moving on. At first we were all busy with school, then finding a place to be on this earth, and then raising our families in other places. I somehow believed you would always be there, each spring and summer tending your garden, raising the tomatoes for Mommy's special spaghetti sauce. Strong and alert, you would wait for me to return home to ask you how best to plant the bell peppers and how close to space the corn plants, and how best to live this life through. Now that I have a moment, I find that for the first time ever, you no longer have the energy for a garden. Brother Joe planted five tomato plants and a friend brought over three bell pepper starters to keep the land alive. Now much of your time you spend in quiet dreaming between the life before and the hereafter. When I return from this trip, I will come and sit by you and listen to your dreaming. And then, I will walk out into the summer heat and water the garden.

French Dressing

JOANNA BIGGAR

༷

On a tree-shaded square in the Southern French city of Carcassonne, I said to my friend and traveling companion, Barbara, "If I ever dress like that, shoot me." We both laughed, but the remark hung in the warm summer air and kept buzzing around me like an unrelenting mosquito. What did I mean, anyway?

By "that," I was referring to two older French ladies who had come in and sat near us in an open-air café. One sported a cap of short brown teased hair and lipstick, while the other wore her grey hair straight with bangs, her face hidden behind large spectacles. But they both had on what I off-handedly call "the old-lady costume" — the plain knit or cotton top in beige or black atop a large floral print skirt of un-pedigreed fabric. In summer the required accessories include open-toed, low-heeled sandals or comfortable walking shoes, a light cardigan in case of a shift in the weather, and perhaps a small shopping cart with wheels.

It is a kind of uniform in a world where uniforms as visible declarations of one's station and class are rapidly disappearing. It's a world where men with three-piece suits, broad ties and felt hats, and ladies in svelte belted dresses, gloves, matching shoes and bags have given way to form ubiquitous, unisex, and anonymous crowds in jeans and tee-shirts. Hence a uniform, especially a voluntarily adopted one, stands out. Usually it is the young with their too tight or too loose pants, their piercings and dye jobs and backward baseball caps who choose to make a statement by their dress. But in France at least, they are not alone. In France certain old ladies stand in solidarity with them. Yet unlike the young, whose clothes demand *"Pay attention, world,"* the message of the old French lady seems to be, *"I am invisible. Leave me alone."*

So my response was "shoot me." It was, I suppose, a *"cri de coeur"* on many levels. On the one hand, it was a straight shot from the depths of my psyche, wounded for years from being incapable of truly dressing French. My first encounter with this peculiar angst came with my first encounter with France, as a young student at the Sorbonne. I did my best to affect Parisian style. It was all about the artfully tied scarf, the correct heel on the boot, the ever-present black leather gloves. This was all right as far as it went, for university students were famously rebellious, studiously rumpled, and suspiciously tainted with foreigners anyway. But at the same time I did discover a true and disheartening "uniform" nearby in a *lycée*, a girls' high school, close to the university.

As best I could tell, to even attend high school there was a pulchritude requirement that was both breathtaking and daunting. These *lycéennes*, like fashion models pointing the way to some unblemished future, wore sleek chignons, make-up, fashionable suits with skirts just to the knee, hose and high heels — and wore them to school! Another disconcerting fact about these darlings was that they all appeared to be a size 4. Since I was probably born a size 4, seeing these paragons of stylish girlhood, who were soon to burst onto the scene as the next generation of Parisian womanhood, made me realize, uncomfortably, that attaining their particular level of chic was probably never going to happen in my present incarnation.

Indeed, the decades to follow only increased my French fashion angst. The imprints of Dior, Hermes, Yves St. Laurent, Chanel, and Givenchy on American female consciousness following the Kennedy years, and the dazzling women, like Catherine Deneuve, Jeanne Moreau, Audrey Hepburn and la Jacqui herself, who represented the elusive qualities of being *à la mode*, only served to reinforce that angst. Perfection in clothes, accessories, make-up, coiffeur, to say nothing of the unattainable size 4, were clearly and permanently beyond my reach.

But it did form the basis for a life-long existential quest: I was never going to reach the perfection of my role models, and I certainly wasn't going to experience rebirth as a petite, but it seemed to be my fate to keep trying. I kept tying the scarves, looking for the right boot, and weather permitting, bringing out the leather gloves. But over time, the downward slope seemed to be getting slipperier and I realized there was a whole other factor I had never taken into account: age. At the beginning at least, I had that going for me. I had turned twenty in Paris.

However, the years, the decades, had inexorably slipped away, and with them — and the globalized culture of sartorial casualness — my youthful ideals of embodying French style. But now, suddenly, in the South of France I was encountering a whole group of French women who seemed not to care about a svelte silhouette, about clothes of striking cut or fabric, about gorgeous, impossible-to-wear shoes, or the latest color and look from that endless bazaar of Parisian cosmetics. At last, a group of French women whose look I could actually aspire to! And my response was, "Shoot me."

I understand, of course, this reaction had foremost to do with my aversion to becoming an "old lady," regardless of my eligibility to join that club. Now I am reflecting on my own grandmother, and the fact that I have become a grandmother — twice — in the last two years, at precisely the age she was when I was born. I do not know when, exactly, she adopted her "old lady" uniform, but I do know with her neat floral dresses, hats, gloves, and black laced-up shoes, she had one as surely as the French ladies do. I also cannot imagine her at over sixty, as I was, dressed in shorts and hauling lines on a boat on the Canal du Midi. In fact, I cannot imagine her at any age doing this, and therein perhaps lies the rub.

The old lady uniform seems to come with an aura of renunciation. The ladies I saw in the café, as well as so many others I

observed in the deep South of France, seemed to have been remarkably untouched by the sun, just as my grandmother, a Californian,
was. A precondition to adopting the uniform appears to be a life
apart from adventure, athleticism, or exposure to the elements. It
hints of a life of sheltered domesticity. I could, of course, be dramatically wrong, but such overtones I think account for my first,
negative reaction. It is not age itself, but what is implied by such
dress, that spurred my aversion.

However, there is another side to my fascination with these
women, one that I find deeply attractive. Unlike the *lycéennes*, who
I imagine grew into those stylish, worldly, and handsome women
with throaty voices who still command attention on the boulevards
of Paris, these old ladies have, by virtue of their uniforms, announced their invisibility. And by so doing, they have created for
themselves their own private world.

As I watched the two ladies in the café in Carcassonne, I was
filled with wonder and curiosity. They lingered for close to two hours
over their small espressos, chatting, whispering, laughing knowingly.
Their private world was obviously a miracle of shared experiences,
secrets – and perhaps even covert adventure, out of public view, behind the veil of drab appearance. What could they tell, I wondered,
of hidden loves, of life during war, occupation, and eventual victory?
What did they know of passion, daring, betrayal?

I longed to know what they were saying.

Even as I accept that I shall never adopt their mode of "dressing French," my tan from a life in the sun now an impediment as
surely as not being a size 4 was in my youth, I also quietly salute

the private world they've declared for themselves. I embrace them in solidarity as "age-mates" and realize my membership in that group as my eye is now drawn to these French "old ladies" in their imagined lives (and to babies, my other new-found passion) as surely as it used to be attracted by handsome young men. Most of all, I respect their quiet "invisibility": That, too, is the correct dress code for a writer, and a look I think we can both define.

As for the beige top, floral print skirt, dumpy sandals, and shopping cart on the side, well, shoot me.

Alone, But Not Alone

STACIE M. WILLIAMS

)⤚

"Loneliness is the poverty of self; solitude is the richness of self."
— MAY SARTON

"I've never found a companion as companionable as solitude."
— HENRY DAVID THOREAU

As *Lurley* slowly, deliberately motors along the Canal du Midi, we are passed often by *bicyclettes* and their friendly riders. Even at a casual pedalling pace, riders move faster than the top speed of boats. I had a conversation with a woman rider at one of the many *écluses*. She rides her cruising bike bi-annually from Toulouse to Sete on the coast of the Mediterranean. She takes four days

to ride the two hundred forty kilometers that separate the two cities. After this year's ride, she is going to India to volunteer for two months. It will be her third time visiting that country, giving up the vacation time the French government has allotted her to attend to others in more need. After that, she is off to California! She will be staying with the family of a friend, but isn't sure of the city. We spoke of the canal: its beauty and the lovely people we encounter on it. How everyone greets each other with a nod, a smile, *"Bonjour"* or a wave. Often it's a combination of these subtle, yet warm communications. She said of journeying along the canal, "I like it because I am alone, but not alone."

This stuck with me. How true her statement is out on this watery path. Numerous people bike alongside the canal on the dirt and paved roads. The people who pass are of many different nationalities. Some are locals out for their daily pleasure ride, others are dressed in professional sportswear – matching spandex – and fly by with grace and ease. Travelers wear backpacks, side-tied packs, hats and sunglasses, out for a journey from one village to the next. Many are eager to strike up a conversation with those passing through via small boat, yacht or barge.

There is the occasional boat that passes by, but never without *"Bonjour"* and a wave. Even on our small yacht, in cramped and intimate quarters, made so by five of us invading one another's privacy, "aloneness" can still be found.

The breeze from the Pyrenees travels past the French mountain villages and whispers along the canal to provide a fresh respite from the summer heat. Birds sing us to the next *écluse*. Although they are invisible, it is a soundtrack the boat can dance to, the water its dance floor. Sunflowers are our audience. They stand captivated at our dance, our slow waltz under the plane trees. And for me? I am learning the dance, the swaying rhythms, the musical interludes – trying to follow the canal's lead, learning to move and think and feel with grace.

Sitting in quiet contemplation, admiring the pastoral beauty surrounding us, I am silent and still, yet no more than ten feet from two people in conversation. The motor drowns out their voices, but not those of the birds or the water swirling by. The sun closes my eyelids and soothingly caresses my shoulders. I feel alone. Not lonely, which is entirely different, but definitely alone. Even so, I am not alone.

Marie Jeanne: Une Seconde Vie

MARY JEAN PRAMIK

> ⟩⟨

For many years, my daydream was to board any flight to any destination, preferably international, and not inform anyone of my whereabouts. After twenty-five years, my marriage finally ended, my children moved on to establish their own lives. I began to search for something to do for the rest of my life, something to fill the fast approaching void. With one child a professional dancer in Pennsylvania, the second a recent college graduate sorting out life in Maine, and youngest soon to start college, I knew I would soon have my chance to travel, to explore the world I had been missing.

Thus, on a desperate whim and a bit ahead of schedule, I signed onto a boat voyage on France's Canal du Midi, ostensibly billed as a writing conference – and a tax deduction to boot. An attractive quality of the trip was the peaceful demeanor of the ship's captain. Knowing nothing about her, the boat or the Canal, save that all three existed, I conducted a brief telephone interview and discovered the basics – she had sailed solo across the Pacific the previous year, had two daughters in their twenties, was married to an attorney, loved boats, owned this one named *Lurley* and published books. I sent my check in the next day, an extravagant expenditure.

I looked to this trip with a small boatful of writers as a safe space for travel without the plastic feel of a tour. It would add to and encourage my solo movement through the world – an experiment in putting myself out there, validating my existence. The writing conference would expand my work as a science writer. More rationalizations followed each week, as the day of departure loomed.

It began in Paris. Our writing instructor, Linda, suggested viewing an exhibit of the later works of Matisse at the museum in the Luxembourg gardens. I know Matisse. I have always enjoyed his childlike forms and color cutouts that seemed so like my own children's drawings and paintings. In Nice, over a decade ago, I had visited the Musée Matisse that overlooks the city's amble along the Mediterranean. With children in tow, I had made the pilgrimage to a church at Vence embellished by the artist's reverent stained glass windows that soared upward in search of light. Yes, I knew Matisse, which may have accounted for my sense of indifference as I approached the exhibit.

Then our Greek crewmember, Connie, handed me an audio tour guide. I usually avoid the recorded lectures because I want to experience exhibits without being told what to see or feel – experiential viewing. But I was in France, a new environment; this time I listened. A descriptive recitation accompanied each section of the exhibit. I became entranced by the soothing male voice. The recorded host told how Matisse had survived cancer after a serious operation in 1941. Out of this painful time, the artist – now nearly eighty years old – became inspired and extraordinarily productive. He called these years his second chance at life, his *"seconde vie."* He had been given an opportunity to further develop and define his art. He moved into this task with fervor.

The 21 Trees, a series of twenty-one pen and ink drawings of mostly plane trees – stalwarts that line the Canal du Midi – led Matisse to describe the "birth of a tree in the head of the artist" in an intense twelve-year correspondence with his close friend, André Rouveyre. Each tree in pen and ink on paper began with a strong trunk, with Matisse drawing each leaf individually with reverence.

Then my favorite collection appeared: *Jazz*. This group of vibrant paper cutouts, took on a deeper meaning now that my youngest offspring had decided to become a jazz musician, honing his abilities on drums, marimba, vibes and piano. He has repeatedly surprised me on our driving trips with his latest collections of jazz classics. "Mom's Birthday Mix" opened my ears to new colors of percussion and sound. I could hear him accompany Matisse's fourteen works in this suite.

Further into the winding rooms, I realized much of Matisse's attraction grew from the simplicity of his cutouts – how the colors and shapes intertwine and cannot be separated. They express the same spirituality that shines from the Amish quilts I grew up with in eastern Ohio. He cut colored paper and layered restless figures on pages, moving sheets here and there. Much like working on a jigsaw puzzle – if one squints and breathes slowly, the pieces place themselves. Matisse took this technique further. His cutouts left spaces between each other, where a thought or a person could find further definition.

Matisse confided to his friend Rouveyre that this second chance at life upon being cured of cancer, this *seconde vie*, had revealed to him the "space between things."

Hearing these words, I stopped mid-exhibit. The space between things. This was why I had come to Paris, to France, this year, this month, with these people. I had arrived here to try to become comfortable with the space I had developed around myself after half a century of living. To a place where I could possibly reclaim my art and what remained of myself.

Then I saw *Zulma*. Rouveyre loved this painting, describing Zulma as the epitome of a woman. Matisse completed *Zulma* in 1950, when I was two years old. He cut and patched together a seven-foot tall woman with ochre center and black hair, cerulean blue arms and outer legs – not anatomically correct, but psychologically precise and insightful. *Zulma* – so many pieces and stresses pull at this woman. A cutout, she is inorganic – just pieces of paper. But she is human, glued together and holding on.

⋟ ⋟ ⋟

The cutout masterpiece of the woman from Matisse's later years followed me to Toulouse after a rapid five-hour ride on the high-speed train. The Toulouse sky radiated blue hues. The rose-colored bricks heated the outlines of the Canal in the torpid afternoon.

At the train station, someone suggested, "Let's walk." On a cool morning in Paris, the mile trek would have been wonderful. However, my thirty-seven-pound rolling suitcase full of books squashed any fun out of walking more than two blocks. I pulled, twisted, sweated, all the while muttering "Next time, a taxi." We pass *La Purgatoire* bar along the Canal, the neon sign apropos of our prickly condition as we navigated uneven cobblestones and gray gravel.

I could not request help. All the others in the troop laughed and joked. We approached the marina and spied *Lurley*. Our *capitaine*, Barbara, waved a hurrah. One last pedestrian bridge, a melange of irregular concrete stairs, was the ultimate challenge. My companions were far ahead. I was the shortest and the oldest. I felt like Joan of Arc, martyr with a purpose. *"Jeanne d'Arc, c'est moi,"* became my mantra with each struggling step.

Voila! Captain Barbara appeared with her gentle smile. Her welcome hug lightened my load immediately.

Once on board, a survival war began in earnest. Only three berths looked at all comfortable. I went to load my bags and returned to find all berths taken. The two quiet crewmembers, April and I, were allotted the smallest and most difficult to ascend berths. Difficult for short individuals, in particular, and nary a ladder in sight. A new lesson for the *seconde vie*: survival selfishness might be required. *Jeanne d'Arc* the Second accepted the berth "under the torpedo" as my ex-husband used to describe his bunk on a Navy submarine. Neither April nor I had room to unpack our suitcases. But we did have two toilets on board. It could always be worse.

The next morning, while others headed straight to the Sunday market, I searched the streets of Toulouse for an internet café to check e-mails. Refreshingly, none were open, hastening my separation from my "first life" of family, work and worry.

We said *"Au revoir"* to Toulouse high on board the *Royal Destiny* that Sunday afternoon. We were seven sisters, the Pleiades. This plot might work, I thought: seven would-be artists transition the locks to unleash their perimenopausal energy to the universe. Bicyclists and rollerbladers escorted us out of the rose city. We waved and smiled.

A plane passed overhead while a luminous dragonfly hovered and zipped around us close above the deck. The screaming locusts seemed to echo themselves in a steady crescendo. Tensions on the boat reflected the thunder rumbling through the atmosphere. We were on a boat and there was nowhere to turn except into each other. We had ten kilometers before reaching the first olive-shaped lock. My jet lag kicked in after a lunch of country bread, Morbier cheese laced with ash, a petit Saint-Paulin cheese and the obligatory wine-with-every-meal, this one a Chardonnay, pleasingly appelled Sainte-Marie de Pins. A smiling woman played her red accordion on a neighboring boat, lulling me into an afternoon stupor.

We tied up before the lock and awaited the arrival of Cristophe, agent of Sunshine Cruise Lines. He was to instruct the crew on how to navigate the locks. I did not recall reading this section of the trip planner — that I would be part of the crew, that we neophytes were to handle the lines. Judging by the calm, blank looks on the faces of my travel-mates, neither did they. We all were slowly coming to realize not only were we attending a writing conference on a thirty-eight-foot cruiser, we were also the crew.

Cristophe knew only one speed, the stride. He strutted straight-away toward the moored vessel. His teaching technique reflected his gait: He propelled staccato instructions at the six rapt women about how to hang the lines (black ropes) on the side of the boat so as not to pull the railing off when negotiating the locks, how to cast off gracefully and tie up securely with fanciful knots, how to behave in the olive-shaped locks. He introduced us to bollards, the mushroom-shaped pieces of metal bolted onto the ledge of the lock to hold the line. He demonstrated preparing the ropes to toss them up to the crew member who has jumped off to warn (actually, alert) the lock keeper that we wished to — phonetically — 'sweat passay' (*souhaite passer*).

Passing through the first lock resembled a Keystone Cop comedy. Lesson one: Tossing lines UP is more difficult than tossing them DOWN. Our *Capitaine* frowned on our lack of expertise.

"I'll get it," one crewmember shouted.

"No! Toss it here. I'll do it," another parroted.

"Wrap it quick around the bollard," the voice of the captain boomed.

"Oops," someone whispered.

"Here, try it again. Ready, aim, uhhhh. Oops." "Hey, I've got it! Ahhh, missed,"

My melatonin had not kicked in, while the midday wine had. The frenzied scene said to my reptilian brain, *"It will be better in the morning or at least after a nap."* In the confusion, I pulled myself up into my uncomfortable bunk that corralled the engine fumes fed back by banging inside the lock as the water rose. I dreamed I slept through a silent flotation of the Ark, with stupendous bumping and banging and shouting. The captain's seat vibrated hysterically. Fumes and fumes, two by two.

It seemed everything I did was wrong. Crew members grumbled that I had disappeared while *they* labored through the second lock without their noticing that they had highjacked every job on board, leaving me to feel, well, slightly insignificant.

Lightning in the east sliced the early evening sky. Thunder punctuated the tensions after a very long first day navigating the Canal. Rain tapped into our respite as we huddled below in the evening, tied up at Montgiscard. Linda lectured about current travel writing trends, writing about place, third person omniscient narrator. I realized, *"I am very hungry, irrespective of time zone."*

"Find your niche," said the instructor and my mind flew to the isosceles triangle that was to be my sleeping quarters for the next six nights. Covered with a rather warm and fuzzy ochre-colored blanket atop a two-inch plastic-covered mattress, the best term to describe my feelings . . . chagrin. At least the small porthole opened above the waterline.

After class, we had an intense group discussion about dinner.

The sky had cleared and we gathered on the upper deck. We could walk a mile into the nearest town to a restaurant, or we could cross the street and bring home pizza and salad.

I watched the swallows' aerial ballet, diving to the water's surface, darting close, then ricocheting apart back to the twilight sky. On the Canal's surface, water striders skimmed along with their six legs akimbo. Some straddled their paramour from behind for a night of French love. Nearby, a white Labrador retriever rustled his chains lumbering into the shade of a doghouse that had been decorated by a white picket fence and red geraniums.

The vote was unanimous – the path of least resistance – La Pizzeria de l'Ecluse, across the country road from our mooring. Excellent pizza and rosé, a Chateau Trois Moineaux de Gaillac. We sat atop the boat in the fading sunlight, enjoying the warmth of the oncoming evening.

At 3:43 a.m., all was quiet outside. A cat kept guard on the stone fence that bordered the opening to the lock. A red-pink neon circle spun a bleep-bleep-bleep continuously above the door of a video rental shop. Lightning caressed the northeast horizon and the cat walked down the stone fence into the darkness. I returned to my bunk from the prow of the cruiser. Everyone slept.

I began our second day by running – alone – on the tar path bordering the Canal. Gaining strength by finding my body moving through familiar action, I decided to volunteer for tasks on the boat. I asked to take the helm. Under the watchful eye of the captain, I began steering wild S's, first left then right. After three hours of intermittent practice and centering focus, the wheel felt solid and my steering calmed. We had to duck under several low bridges. The Captain took us through the deep double lock. Joel the lock keeper turned the water on full bore to speed the filling. The boat bobbed with the turbulence and the lines demanded amazing strength. I planted my sandaled feet solidly against the railing to keep from flying over the metal balustrade.

The Pleiades were indeed stars, their individual personalities lighting up the stage of the boat. I was still sorting out my melatonin levels and basal cortisol titers. My body normally requires five days to gain sea and land legs after crossing the Atlantic. With this group, I did not have the luxury of time, it was survival or else.

At times, personal interactions grated. "Be gracious," commanded one mate, handing me a bottle of water. "Don't take it personally," said another, not explaining how to take a critical comment impersonally. Joyce Carol Oates and Alice Walker's zeal for solitude seemed most attractive at such moments. I found it difficult to write with all the laughter, singing, chatter, grandstanding and intermingling. The boat's buzz flooded the pathways to what I think and feel and drowned the space between things I sought.

I tried to apply some of the instructor's *bon mots* about writing to living on the boat. "Don't strive to blend in and don't retreat. Don't be shy about how you feel, this is what it's all about." And then, "Don't be fearful, use humor, you can relax and laugh. Stress, release."

We passed the peak of the canal — *le seuil* — where the water begins to flow toward the Mediterranean. We tied up at Le Segala, a small town surrounded by red clay tiles piled high at a tile factory.

Actually, the tile factory was the town. Walking through all four square blocks of the village, I began to gain a clearer understanding of what Matisse described as the space between things, space that sometimes bound people and places together.

We had a jovial supper at Le Relais de Riquet alongside the Canal. "*Josianne pas* (not) *Josephine,*" laughed our hostess. Marquise, the resident canine, welcomed the seven maidens of the Midi, as we began to call ourselves. We shared a cassoulet dessert after our various main courses. With enough *vin du pays d'Oc*, each of us relaxed into her own space.

Our late morning push off allowed me to try one of the bikes. I needed to move faster than eight knots. I had thought the bike too large, but it fit me well enough. Pedaling past fields full of sunflowers again added new space to my trip. Through locks and more locks, I became expert at handling the lines around the bollards on shore.

In Castelnaudary, I found the center, that space around myself, like Matisse's red and black seaweed and azure balls of twine. I could look at the crew with open eyes and still hold onto who I was. This sense of presence allowed me to defend my actions with unquestioning zeal. Pushing back against the star-like Pleiades was slow in coming, goodness, a whole five days. Listening to the conversation, it did not matter that I had no famous friends or PhDs or extraordinary adventures. Why, I was just starting my *seconde vie.* Enjoying each of these six individuals for herself ironically strengthened my sense of who I was. I laughed as I watched two crewmembers share an iPod, programmed with '60s favorites, dancing home to the *Royal Destiny.*

It was time for the return. We aimed to reach Toulouse in about one-third the time it took to dock at Castelnaudary. Retracing our kilometers, it was difficult to steer into the headwind. I found the boat did not respond as before, the zigzag wide S's returned. *Capitaine* vibes said *"Please shape up."* My new sense of space said *"Hey, I can only do what I can right now."* We passed wildflowers that mimed the Queen Anne's lace of my childhood in Ohio. The roots of the plane trees lining either side of the Canal resembled claws of ancient birds holding the shores together. Duck families hid among the talons. Green leafy vegetation bowed overhead.

Later that day, I rode the bike nearly twenty kilometers along the path. The surge of power on the old bike felt tremendous. I was the messenger to the lock keeper at *Ecluse Négra*, where we would dock for the night. As I staked out a dock site, Jean the lock keeper, with his wry smile and twinkling eyes, walked over to where I rested against the bike. We chatted in his excellent English and my half-French. He had been lock keeper for five years. He cared for the gardens around the lock as well, and the Chapel with its beautiful woodcarvings.

Did he like this job? I loved the way the French say *"pfooot"* and roll their lips to answer such questions. Further explanations would have to wait as the *Royal Destiny* rounded the bend with our stalwart *capitaine* at its helm. I felt so present in that moment, only the word "joy" could describe my sense of place and space.

In the early morning, Linda and I ran and talked, past the fields of sunflowers with freeway noise rising in the distance. As we cast off at Négra, lock keeper Jean, with his wide grin and enchanting scar on his left cheek, quickly picked a bouquet of his cultivated lavender and handed it to me as the boat sank into the lock. Later I divided the stems among my fellow travelers to press among the pages of our writing notebooks.

In six days, traveling from Toulouse to Castelnaudary and back interrupted the frenzy of my American way of life. I focused in the moment. It was yoga on a moving floor. The locks served as metaphors. They were like our newfound relationships, up and down, growing as long as we worked together navigating the Canal du Midi. We toasted each other as we neared our destination, "May the Pleiades, the Seven Sisters, shine on the Canal du Midi."

Rather than outlining a new life path or acquiring another personality during this maiden voyage on the Canal du Midi, I found, instead, the space between things, where I firmly resided. And for now, that is enough.

Trying to Punt

ETHEL F. MUSSEN

⟩⟨

We motor purposefully from lock to lock on the Canal du Midi, an historic canal I've long wanted to explore. Now I find myself one of five strangers crewing a thirty-five-foot yacht from Toulouse east to Castelnaudary and back. We count the families of paddling ducks as we pass on waters dappled by the reflections of poplars lining the banks. Early mornings we wait for the fields of drooping sunflowers to become golden and open to the warming sun. We duck under arched brick bridges filled with onlookers leaning over the walls and waving us on as we glide, dock, moor, and wait for the green waters to rise or drop until the gate is ready to open at each lock on our journey.

The captain has assigned us our duties. She steers her craft and maps the route and the stops for she knows the canal and the guardians of the locks. Larry, the only male, takes one bicycle and the two girls alternate with the second bike. Shortly after breakfast, the riders take to the path along the canal to ride to the next lock and meet us when we moor. Either nimble Stacie or willowy Lynn and I are left to coil the lines and toss them to the waiting riders when we approach the next lock. On shore, they grasp and pull the ends taut around the bollards and hold us fast while the lock keeper sends his waters rushing in.

We on board watch the fenders tied to the sides of the boat and push away when necessary to make sure we do not scrape the wet walls. Barbara, our mariner, leaps from behind the wheel as we make fast to direct the mooring. I try to flatten myself as she rushes past, always politely murmuring, "Excuse me, Ethel." I would like to be more helpful, but apparently in deference to my advanced years, I have been relegated to coiling lines, watching fenders and pushing off walls. Of all crew jobs, my one area of expertise is washing the dishes after breakfast and lunch. Here I excel, since the girls from the Midwest and East know little of washing in desert conditions, that is, the fine art of rinsing and washing without wasting the precious hot water in the instant heater. I take solace in my galley duties, though I would like to master the art of flinging the rope upward and having it caught easily by my fellow sailors.

I am reminded that over the years, my husband and I took occasional canal and river trips. Wryly I recall another waterway:

the River Cam in England. Today on the Canal we encounter occasional boats, but on that summer day in 1969, the Cam was bustling. The river was a little wider at the boat dock there, not far from the sloping fields of Cambridge University. We gazed at the punters on their crafts and both our children shouted immediately "Daddy, let's do that, let's go out there too!"

Paul hesitated, tried to say no. I agreed, since I had doubts about his boating skills. He had served in the Navy, but his wartime stint was spent behind desks. Michele and Jimmy hopped in place and insisted, begging until Paul at last consented.

We paid our five bob to the boy in charge of the punts and soon we gingerly boarded the long narrow floating object that was neither canoe, raft, nor gondola, but some combination of all three. The children sat upright, anticipating our journey. Other punters poled their way by us in both directions on the river. A wide grassy bank beckoned to us on the other side where lovers lolled, gazing at our little family. Alongside us, lively couples dashed or swung around us, skillfully manipulating their poles as they moved from shallow to deeper waters.

We waited breathlessly as Paul adjusted his grip up and down the pole, trying to get some purchase from the bottom of the river to move us out from the dock. We leaned empathically with him in each direction as he tried to move. "Left," we urged and leaned all together to help him. Nothing changed. Right we leaned, and then tried rotating a little to see if our movements could coax the flat bottom to turn.

"Stand back!" "Make an angle with the pole!" "Shove off!" Each shouted a solution.

At last the punt angled away from the dock and seemed to feel the middle of the river before embracing it. "We're turning!" the kids shouted joyfully, and indeed we turned in a fine arc away from the dock.

Other craft passed us, some left, some right; women sat back on their cushions, trailing delicate hands in the golden waters as they rippled by. It was a scene stolen from *Masterpiece Theatre*.

Paul leaned again on the pole and tried to move us straight down river. We leaned with him but the boat slowly circled back toward the dock.

"Push away!" Michele directed, but the circle persisted; neither bow nor stern had a nautical vision of where they were or should be. Paul tried again. His long arms strained, his face dripped with effort in the sunny afternoon.

"Push the other way!" we chorused, but no matter how he tried to place or move the pole, the boat remained in its orbit one length away from the dock, circling, circling. Too far to step off, too inept to move away, we finally gestured to the boy on the dock, who extended a grappling hook to Paul and graciously refrained from smiling or laughing. He motioned to Paul to raise his pole from the river bottom, towed us into the dock and helped us step off onto the landing. We had been punters for just thirty minutes. The boy refunded a share of our hour's deposit.

Silently we left the river and walked a block towards town before anyone spoke. While Paul gathered together his bruised ego and worn body, I ushered the children ahead of me. I knew that Paul had never mastered the art of the bicycle and had only recently learned to drive. I had ceased asking him to do any household carpentry after he hung six cup hooks in our cupboard at forty-five degree angles, rather than plumb and flat against the shelf, and never even noticed.

"One thing you have to learn about Daddy is that he wants very much to please you and try fun activities, but some tricks he just can't do very well, and it really upsets him to try and not be able to finish." I tried to console us all. "Think of all the wonderful things we did do this summer. He took us to the tops of the coliseums in Rome and Arles, to the aqueduct at Nimes and the tops of San Marco, St. Paul's, Notre Dame, and the Eiffel Tower. We went swimming in the Mediterranean at Cannes and even managed a *pedalo* on the Lake near Fayence. Everything was an adventure. Maybe we can stick to asking Daddy to do what he's good at."

Thirty-six years after our punting experience, Paul has passed away; our children are adults. I am voyaging on *Lurley* on the Canal du Midi with shipmates the ages of my children and grandchildren. I was never a biker. My back is too stiff to allow me to leap quickly from the boat to the quay. My once-firm arms are no longer strong enough to haul in the lines as water surges into the locks. As much as I want to participate in the adventure, the challenge of ascending and descending the locks, these are tricks I can't do very well. It would upset me to try and fail. Standing discreetly aside on the deck, I understand Paul as I never did before. May my shipmates – and my children – do the same for me.

Le Relais de Riquet

Il y a du vrai dans ce que vous dites,
Oh yes, there is some truth to what you say,
Marinated scallops bedded in leeks,
Grilled scampi, sanctioned special of the day.

Il y a du vrai dans ce que vous dites,
Encouraging your Midi-an menu,
By suggesting delicacies without meat,
Like garlic mussels and sea snails for two.

Il y a du vrai dans ce que vous dites,
Recommending a pleasing chilled Corbières,
Speaking your English phrases while we eat,
There, in Le Segala, a French affair.

Josianne, there is truth to what you say,
Your Inn, an honor to Monsieur Riquet.

– CONNIE BURKE

Vignettes

LARRY HABEGGER

The Canal du Midi flows as lazily as time, gently descending its tree-lined way to the Mediterranean or the River Garonne to link with the Atlantic. Days spent on the canal move with the same easy rhythm, allowing the soul time to drift and form impressions.

Cruising

In the cabin the motor rumbles like a snoring beast, humming up through my bones, exhaling in oily breaths. From there I see the canal the way the captain sees it, rolling along in a steady green stream sparkling in the sun, the trees forming a leafy tunnel. On the bow the motor is muffled and far behind, the odor of burned fuel too distant to notice. There the canal waters greet me silently, the smells of the muddy banks and dry fields merge and dance in an earthy stew. Songbirds warble morning greetings, announcing their presence and marking territory with pure aural poetry. And the world glides by on all sides, unaware of our passing.

Boats and Traffic

A lot of boats cruised the canal, but we didn't see any working boats. The barges and *peniches* – all so large they'd fill each lock themselves – were all moored near Toulouse. We saw sailboats with their masts dismantled and strapped to their decks on their way to the sea or ocean; private boats owned by locals or others who spend their summers on the canals; rented boats from Sunshine Cruise Line and Locaboat and Crown Blue Line and Navi-Canal. With them we saw a wide variety of sailors. One crew of two repeatedly lost control of their boat in the locks, less through poor boating skills than pure lack of attention. They were trailed by an aggressive boatman who, for all his arrogance, handled his boat well, and without his skills at avoidance would have had several collisions.

The renters tended to use the technique of scraping along the side of the lock to help them make a safe exit when they left – not recommended, especially if you don't have full rubber stripping along the hull of your boat. But they did it just the same.

Tow Paths and Cycle Routes

A father with a toddler in a bicycle seat rode alongside our boat at our exact speed, staying with us from one lock to the next so his son could keep a close watch on us. I didn't appreciate how hard it was to do until I got on a bike myself. To cycle at the boat's pace I felt I was standing still. But there were many paces along the tow path. Local octogenarians shuffled along with canes and dogs; younger folk strode for their daily exercise; cyclists out for an easy spin rolled by in conversation; other cyclists whooshed past almost like ghosts, their bikes as silent as the canal; others still, a mob of racers attired in yellow and black carrying flags as if members of the flying bumblebees, shouted at each other and forced everyone else out of their way. Yes, there was a lot of traffic on the tow path, even children looking for butterflies.

Cycling

The bicycle was a hybrid – not a racing bike nor a mountain bike, more a throwback to the broad high handlebars and comfortable wide seats of the bikes I'd grown up on. Like the old Schwinn Cruisers of the 1950s, it had the feel of a bike built for observation, meant for idling along lakes and parks and taking everything in. Except this one had many gears to make the occasional hump in the path easier to handle. Cycling provided a relaxed alternative for navigating the canal. From the bike I could stop at will to admire the girth of a tree or the puzzle-pattern of its bark – the yellows and greens and browns where bark had sloughed off or still adhered. I could take in the full breadth and depth of a sunflower field or seek out the ideal vantage to frame the canal and plane trees with the eye of a painter. I could stop and admire the flow of water over the locks before the boat arrived and imagine I was in a mini Versailles or Vaux-le-Vicomte, and I could do it all almost without effort because the bikes ran so smoothly and the path was so flat. It was a ride in the park.

Walking

We had only a kilometer to the next lock, so rather than get the bike off the boat I strode off, knowing that I could easily walk three miles per hour while the boat moved at five. With an adequate head start I could beat the boat there. Soon I fell into a rhythm completely different from cycling or cruising on the boat. The world was utterly silent. No motor rumbled through my body, no cycle beneath me crunched gravel or rattled over bumps. The only sounds were my breathing, the faint rustle of my clothing, the light touch of my sandals on the path. The water made no sound. The trees were still, as if holding their breath in the windless morning. The only being moving in this dreamy green world was me, and it felt as though I were walking through time.

The Locks – Gardens and Houses

The *écluses* (locks) give the canal its personality – sturdy stone, fish-shaped ovals with iron gates that open and close on gear-driven hinges. They hold back the canal but spurt and spray as if engineered as fountains rather than sealed doors. The ivy-covered arch at *Ecluse de la Méditerranée* welcomes you as if you're coming home, a leafy green portal into a tranquil world. *Ecluse l'Océan* marks the boundary between the present and the past, drifting away from the roads and remnants of our times, broad sunflower fields giving way to sweeping, terraced fields of wheat. On one side you drop toward the Atlantic, the other side toward the Mediterranean.

Every lock has an elegant stone house flanking it, often on both sides of the canal. Many are festooned with flowers: petunias lining the tops of the lock gates, geraniums on window sills and lawns, oleanders marking boundaries for the pathways, even hibiscus pruned to grow tall like trees. Some of the *éclusiers* take deep pride in their gardens, treating their dominions as their own little patches of France where they nurture beauty between opening and closing the locks, beauty for themselves and all who pass by.

Friends

Time passes, sometimes unaccountably. I left Languedoc and returned to Toulouse and the Midi-Pyrénées to visit friends who live in the country a short distance from Gaillac. Their house — a two-story converted stone pentagon of uncertain vintage and even less certain function — they converted into comfortable living quarters and are hard at work on expansion. They took me in and showed me around the nearby villages — Castelnau de Montmiral, Puycelci,

Penne — all picturesque medieval hill towns where it was impossible not to think of life in those times when marauders came to lay siege, or worse, when crusaders launched by a venal church hierarchy rolled through, and unable to tell a heretic from the holy, were told to slay them all.

I've known my friends for twenty years. We've lived in privileged times, with no worries about inquisitions, persecution of nonbelievers, or barbarians overrunning our towns. Their home looks over a valley and on a clear day they tell me you can see the Pyrénées. As we sat in the evening light and watched darkness gradually drift over the land, the silence grew so deep it seemed to reflect the quiet of those thousands of lost souls murdered by the keepers of their own faith. Lights began to twinkle on the horizon and I asked if it was a town.

"No, it's the autoroute. Those lights are the cars. If you watch carefully you can see they're moving."

Cars on the autoroute. People moving from place to place. Life goes on. I watched the twinkling lights, barely perceptively moving, and saw not cars, but the souls of the innocent.

Anything But Plain

STACIE M. WILLIAMS

ᢞ

"When the root is deep,
there is no reason to fear the wind."
—CHINESE PROVERB

There are more than 20,000 plane trees along the banks of the Canal du Midi in the South of France. Planted there prior to the canal's opening in 1681, they provide lanes of shady cover for those traversing the waterways beneath them. Between the locks *Ecluse La Domergue* and *Ecluse La Planque,* the trees lunge across the canal towards each other so far they appear to be lovers parted and straining for one last kiss. The space between their leafy arms and fingers provides for the sun's occasional bursting forth to warm and bronze our skin.

Who knows how old some of these friends may be? Most of the plane trees are so thick I would be unable to circle my arms around their circumference. Are they the originals? Have they managed to survive over three hundred years? Some appear quite young as though they could be re-planted versions of their forefathers. They don't extend nearly as far across the canal nor do they provide as much cool shade as the older generations standing tall and strong.

Even as I gaze at their height and expanse, wondering about their ages, I find it is their roots that most fascinate me. They are plentiful: an abundance of gnarled, twisted, snaking pieces for each tree. They creep and slither towards the water, grasping the ground and then delicately dipping in their toes. It is no wonder these trees flourish. They can drink all day and night from a ready glass of water kept filled for their refreshment.

Beneath the trees, covering the ground between bike path and canal, greenery thrives: a variety of grasses, small plants and simple ground cover. In some spots this verdant carpet has been reduced by something that has ripped their roots from the ground leaving primarily dirt. Yet in these spots, new growth can be seen making its way through the earthy dust. Despite having been uprooted, destroyed, nature cycles forward to create anew.

Trobairitz – Tracing the Songs of Uppity Women

Joanna Biggar

ᕱ

Some of my earliest and fondest memories of childhood are those of walking hand-in-hand with my father through the naves or down the winding staircases of various Anglican churches. There was something deeply moving to me about the beauty of gothic form and structure, about the oddly distorted, multicolored figures in stained glass – especially the elongated women who seemed to be every girl's vision of the beautiful princess. If my father's intent was for me to follow in his footsteps, he was successful in ways he could not then have fathomed. I did not follow him into the conservative and financially promising profession of banking; I became a medievalist.

My memory of the decade of my twenties is that of juggling babies on my hip while squinting interminably over some medieval manuscript as I pursued a Ph.D. in French literature at Rice University. My declared specialty was the Middle Ages, and while I wrote my dissertation on the fifteenth century poet Charles d'Orleans, a royal duke in whose name Jeanne d'Arc lifted the siege of Orleans, my fascination with the rich literature of Languedoc, the land of the South, in the Provençal (or Occitan) language grew over time. I became enamored with the lyricism and sound and the startling content of the poetry of the troubadours. For a time, I was actually pretty adept at reading them in their original tongue.

Jaufre Rudel, Peire Vidal, Arnaud Daniel, and Bernart de Ventadorn, these and others were my familiars and my guides as I explored the land of Midi and the legacy of its astonishing, vanquished high culture. These troubadours were practitioners of an art form and a sensibility, courtly love, new to the Western World. Borrowing heavily from the poetry and civilization of Islamic Spain, the new sound of the troubadour distinguished itself by singing the praises of a beloved who was basically unattainable to the poor poet. This was for two reasons: the troubadour was of a lower station than the lady (many were commoners or lesser gentry), and the high-born lady was always married. Thus courtly love was by nature unrequited and unfulfilled, and the lady therefore rarified, distant, and idealized, while the love the poet felt for her was comprised of joy and torture (often compared to sickness), probably in unequal parts. Eventually — as can be seen in the work of Dante and Petrarch, direct descendents of the troubadours – the lady in question (Beatrice and Laura respectively) became increasingly an idea and less a real person, and in Petrarch's case some scholars have suggested she never existed at all. So the quest for courtly love, a concept as profoundly male as was crusading warfare, evolved into a spiritual quest – the pursuit of a virtuous ideal – whose purpose was to elevate the adoring, heart-struck lover. In fact, placing the idealized lady on an untouchable pedestal was in sharp contradiction to the actual status of women, who were controlled by fathers, husbands, or the "lords" for whom they worked, and a highly misogynistic church. In a final incarnation, after the Albigensian Crusade instigated by the church to wipe out the heretical Christian sect of Cathars and also the flourishing culture of Languedoc – epitomized by troubadours and the flowering of courtly love – the idealized lady was transformed into Mary and the cult of the Virgin.

These notions were deeply embedded in me through all those years of study in my youth. But in the end, perhaps not surprisingly, there was not a huge demand for medievalists, so I left my beloved poets behind to pursue other, if equally impecunious, careers. Therefore, I was unaware until about fifteen years after its publication, of a book that still astonishes me and completely upended some of the most basic things I thought I knew about the nature of the Middle Ages. *The Women Troubadours*, published by Paddington Press, Ltd., in 1976, by author Meg Bogin is dedicated *A totas las valens femnas/ qu'an cantat ses estre cantadas* – *To all the valiant women/ who have sung and gone unsung.*

Women Troubadours, or *trobairitz* in Occitan! The very title seemed a contradiction. And so those *unsung* singers – the women – entered my consciousness and names such as Castelloza of Le Puy, Lombarda from Toulouse, the famous Countess of Dia, and Bieiris de Romans became my new guides to the Midi.

We still know tantalizingly little about them and their sisters in song. While there are some four hundred known male troubadours, the names of only twenty women have survived, all of them from the Midi, and all of them noblewomen – the only ones who would have had access to courtly tradition, whose lives would have been important enough to record even fragmentary data about, and who might have been literate. There is some debate as to whether the troubadours, male or female, actually wrote down their own songs or merely composed them. For most of the *trobairitz* only one poem, or some fragments of a poem, a total of twenty-three altogether, still exist. Yet theirs are strong, independent and unique voices to give us some glimpse of a larger whole that has been lost and a female point of view of a pivotal time in Western Civilization that has profound reverberations in our own.

Meg Bogin tells us that "the most striking aspect of the women's verse is its revelation of the experience of emotion. Unlike the men who created a complex poetic vision, the women wrote about their intimate feelings." They also, she notes, speak in *their own voices,* not in the stylized persona of the knight or lover, as is often the case with the men.

In other words, they speak with an amazing honesty, laying bare not only their own feelings and lives, but giving us an alternative view of reality behind the finesse of courtly love (which would evolve into romantic love, an ideal still much with us). Like the men, they had much to say about love. In some instances, it is sweet. Hear the lady Tibors from Orange:

Sweet handsome friend, I can tell you truly
that I've never been without desire
since it pleased you that I have you as my courtly lover;
Nor did a time ever arrive, sweet handsome friend,
when I didn't want to see you often;

And sometimes, unlike most of the verse composed by the troubadours, blatant desire seems a better alternative to smoldering repression. No one says it better than the Countess of Dia:

I've lately been in great distress
over a knight who once was mine,
and I want it known for all eternity
how I loved him to excess.
Now I see I've been betrayed
because I wouldn't sleep with him;
night and day my mind won't rest
to think of the mistake I made.

How I wish just once I could caress
that chevalier with my bare arms,
for he would be in ecstasy
if I'd just let him lean his head against my breast. . . .

In addition to wanting her man, the Countess de Dia also laments that she's been betrayed by him — a common refrain for our ladies. But the response often is startlingly bold, as in "don't get mad, get even." Listen to Isabella about whom little is known, but that she exchanged alternating verses in this poetic form called a *tenson* with a troubadour lover named Elias Cairel.

Elias Cairel, you're a phoney
if ever I saw one,
like a man who says he's sick
when he hasn't got the slightest pain.
If you'd listen, I'd give you good advice;
Go back to your cloister,
and don't dare pronounce my name again . . .

Or how about this response from Castelloza of Le Puy, who like others, makes the case for women doing the courting.

It greatly pleases me
when people say
that it's unseemly
for a lady to approach
    a man she likes
and hold him deep in conversation;
But whoever says that
    isn't very bright,
and I want to prove
    before you let me die
that courting

> *brings me great relief*
> *when I court the man*
> *who's brought me grief.*

There's more, too, in this slim collection of verse that speaks directly to the real lives of women. There is the poem authored by three women of unknown origin, Alais, Isleda and Carenza, which is like a conversation among friends where the subject of marrying and having babies is discussed – and largely rejected. One of them asks:

> *. . . shall I stay unwed? that would please me,*
> *for making babies doesn't seem so good,*
> *and it's too anguishing to be a wife.*
>
> *Lady Carenza, I'd like to have a husband,*
> *but making babies I think is a huge penitence:*
> *your breasts hang way down*
> *and it's too anguishing to be a wife.*

If that weren't shocking enough, there are the lyrical words of praise Bieiris de Romans sings – of the "merit, distinction, joy, intelligence and perfect beauty," the "merry disposition, sweet look and loving expression" – that belong not to a man, but to a certain Lady Maria. To my knowledge, this remains the only extant medieval poem expressing lesbian love.

So with their direct, bold, daring, fresh and beguiling poetry, this small and fragmentary collection by the *trobairitz* represents an affront, if not an outright assault on the established world-view of the troubadours. But the tensions between them were carried out in verse, as well as, I presume, in court, in castles, and in bed.

The real danger they posed, I can only imagine, was to the established order and the church. Here were high-born, powerful women openly singing of lust, of pursing men, of loving other women, of eschewing marriage and motherhood, and of mocking the low-lifes who betrayed them ("get thee to a cloister," to paraphrase Isabella). By the lights of the church, in a land that was already morally loose, and where noblewomen already had too much power — they could inherit property, for example — these women were no doubt over the top. They were uppity women. And they were brought down, as was the whole world around them, by the awesome wrath of the church in its bloody twin pursuits of crusade and inquisition.

Or were they?

Just as I believe the culture of Midi with its inherent *joie de vivre* went underground but survived, I believe the spirit of these proud women still haunts the southern landscape. I hear their refrains yet in the ruins on the hills and in the persistent winds of Languedoc. Just as they appear to have transcended the ethereal ladies in the stained glass I so admired in my childhood and stepped out to become real flesh and blood women with sorrows and passions I can understand, their few songs seem to have floated down the centuries into the thousand thousand voices of the women who came after. The conversations they began about love, lovers, betrayal, deceit, rank, and marriage, about getting down, getting laid, getting even, getting one's own, and especially getting real have continued. Folk music, sonnets, pastourelles and rounds, operas, ballets, ragtime and honkey tonk, blues, jazz, soul, pop and rock, all seem to have added their own notes to those ancient themes. But of course, these no longer belong exclusively to a select well-bred elite in command of a rarified courtly tradition. They have become the territory of down-and-out, poor, rags-to-riches heroines, the blues-belting Big Mamas and the hard rockers and rappers with attitude.

I'm sure we all carry a soundtrack in our heads of well-loved favorites. My own would feature Edith Piaf with her *cri de coeur, "je ne regrette rien"* – no regrets – a refrain I can well imagine she might have sung in two-part harmony with Tibors. It would also include Billie Holiday and Ella Fitzgerald in a kind of call and response over the centuries to the likes of the Countess of Dia, Castelloza and a dozen other *trobairitz* who lamented that "her man had done her wrong." Then of course there would be Bonnie Raitt belting out her anthem of "Fearless Love," and Janice Joplin's wail, as always telling it like it is: "Bye-bye, baby . . . I've got a lot of things I gotta do." Surely this would hit a responsive chord with the likes of Garsenda, wife of Alphonse II, Lord of Provence, who called out her timid suitor this way:

You're so well-suited as a lover,
I wish you wouldn't be so hesitant;
but I'm glad my love makes you the penitent,
otherwise I'd be the one to suffer . . .

This is an incomplete playlist, of course, but it does serve to let me know that, having discovered the *trobairitz*, whatever else I might say about my years lost to studying obscure medieval texts, they weren't completely in vain. These unsung singers have helped me understand the connections between that time and our own, through the real lives of women, in ways I never had before.

In one aspect above all others, I see the struggle for equality between the sexes as *the* battleground common to that distant age and our own. None of the singing ladies lays out this struggle better than Maria de Ventadorn, a struggle which in her time was also about the assumed higher rank of the beloved over her suitor. In a *tenson* exchanged with troubadour Gui d'Ussel, he proposes the fairly "liberated" view that they should do for each other, "without regard for rank/ for between two friends neither one should rule." To which she replies that it's "nothing short of treason/ if a man says he's her equal *and* her servant." In other words, forget that. He can love (serve) her if he likes, but she's got power and she's not about to give it up for "equality" with him — or any man.

Uppity? No doubt. But also bold, proud and strong? Absolutely. In our own time Maria's quest for not just equality, but power might be responded to by Aretha Franklin in her oft-sung, single and mighty word, delivered like a thunderbolt: *RESPECT.*

Appendix:
How to Cruise the Canals

Individuals may rent boats to traverse the canals of France from a number of commercial companies. These boat rental companies rent boats *sans permis,* which means that the person renting the boat is not required to have either previous experience or a special operator's permit. Each company offers a short introduction to handling the boat and to the operation of the locks. Boats are designed with inexperienced boaters in mind. This includes being equipped with rubber guard rails and extra fenders to keep the boats from being damaged in the locks. The commercial companies offer support service in case anything goes wrong with the boats during the rental period. Rental prices vary widely depending on the month and week of the rental.

During the summer of 2005, I rented the *Royal Destiny,* the boat which figures in a number of essays in this anthology, from **Sunshine Cruise Line.** In France, Sunshine Cruise Line rents boats on the Canal du Midi and the Lot and Garonne Rivers, as well as on the Saône River. Their telephone number is 33(0)6 10 28 88 08.

Other boat rental companies include:

Crown Blue Line has one rental center located at Castelnaudary on the Canal du Midi. Crown Blue also offers yacht-style boat rentals in Germany, Holland, Ireland, England, Scotland and Italy.

Crown Blue Line
Le Grand Bassin – BP 1201
11492 Castelnaudary CEDEX France
Tel: 33 (0)4 68 94 52 72
Fax: 33 (0)4 68 94 52 73
www.crownblueline.com

Locaboat Holidays specializes in penichette-style boat rentals. On the Canal du Midi, Locaboat has a rental center at *Ecluse Négra.* Locaboat also rents boats in Germany, Holland, Ireland and Italy.

Locaboat Holidays – BP 150
89303 Joigny CEDEX France
Fax: 33 (0)3 86 62 42 41
www.locaboat.com

About the Contributors

JOANNA BIGGAR is a teacher, writer and traveler whose special places of the heart include the California coast and the South of France. She has degrees in Chinese and French and, as a professional writer for twenty years, has written poetry, fiction, personal essays, features, news and travel articles for hundreds of publications including the *Washington Post Magazine, Psychology Today, The International Herald Tribune,* and *The Wall Street Journal.* Her book *Travels and Other Poems* was published in 1996, and she and photographer Ann Hawthorne are currently working on a collaborative book of their adventures on the road in America entitled *Roadkill.* She has taught journalism, creative writing, personal essay and travel writing at The Writers' Center in Bethesda, Maryland since 1984 and "Spirit of Place" at the Writers' Center of Marin in San Rafael, California.

LYNN BRANECKY is a New York based freelance writer. Originally from Texas, she has traveled the world in search of a story. Her observations range from hailstones the size of tennis balls in South Africa to the nesting habits of orangutans in Borneo. Her last article was published in *Vogue Australia.*

CONNIE BURKE left San Francisco, California in 1979. She set out for *Ithaka*, hoping to make her journey a long one, full of adventure, full of discovery. She has yet to return. On the way, she joined the English Faculty of the University of Maryland, European Division and The American College of Greece. Then she went on to establish and direct The Burke Institute for English Language Studies in Piraeus, Greece. Retired from academia, Connie resides in Piraeus and serves as the first President of Habitat for Humanity, Greater Athens. When she is not hammering nails and cleaning paintbrushes, she spends her time reading, writing, and celebrating life in the southern Peloponnesus.

LARRY HABEGGER is a writer, editor, journalist, and teacher who has been covering the world since his international travels began in the 1970s. A freelance writer for more than two decades and syndicated columnist since 1985, he has written for many major newspapers and magazines, including the *Los Angeles Times*, *Chicago Tribune*, *Travel & Leisure*, and *Outside*. In the early 1980s he co-authored mystery serials for the *San Francisco Examiner* with James O'Reilly, and in 1993 founded the award-winning Travelers' Tales books with James and Tim O'Reilly. He has worked on all of the company's more than 80 titles and is currently executive editor. Larry's safety and security column, World Travel Watch, has appeared in newspapers in five countries and on Internet sites, including WorldTravelWatch. com. He regularly teaches the craft of personal travel writing at workshops and writers conferences, and he lives with his family in San Francisco.

LINDA WATANABE MCFERRIN, poet, travel writer, novelist and teacher, is a contributor to numerous journals, newspapers, magazines, anthologies and online publications including the *New York Times*, the *Washington Post*, the *San Francisco Chronicle Magazine*, *Modern Bride*, Travelers' Tales, Salon.com, and Women.com. She is the author of two poetry collections and the editor of the 4th edition of *Best Places Northern California*. A winner of the Nimrod International Journal Katherine Anne Porter Prize for Fiction, her work has also appeared in *Wild Places* and *American Fiction*. Her novel, *Namako: Sea Cucumber* was published by Coffee House Press and named Best Book for the Teen-Age by the New York Public Library. Her collection of award-winning short stories, *The Hand of Buddha*, was published in 2000. She is also a co-editor of a prize-winning travel anthology and the recently published *Hot Flashes: Sexy Little Stories & Poems*. Linda has served as a judge for the San Francisco Literary Awards and the Kiriyama Prize. She holds an undergraduate degree in Comparative Literature and a Master of Arts degree in Creative Writing and is the founder of Left Coast Writers (http://leftcoastwriters.com). When she is not on the road, she directs art, consults on communications and product development and teaches Creative Writing. (http://lwmcferrin.com)

C.J. MARCUS is a northern California native. As a young adult, she was intrigued by the emerging music/media community in the Bay Area, where she soon joined the staff of the legendary FM radio powerhouse, San Francisco's KSAN. She found herself surrounded by not only world famous musicians but literary icons such as the late Hunter S. Thompson. Drawn to the music business, she became the first woman to hold an artist relations and marketing position with EMI Records. C.J. also enjoyed acting and performed in various films and commercials. As an avid traveler, she has visited much of the world accumulating a considerable repertoire of experience and inspiration for her persistent interest and true passion – the craft of writing. Upon settling in the Sonoma County Wine Country, she turned to the real estate business and became actively involved in the area's economic development as an investor, entrepreneur and investment counselor. These days when she is not in Santa Rosa, she can be found diving a variety of islands in the Pacific, shushing down snow-covered mountains or cruising the bucolic canals of Provence. She remains tattoo free and enjoys spending time with her faithful pup, Cosmo.

ETHEL F. MUSSEN was born in the Jazz Age in Los Angeles where the ubiquitous tinkling background music changed to marches and swing during WWII. Ethel's youthful artistic aspirations also changed to wartime nursing and a subsequent fifty years in health care, mostly as a speech pathologist and audiologist. Married to a Berkeley professor in demand around the world, the family traveled widely both professionally and as tourists. They returned most often to Florence and Provence, regions which became second homes, deepening her acquaintance with the people, history, and more specifically the ceramics produced by both cultures. Retirement from audiology and the subsequent death of her husband freed the peripatetic adventurer to revisit old haunts and seek the new. She is still learning to write non-academically in order to share her experiences and mishaps over the years. Tales have appeared in *A Woman's Europe, I Should Have Gone Home,* and *Travelers' Tales Provence.* Taking a chance on the Canal du Midi proved to be summer camp afloat in the company of hardy mariners with a dose of youthful angst – a prelude to more watery adventures in Northern canals amidst a stiffer and grayer cohort.

APRIL ORCUTT has been a writer and producer of public affairs, documentary, and science television programs, a college professor who taught broadcasting and created and chaired a multimedia/ web design program and department, a contributor to two books about broadcasting in Eastern Europe since the fall of the Soviet Union, and a travel writer and photographer who's been published in newspapers and online in the U.S. and Canada, including in the *Los Angeles Times, San Francisco Chronicle Magazine, Denver Post, Kansas City Star, Montreal Gazette,* and others. She was a winner in Lonely Planet's 2003 "The Kindness of Strangers" writing contest. April has traveled on a shikara in Kashmir, a ferry in Greece, a sailboat in San Francisco Bay, a kayak in Tomales Bay, a catamaran in Newport Harbor, an oar boat in the Sierra Nevada, a rubber raft in the Rocky Mountains, a makeshift driftwood raft on a lake in the San Juan Islands, a canoe in Michigan, a cruise ship off Mexico, a paddlewheeler at Disneyland, and, most recently, a yacht on the Canal du Midi in Southern France.

MARY JEAN PRAMIK, a coalminer's daughter and a great, great grandniece of the Mongolian plain, has published copiously in classic medicalese, mined technical metaphors on end and raised three children. For nearly four decades, she has worked as a science and medical journalist, edited medical school texts, and penned a myriad of published medical journal articles. A graduate degree in biological sciences and another degree in creative writing opened up both the fields of science and literature to Mary Jean. She served as editor (a.k.a. ghostwriter) of the pharmaceutical thriller *Norethindrone: The First Three Decades* relating the tortuous development of the first birth control pill, which can be found in most medical libraries. She published in *Nature Biotechnology, Drug Topics* and *Cosmetic Surgery News* as well as mainstream magazines like *Good Housekeeping* and the *National Enquirer.* Her poetry appeared in literary journals such as *Transitions.* Mary Jean lives in the San Francisco Bay Area where she moonlights as a political activist and fledgling triathlete. She is currently at work on a novel entitled *The GEM of Egypt* and a book of personal essays, *Know It All.*

ANN KATHLEEN URE lives in Mill Valley, California. By day, she directs a non-profit organization affiliated with Levi Strauss & Co. in San Francisco. By night, she dreams about becoming the next Erma Bombeck. She loves animals, singing, dancing, games, and hanging out with friends. Throughout her varied career she has written advertising copy, product flyers, song lyrics, grants, business proposals, witty e-mail messages, and first-person essays. An essay about her 1994 bout with cancer was published in "Ways of the Healer" by the Institute for Health and Healing at California Pacific Medical Center.

STACIE MICHELLE WILLIAMS, daughter of an author, wrote her first story at the age of five and never stopped. Traveling the world was an obsession that began even before she got a chance as a teenager to visit such places as Sweden, Switzerland, Fiji and Australia. After embarking on the Canal du Midi, her first visit to France, Stacie spent a week alone in Paris practicing her rusty French. Stacie was born and raised in California, living there until the crazy notion came up that she should move to Milwaukee, Wisconsin – the home of cheese, brats, and beer: the first she loved, the second she'd never tried, the third she couldn't stomach. She continues to reside in the heart of Harley/Packer country with her two crazy Siberian Huskies, three cats and a man who follows her everywhere claiming to be her husband. She is biding her time until her next trip by working in an independent bookstore, riding horses and, of course, writing.

About the Editor

BARBARA J. EUSER is a former political officer with the Foreign Service of the U.S. Department of State. In 1993, she sailed her family's boat *Islander* across the Atlantic to take her post in the political section of the U.S. Embassy in Paris. When she and her husband took *Islander* through the rivers and canals of France, she began dreaming of traveling through the canals in a boat built for that purpose. She realized her dream and now plies the Canal du Midi in *Lurley*. As a director of the International Community Development Foundation, she has worked on projects in Bosnia, Somaliland, Zimbabwe, India and Nepal. Her articles and essays have appeared in magazines and anthologies. She is the author of *Children of Dolpo*; *Somaliland*; *Take 'Em Along: Sharing the Wilderness with Your Children*; co-author of *A Climber's Climber: On the Trail with Carl Blaurock*; editor of *Bay Area Gardening* and the forthcoming *Gardening Among Friends*. She lives near San Francisco with her husband. They have two grown daughters.

Index

GOSPEL of PEACE

no more shame…no more fear!

no more shame…no more fear!

DR. JAMES B. RICHARDS

Editorial note: Even at the cost of violating grammatical rules, we have chosen not to capitalize the name satan and related names.

THE GOSPEL OF PEACE

Published in the United States of America
© 1990 by Dr. James B. Richards

Milestones International Publishers
An imprint of True Potential, Inc.
P.O. Box 904
Travelers Rest, SC 29690
http://truepotentialmedia.com
www.milestonesintl.com
864-836-4111

ISBN13: 978-0-924748-94-3

Library of Congress Cataloging-in-Publication Data

Richards, James B. (James Burton), 1951–
  The Gospel of peace / by James B. Richards.
    p. cm.
  Includes bibliographical references.
  ISBN 0-88368-487-X (pbk. : alk. paper)
  1. Peace—Religious aspects—Christianity. 2. Bible. N.T.
Gospels—Criticism, interpretation, etc. 3. Jesus Christ—Person and
offices. I. Title.
  BT736.4 .R493 2002
  234—dc21   2002005232

Dedication

ജ

This book is dedicated to Bobby C. Goode, my uncle. Thank you for being a role model, a friend, an example, and the only real father I ever knew.

Because you believed in me, I was able to believe in myself and come out of what would have been a disastrous lifestyle. In you, I saw high standards without rejection. You helped me to see God as a Father.

Other Books by James B. Richards

Apocalypse: A Spiritual Guide to the Second Coming

Moving Your Invisible Boundaries

Anatomy of a Miracle

Becoming the Person You Want to Be

Breaking the Cycle: The Ultimate Solution to Destructive Patterns

The Lost Art of Leadership

The Prayer Organizer

Satan Unmasked:The Truth Behind the Lie

Take Control of Your Life

Taking the Limits Off God

Wired for Success Programmed for Failure

Contents

ও৩

Visit http://www.impactministries.com/gospel-of-peace

to view the complete video series

"The Way of Peace: The Place of Power"

One

❧

Experiencing the
"Peace of God"

One

ஐ

Experiencing the "Peace of God"

*H*undreds of times in the Bible God, or an angel, tells man not to fear. When Jesus appeared to His disciples after His crucifixion, He said, "Fear not!" There should be no fear of God in the heart of a believer. There should be only a deep and powerful realization of being loved and accepted by God the Father, the Creator of the universe.

When fear is in a person's heart toward God, it is clear that the person in question does not really believe that God loves him with a perfect love. If there is fear, it is because that person is afraid of what God will do to him. He is afraid he will be hurt or rejected by God.

First John 4:18 is best expressed in *The Living Bible:*

> *We need have no fear of someone who loves us perfectly; his perfect love for us eliminates all dread of what he might do to us. If we are afraid, it is for fear of what he might do to us, and shows that we are not fully convinced that he really loves us.*

The earmark of the Christian who believes what Jesus did through His death, burial, and resurrection should be a life of confident acceptance that is permeated with peace. There should be no torment. There should be no nagging sense of guilt and rejection. There should be only peace.

Every religion in the world offers peace to man. Christianity is the only one, however, that delivers. For we are not a people that is attempting to achieve a state or status that will give us peace; we are a people that has been made right with God through the finished work of one Man, Christ Jesus. And because of His finished work, we have been granted peace with God.

Because not every Christian knows or believes this wonderful reality, not every Christian lives in a continual state of peace. Far too many Christians live in torment and turmoil, always fearful that things are not right between them and God.

My involvement in ministering to people in mental wards has proven this time and time again. I have repeatedly seen the emotionally unstable and the mentally tormented struggle with the fear of not being able to please God. The world is right when it says, "Religion will drive you crazy!" Religion is man's attempt to find peace with God. Christianity, on the other hand, is man's accepting peace with God through the Lord Jesus Christ.

A great percentage of people in mental hospitals feel they have done something that is beyond God's ability to forgive. They are awaiting judgment from an angry God. Many times they have no idea what they could have done; they just have a sense of fear and impending judgment. This is what the Bible calls condemnation, or the expectation of damnation and judgment. In Christ. though, we are free from condemnation!

What is so sad is that this portrait of fearful people also describes many of the faithful who sit in church every Sunday. Fear seems to be the motivating factor in the lives of many Christians. Where would these people get such an idea about God? How could someone become so afraid of God that he would end up in a metal institution or chronically fearful and depressed? Who represented God so negatively that an entire world is turned off? It has not been some force outside the church that has so destroyed the reputation of God. It has not been some evil, demonic group. Unfortunately, it has been the voices of well-meaning people within the church.

Fear has been passed down from generation to generation in the church. From the earliest of times, the church has struggled with believing the truth about the finished work of Jesus. This failure to believe the truth has been the root of the fear, anxiety, and sometimes outright meanness of the church down through the ages.

When Isaiah prophesied about the great work of the cross, he also prophesied, *"Who has believed our report?"* (Isaiah 53:1 NKJV). There is a report about God that is so good, so freeing, so loving, so kind, so merciful, and so generous that man refuses to believe it.

Those who reject this wonderful report either spend a lifetime trying to please God or ultimately walk away from God. In my years of ministering on the streets, more people were angry at God because of the unbelieving report they heard in church than for any other reason.

In his introduction to the book of Galatians in *The Message*, Eugene H. Peterson says, "When men and women get their hands on religion, one of the first things they often do is turn it into an instrument for controlling others, either putting or keeping them in their place." This control seems to have become the goal of the church. Rather than setting people free with the good news about Jesus, they use it as a way to bring people under their control.

Early in Christian history there arose those who would pervert the Gospel. There were those who followed Paul around and proclaimed, "Believe on Jesus! He is the Messiah. He is the way of salvation. But the way of righteousness is works of the law." The deceit in this message is subtle. It is obvious that God has called us to live a righteous life. It is obvious that righteousness should be the fruit of being a Christian. So it would seem only logical to accept this message. However, what you believe about righteousness is really what you believe about how you relate to God.

If keeping the law is our basis for righteousness, then it is also the basis for receiving the promises of God. It is the basis of getting our prayers answered. It is the basis of God's protection. If keeping the law is the basis of righteousness, then our ability to have peace is determined by our ability to keep the law. Ultimately, keeping the law becomes our basis for salvation.

While proclaiming belief in Jesus as the way of salvation in one breath, we have totally excluded Jesus in the next breath. Of course, none of us denies Jesus as Lord. In experience, however, we look to our performance to provide everything that Jesus died to provide. Intellectually and theologically, Jesus is still the center of our faith, but emotionally and functionally, *we* have become the center of our faith.

Romans 8:5–8 in *The Message* says it this way:

> *Those who think they can do it on their own end up obsessed with measuring their own moral muscle but never get around to exercising it in real life. Those who*

trust God's action in them find that God's Spirit is in them—living and breathing God! Obsession with self in these matters is a dead end; attention to God leads us out into the open, into a spacious, free life. Focusing on the self is the opposite of focusing on God. Anyone completely absorbed in self ignores God, ends up thinking more about self than God. That person ignores who God is and what he is doing. And God isn't pleased at being ignored.

This self-obsession is not the product of a person who desires to reject God. Rather, this is the person who is trying to please God by his own efforts. This is the person who has ignorantly rejected the finished work of Jesus and has become obsessed with earning righteousness by his performance; thus he has an obsession with self.

Every letter Paul wrote was aimed at bringing believers back to the finished work of Jesus. One by one, church by church, city after city, many believers forgot the message and were seduced by others into returning to their own performance as their source of righteousness and ultimately their source of peace with God. They just would not believe the report about Jesus.

In the book of Galatians, Paul pointed out the motivation of those who pervert the Gospel: control! Leaders who don't trust Jesus don't believe the Gospel will work by its own power. Because they themselves do not believe in the power of the Gospel, they feel it is their job to control you, to "put you in your place."

What makes this so undetectable is the motive. Many of the most destructive forces in the church are people with good motives. The most dangerous person is the one who has a deep passion to help people but who does not believe in the power of the Gospel to produce change. Instead of proclaiming the finished work of the Lord Jesus and entrusting the people to the work of the Holy Spirit, that person will resort to carnal methods of control. When people are controlled, it appears that they have changed. So the deep motive to help people justifies the desire to control.

The main tool for control is fear. If you are not confident in your relationship with God, you will have fear. Fear will rob you of confidence. It will restrict you. It will make you angry. It will make you emotionally unstable. Fear will strip you of the new identity you have in Jesus. It will leave you stripped of the God-ordained dignity and worth that belong to you as a priest and a king. It will make you feel the need for an intercessor.

The intercessor who will come between you and God will not be the Lord Jesus, however. After all, you have rejected the peace He gives for the peace that someone else is offering. Instead, this intercessor will be someone who offers to show you the way—the formula. It will be someone who will know all the rules and requirements for staying right with God. You will be saved but never secure. Your sin will be forgiven but never forgotten. You will have the promises but never the qualification to receive them. You will be given the family name but never the family inheritance. You will forever strive to attain what Jesus has freely given. You will be offered peace but never have peacefulness.

This is not the plan of God for you. God desires for you to know and experience His great love, acceptance, and peace. But you must believe the report God gives about the finished work of Jesus. It is a good report. It is a report of peace!

Two

&

A Relationship with God

Two

❧

A Relationship with God

*T*he ultimate goal of the Gospel is a loving, meaningful relationship with God. Until people understand this goal, they will pervert the process. Because we fail to realize what God desires, we spend much of our time and effort pursuing an entirely different goal than that which God desires.

Jesus did not come to build an army. He came to recover a family. Through His work we are adopted, not inducted. Adoption is acceptance into a family. Induction is enlistment into an army. God is our Father, not our general. Although Jesus is our Lord, He is also our Elder Brother. The ultimate goal of God is not a labor force or a warring force; it is a family.

God wants us as His sons and daughters. He wants us to be a part of His family. He wants our involvement. He wants a relationship with us. Therefore, He initiated the plan that could bring all of this about. He dealt with the one thing that stood between us and Him: sin!

Sin had separated man from God. Sin had created a bridge that we could not cross. Sin introduced the one thing that would keep us from loving, trusting, or being involved with God. It began to reign with Adam, and it has continued until this very day.

Genesis gives us some insight into the way sin affected man's relationship with God. Genesis 3:8 is one of the saddest verses in all the Bible.

> *And they heard the voice of the LORD God walking in the garden in the cool of the day: and Adam and his wife hid themse lves from the presence of the LORD God amongst the trees of the garden.*

Just as God had initiated this whole plan of man, just as He had initiated every aspect of Creation, just as He had initiated a relationship with man to start with, this day He initiated a visit with Adam. But for the first time, man didn't respond. He hid from God. From that day until the present, man has continued to run from the invitation of God. Man has refused to draw near and experience God.

Genesis 3:9 says, *"And the LORD God called unto Adam, and said unto him, Where art thou?"* There is every indication from the original language that when God called, it meant He "called to make peace." God wanted peace. Adam assumed God called for judgment. That assumption is perpetuated in fearful men to this day.

Unfortunately, this fear of God is not experienced exclusively among the lost. Even after people are saved, they have reservations about intimacy with God. Among believers, there is a lack of confidence concerning God's desire to be intimate with us. There is a low-level, nagging fear in most people. They do not really believe that they are acceptable to God.

We have the illusion that we are trying to get holy enough to have involvement with God. But our attempt to be made acceptable is like Adam's. Adam had always been naked before God. Now Adam, through his newfound abilities, determined that God should not see him naked. So Adam made a covering out of fig leaves. Thus when God came looking for Adam in the Garden, Adam didn't think he could stand before God, and he did what he thought would make him acceptable. Adam, like us, missed the point. If God did not want to fellowship with Adam, He would not have come to the Garden looking for him.

Our fears, like Adam's, affect our behavior so dramatically that we cannot have meaningful involvement with God. We do not accept the reality that God pursued us in Jesus. He made us acceptable. He wants a relationship so much that He has done everything to make this relationship possible.

Meaningful relationships are the product of love, trust, and personal involvement. Relationships grow to the extent that each of these factors is present. When there is no love, trust, and personal involvement, it is not a relationship. At best, it might be considered an arrangement or a "working relationship." It is not a personal, family relationship.

We need time with God in order to develop and experience these factors. When you spend time with someone who is kind to you, you grow in your trust for him. All positive involvement is part of developing the relationship. However, you will not spend time with someone if you do not realize that he accepts you. You will never have the opportunity to experience God until the issue of peace is resolved.

The one element that hinders a real relationship more than anything else is fear. Fear breeds all sorts of negative emotions and actions. It is the root of deceit. You can never be honest with someone when you fear what he will do to you or how he will respond. You can never be real. You are too busy trying to cover your faults to develop a relationship.

This all began in the Garden. Man started running and has never stopped, because we are afraid of God. We don't really believe how God feels about us. We have not allowed love to deliver us from the power of fear.

There is a real possibility that the sin nature is not necessarily a nature that just craves sin. There is every indication that the essence of the sin nature is fear. Fear was the first emotion mankind displayed after Adam ate of the Tree of Knowledge of Good and Evil. It was fear that made Adam hide from God. It is fear that makes us turn to sinful actions instead of trusting God.

Fear and unbelief go hand in hand. Where there is one, there is always the other. Because we are afraid of God, we do not trust Him. Because we do not trust Him, we do not come to Him to receive strength and help in our time of need. We do not believe He will really give us the promises He has made, because we are afraid.

What do we fear? We are afraid that we are unacceptable to God, that He does not approve of us. We are afraid that we do not measure up and that He will find fault in us and punish us. We are afraid because we do not believe that we are righteous.

This fear prevents us from having an open, honest relationship with God. It keeps us from all honest and open communication. It destroys all possibility of knowing God. It makes us emotionally unstable. It brings all matter of torment into our lives. There is an endless list of the negative effects of fear.

Some might say, "I thought you were supposed to fear God." In the King James Version, numerous Scriptures tell us the value of having the fear of God. Let's take a closer look at the admonition to fear God.

On the one hand, you have Scriptures that tell you to fear God. On the other, God often begins speaking with the words, "Fear not." When there are obvious contradictions like this, I have found that there is usually something I am not understanding.

First John 4:18 tells us, *"Perfect love casts out fear"* (NKJV). This means that fear and love cannot coexist. If I grow in the love of God, the fear of God will diminish in my life. I know God is love. I know God wants me to experience His love. But what about the fear of God?

When Jesus was tempted, He quoted an Old Testament Scripture: *"Then saith Jesus unto him, Get thee hence, Satan: for it is written, Thou shalt worship the Lord thy God, and him only shalt thou serve"* (Matthew 4:10). Jesus was quoting from Deuteronomy 6:13, where it says, *"Thou shalt fear the LORD thy God, and serve him, and shalt swear by his name."* Jesus translated the word *"fear"* as *"worship."*

Actually, the word for *fear* in the Old Testament is better understood as "awe, respect, and love that produces worship." We should have an awe of God that produces worship, not fear. God does not want you to be afraid of Him.

To be afraid of God would contradict all we know about Jesus, His life, and His ministry. It makes an honest relationship impossible. It prevents everything that Jesus came to establish. He came to restore us to the Father. He brought about our adoption into the family of God.

The religious leaders of Jesus' day had completely misrepresented God. They had portrayed God as hard and judgmental. They had perverted the meaning and purpose of the law. They had put God completely out of reach of the people.

Jesus came and properly represented God to the world. He said, "If you've seen Me, you've seen the Father." (See John 14:9.) Hebrews 1:3 in *The New International Version* says that Jesus was the exact representation of God. Jesus was approachable. He was merciful. He was open. He was relationship-oriented. This was the complete opposite of the God represented by the Jewish leaders and is somewhat contrary to the God the church has frequently presented.

Jesus showed us God so that we could have boldness to enter into a meaningful relationship with Him. God desires our presence. He desires our hearts. He wants a relationship with us.

Three

☙

The Good News
of Christ

Three

ॐ

The Good News of Christ

W hen Jesus appeared on the scene, He preached the Gospel of the kingdom of God. The word *gospel* simply means "good news." It is not complicated. Everything Jesus preached was good news. When the masses were healed, it was because they had heard good news. When there were miracles, it was because the people had heard good news. When people turned from their sins, it was because they had heard good news.

The religious leaders of the day preached to the people, but they never brought them good news about God; they always brought bad news. They didn't set people free; they loaded them down with more rules and regulations. They made the people afraid of God. They caused the people to view God as mean, hard, and judgmental. Because they never preached good news, they never saw good results.

When people are afraid of God, they not only fail to establish a relationship with Him, but they also never have real productivity in their lives. In Jesus' parable about the talents, the man who had only one talent refused to utilize that talent because he was afraid of God. Fear binds, destroys, and restricts.

Despite the best attempts of the religious leaders of that day, what they had was not working. It did not set people free; it bound them. They all knew about God, but they did not know the Good News about God. The Pharisees had burdened the people with negatives—law and works—but they did not lift one finger to lighten their load.

Jesus came reading the same Scriptures, praying to the same God, but proclaiming good things and good news. It rang in my heart like a bell of freedom: Jesus preached good news to the people. By His preaching the Good News, their faith was established, their hunger for God was heightened, and their trust for the One who had once seemed so far away and unconcerned was revived. When they found out God was a good God, miracles happened.

Galatians 1:8 says, *"But though we, or an angel from heaven, preach any other gospel unto you than that which we have preached unto you, let him be accursed."* We have departed from the Good News. Our religious system of today is built on the premise of an angry God. When people go to church, they are often "beaten" instead of fed. I was as guilty as any other minister. One day while reading these words in Galatians, the revelation exploded in my heart: "If it is not good news, it is not Gospel."

At one time, I was winning a few hundred people per year to the Lord. Then God spoke to me and said, "When you start preaching the Gospel, you will really do something for Me." I was insulted. "What do You mean, 'When I start preaching the Gospel'?" I thought I was preaching the Gospel. I began to look at what I was telling people. It was mostly bad news. When people presented their problems to me, I was not mean or condemning, but I did not have a sure word that was always good. I did not have a word that always gave freedom. I did not have good news. Paul said in Romans 1:16, *"For I am*

not ashamed of the gospel [the Good News] of Christ: for it is
the power of God unto salvation to every one that believeth."
The good news of Jesus is the power of God. Without good
news, there is no power.

The word *salvation* comes from the Greek word *sozo*. *Sozo*
is more than the new birth. It means healing, protection, deliverance, safety, and a host of other good things. If I do not
preach the Good News, the power of God cannot come and
bring salvation (*sozo*) into the lives of hurting people.

The Good News is not life for everyone—only for those
who believe it. When Jesus began His public ministry, He proclaimed the purpose for which the Spirit of the Lord was upon
Him—to preach good news (Luke 4:18). He had good news
for the poor, the brokenhearted, the captives, the blind, and
the bruised. The Good News is found in Luke 4:19: *"To preach
the acceptable year of the Lord."* What could He possibly have
meant by that?

"The acceptable year of the Lord" is the Year of Jubilee. Every
fifty years all debts were canceled. Regardless of how legitimate
a debt might be, it was canceled. The individual was free from
the debt without any effort or merit on his part. The debt was
canceled. By the debt being canceled, the penalty of the debt
was also canceled. Every good Jew knew the penalty for breaking the law was the curse, as described in the old covenant.
When those curses came, he knew he deserved it. He could in
no way hold God responsible for the curse of the law. But to all
those curses—poverty, brokenheartedness, captivity, blindness,
and bruising—Jesus was saying, "The debt is now canceled."
That is the Good News to those in need. The debt of the law is
canceled. You can now be free from the penalty of your sin.

Jesus repeatedly proved that this applied to the forgiveness
of sins as well as to the curse of the law. The Pharisees never

believed that, and they never partook of it. They may have loved God, but they were offended by the Good News. Despite what we might think, some of those Pharisees had something in their hearts for God. It may have been twisted and perverted, but they must have wanted God very much in order to live the rigid lifestyle they lived.

In the *Archko Volume*, the Pharisees revealed some of their fears concerning Jesus' message. They were afraid that when the people believed in the Good News, they would fall into sin. They failed to understand that the law affects the outer man, while mercy and love affect the inner man. Jesus' message of forgiveness was accused of promoting a loose and lascivious lifestyle.

Contrary to this unfounded belief, the Good News that Jesus preached caused people to fall in love with God. It caused people to trust the God they had grown to dread. It caused them to draw near to the One from whom they had been hiding. It caused them to come out of the stronghold of sin by entering into intimacy with God.

Jesus' preaching of the Good News succeeded where law had failed. By His preaching and demonstrating the goodness of God, the people were able to respond properly. The natural response to goodness is appreciation, thanksgiving, commitment, and relationship. Thus, we see the reality that the Gospel (Good News) is the power of God unto salvation, healing, deliverance, and every other promise that God has made.

Four

❦

The Cross of Christ

Four

✌

The Cross of Christ

*For I determined not to know any thing among you, save Jesus
Christ, and him crucified. And I was with you in weakness,
and in fear, and in much trembling. And my speech and my
preaching was not with enticing words of man's wisdom, but
in demonstration of the Spirit and of power: that your faith
should not stand in the wisdom of men, but in
the power of God.*
—1 Corinthians 2:2–5

*T*hese words haunted me for years. What did this really mean? Did Paul preach only a salvation (born-again experience) message? Did he preach only about the cross and nothing else? I had to know what this meant.

Sometimes the simple and the obvious is the most difficult to grasp. As I developed my understanding of the Word of God, I came to realize that all understanding, all revelation, all that God has done for us can be understood only in the finished work of the cross. I realized the Gospel was understood only in the death, burial, and resurrection of the Lord Jesus.

The rest of the New Testament teaching simply explains and points back to what happened on the cross. The cross is

the basis of the entire new covenant. It is the basis of my relationship with God. It is the basis of all of Christianity. All
truth has its basis in the cross. Any message that is not consistent with what Jesus accomplished at the cross is simply not
true.

Hebrews 1:1–2 says,

> *God, who at sundry times and in divers manners spake
> in time past unto the fathers by the prophets, hath in
> these last days spoken unto us by his Son, whom he hath
> appointed heir of all things, by whom also he made the
> worlds.*

Prior to the cross, God had spoken in many different ways,
through many different people, in many different situations.
Now, however, He has said all He has to say in the Son—
specifically, in the death, burial, and resurrection of His Son.
God has no other message. What happened at the cross is the
basis of the Good News that God has for the world.

The cross must become my focal point for understanding,
interpreting, and judging truth. In other words, anything I
find in the entire Bible must pass the test of the cross. Is it consistent with what Jesus accomplished on the cross? Or does it
contradict the cross? A failure to interpret doctrine in light of
the finished work of the cross has been the major cause of confusion and contradictory teachings.

In our failure to base our entire belief system on the cross,
we have erroneously looked back to the old covenant to relate
to God. Because the message of the cross seems too good to
be true, we have, in our unbelief, looked other places to know
and experience God.

At the cross, Jesus paid the price for sin and delivered us
from the curse of the law. Yet we still look to the law and

assume that our standard of conduct will protect us from the curse. At the cross, Jesus was chastened so that we could have peace. In our unbelief, we live in expectancy of God chastening us. At the cross, Jesus was bruised with sickness so we could have healing. But again we look to some stipulation of the law to give us healing. At the cross, Jesus conquered sin. We try to conquer it in our own strength. At the cross, Jesus conquered death by the Resurrection and obtained righteousness, yet we still try to obtain righteousness by our own works. We have abandoned the cross.

Although the cross is the central message of the Gospel, we have failed to embrace it as Paul and the early church did. We have verbally acknowledged it as the apex of Christianity, but in reality our doctrine and practical application totally deny the cross. Rather than our Christianity revolving around and depending on the finished work of the cross, it depends on us. We are more aware of our works than we are of His work. We erroneously place ourselves, instead of Jesus and His finished work, at the center of our relationship with God.

In short, we will never experience the power of God until our faith stands in the cross instead of the wisdom of men. The simple realities of the cross are the basis for real Bible faith. To live by faith is to live dependent on, trusting in, adhering to, and deriving power from what Jesus did at the cross. All else is simply vain imaginations.

Our faith as Christians is obviously in the person of Jesus. Yet there is no separating who Jesus is from what He has done. There is no operation of faith apart from faith in His finished work. This is the basis for faith. Faith (trust) based on anything else is vanity. It is a denial of the cross of Christ.

This causes us to ask some hard questions of ourselves. Do we really even know what Jesus accomplished at the cross? If so, do we really believe it? Has the cross of Christ become the pivotal point around which our lives revolve, or is it just an addendum to the Old Testament?

Paul said this in 1 Corinthians 1:17: *"For Christ sent me…to preach the gospel: not with wisdom of words, lest the cross of Christ should be made of none effect."* We preach Christ, but we don't preach the cross of Christ—at least not the way Paul and the early church understood it. For that reason, we don't see the same results he saw.

Some of the deepest, most profound, most challenging sermons I have ever heard were not based on the cross. They had a show of wisdom. They were logical. They were about Jesus. They were about loyalty and commitment to Jesus as a person. Yet, in the maze of man's wisdom, those messages never brought one to the place where his confidence before God was based on what Jesus accomplished in His death, burial, and resurrection.

On the other hand, I have heard many heart-moving messages of the cross. I have wept because I was so stirred. Yet, when I walked away and reflected on what I had heard, I realized it never acknowledged the provisions that God made through the cross.

Today I have so committed myself to the message of the cross that I can understand something in the Bible only when I understand it in light of the cross. If what I believe is not consistent with the cross, I must realize that I do not yet understand it. I am only beginning to understand why Paul preached nothing but Jesus and Him crucified.

Five

୫

Peace on Earth

Five

❧

Peace on Earth

*J*esus is the Prince of Peace. God the Father is identified as the God of Peace. The fruit of the Spirit is peace. We are told that we should allow the peace of God to rule in our hearts. Why then are so few Christians experiencing peace?

Instead of being filled with peace, the Christian life for many is brimming with fear, guilt, and condemnation. They should be experiencing freedom from these negative emotions. It seems, however, that quite the opposite is true. Many Christians feel afraid and insecure. They feel that they are continually failing to measure up. According to one study, evangelical Christians have incredibly low self-worth. The legalistic, unscriptural tendency to reject righteousness as a free gift creates guilt and low self-worth in the presence of a holy God.

Low self-worth among Christians is the product of fear in our relationship with God. Instead of accepting and believing the truth about our new identity in Jesus, instead of believing what God has made us to be, we are trying to become what we think God would have us to be.

We are like Adam. God had created Adam in His own likeness and image. Then Satan came along and told Adam, "If you'll do this, you will be like God." Adam already was like God, but he fell because he simply did not believe it. In the same way, we have been made righteous in Jesus. The tempter says to us, "If you will do this, it will make you become like Jesus." We are like Jesus already; yet we fall into his trap because we just don't believe it. So instead of what we *do* stemming from who we are, we try to make who we are the *product* of what we do.

If I think I must become something to be acceptable to God, then I must also believe that I am not acceptable to God in my present state. Hence, low self-worth, rejection, and fear rule in my heart instead of peace. I find myself striving instead of resting, doubting instead of believing.

Colossians 3:15 tells us, *"And let the peace of God rule in your hearts, to the which also ye are called in one body; and be ye thankful."* My heart should always be ruled by peace. There should never be a time when another emotion is allowed to dominate my thoughts, feelings, and actions.

But the truth is, if I believe what mainstream Christianity teaches about God, I will never be at peace. I will never have an abiding peace that dominates my every decision and thought. I will, instead, live in dread and fear of what God might do to me. I will forever be striving to measure up to the standards of behavior imposed on me by the religious system.

Jesus came to establish peace. As He was preparing to leave earth, He said, *"Peace I leave with you, my peace I give unto you: not as the world giveth, give I unto you. Let not your heart be troubled, neither let it be afraid"* (John 14:27). According to Colossians 3:15, I must allow peace to rule my heart. His perfect peace will protect me from fear and guard my heart from trouble. Isaiah 26:3 promises, *"You will keep him in perfect peace, whose mind is stayed on You, because he trusts in You"* (NKJV).

As with all my beliefs, I must look back to the cross to find the basis for my peace with God. I do not want a false peace that is not based on reality. I do not want to look to myself and my performance to determine my level of peace. I want to look to the work of Jesus. I want a peace that has its foundation in what He has done for me.

When Jesus was born, the angels appeared to the shepherds in the countryside around Bethlehem. Their announcement of the birth of our Savior and Lord was magnificent. There was joy in heaven that could not be contained.

> *And the angel said unto them, Fear not: for, behold, I bring you good tidings of great joy, which shall be to all people. For unto you is born this day in the city of David a Saviour, which is Christ the Lord....And suddenly there was with the angel a multitude of the heavenly host praising God, and saying, Glory to God in the highest, and on earth peace, good will toward men.*
> (Luke 2:10–11, 13–14)

This announcement was so glorious that it could not be contained in heaven. There was good news coming to man from God. This would be the most valuable announcement God had ever made to fallen man. For the first time since Adam tried to run from God's presence in the Garden, there was going to be peace between God and man.

Man had already experienced miracles. He had seen healings. Actually, every miracle of the New Testament had been seen in the Old. It was not the message of miracles, signs, or wonders that was too good to be contained; it was the message of peace between God and man.

All my life I saw the Christmas banners that proclaimed, "Peace on earth and goodwill toward men." Those words were always placed in a setting of men having peace and goodwill for one another. Although that is a noble admonition, it is not the true message that was being sent to earth.

For the first time, there would be peace between man and God. Because of the arrival of the Savior, something was going to happen that would make peace between God and man possible. There was going to be a reconciliation. Man was going to be restored to God.

God always wanted peace between Him and man. He put man here in a garden called Paradise. There was perfect harmony between God and man. When man sinned, he did more than disobey God; he acquired a new capability: the ability to determine good and evil for himself. Along with that ability came a self-imposed standard of righteousness and unrighteousness. Through that self-imposed standard, man became fearful of God. He stopped trusting in God's standards of truth and began to develop his own standards. When he failed to meet up to his self-imposed standards, there was self-imposed fear. Man assumed that fear to be from God, and he related to God accordingly. Thus, there was no peace between God and man. This terrible syndrome has continued in the hearts of men until this very day.

With the arrival of the Savior, that fear problem would be resolved; and for the first time since the Garden, there would be peace between God and man. This fear problem was so powerful that man could not be delivered from sin unless he was delivered from fear. Hebrews 2:15 says that Jesus delivered us from the power of evil by delivering us from the fear of death: *"And deliver them who through fear of death were all their lifetime subject to bondage."*

After man sinned, God still wanted man to have the very best, so He gave him the law. The law was not given to make man righteous; there has never been a law that could make man righteous. Rather, the law was given by a loving Father so that man would have a way to avoid falling under the curse of sin. Likewise, it was given so that a sinful, undeserving man could receive the blessing of God. Even when we were dead in sin and enemies of God, He loved us so much that He wanted us to experience the best.

Righteousness demands that sin be paid for in the flesh of the one who commits the sin. Under the law, at best, man could divert the curses. Yet there was never peace under the law. Man was always fearful of judgment. Man was always struggling to measure up. Because man's nature was sinful, there was always the consciousness of sin. There was always fear. There was always enmity between God and man.

Under the law, man feared and therefore did not trust God. All the imaginations of his heart were continually wicked. Thus, under the law, God was angry. As it says in Psalm 7:11, *"God is angry with the wicked every day."* When sin reigned, God was angry. God was required by righteousness to judge sin in the flesh of man.

With the coming of the Messiah, there would be a new day for man and God. Keep in mind that God's plan for man had not changed. God did not change from the old covenant to the new. He had worked every day for four thousand years to bring man into a place to experience His love. But now, through Jesus, it would happen. Finally, a loving relationship between God and man would be possible. There would be peace.

Today, Christians can have what no generation prior to the cross ever had. We can have peace with God. He has dealt with sin. He has made us righteous. He finds no fault with us because we have been washed clean by the blood of the Lamb.

In this environment of peace and acceptance, we can come to God without fear. We can establish a real relationship with Him. We have no need to be afraid that He will reject or hurt us. We are at peace.

Six

&

The Chastisement
for "Our Peace"

Six

❦

The Chastisement for "Our Peace"

*O*nce a man is delivered from unrighteousness, he can have peace with God. Because he has peace, he can have fellowship. Fellowship can happen only when enmity is resolved.

"Therefore being justified by faith, we have peace with God through our Lord Jesus Christ" (Romans 5:1). The word *"justified"* has the same root as *righteous*. It could read, "Therefore, being made righteous by faith, we have peace with God." If one knows he is righteous, he will be at peace with God. More importantly, God will be at peace with him. And the person will no longer live in fear of judgment and death.

Isaiah 53:5 says, *"But he was wounded for our transgressions, he was bruised for our iniquities: the chastisement of our peace was upon him; and with his stripes* [bruising] *we are healed."* Jesus did not suffer for His sin; He never sinned. He suffered for our transgressions and iniquities. Was this a mere show or type? No. He died for mankind, but He was more than a "sin offering."

For thousands of years, the Jews had gone to the priests and presented an offering that was symbolic of Jesus. Their offering was a type, a shadow; it had no real power to cleanse. Jesus was the real thing. His death was not symbolic; it was the fulfillment of the shadow.

For years, the Jews had stood over their offerings and confessed their sins. Then they would witness and participate in the killing of the sin offering. With their own eyes, they would see this innocent animal receive the death of which they were worthy. Next, they would watch this animal undergo mutilation and burning as payment and appeasement for their sin. They exercised their faith and believed that God would turn His judgment from them because judgment was satisfied in the death of the animal. The blood of the animal did not bring forgiveness, but it did turn away, or appease, God's wrath. Thus the blood signified the judgment of the sin. The sentence of death was passed upon this animal that died as a substitute for the sinner. *"And without shedding of blood is no remission"* (Hebrews 9:22).

An important part of presenting a sacrifice in the old covenant was confessing sins over the offering. Matthew Henry said, "They had to be very specific in their confession, and it had to be done in faith, or God would not receive it." There was never any doubt about this animal being judged for the sins of another. All of this was a symbol of the actual event that would one day take place in the Lord Jesus. While this was the type, the real thing happened at the cross.

At the cross, God made peace with man through a new covenant. This covenant was not secured by the blood of an animal, but by the sinless blood of the Lord Jesus Christ. This covenant was established in His blood. But what does that really mean? In 2 Corinthians 5:21 the Bible says, *"For he hath made him to be sin for us, who knew no sin"; "Him who knew no sin he made to be sin on our behalf"* (ASV); *"For God caused Christ...actually to be sin"* (PHILLIPS). Jesus literally became sin! He was not a mere offering. He literally became sin.

Isaiah 53:6 says it this way: *"And the LORD hath laid on him the iniquity of us all."* In the old covenant, sinful men confessed their sins over their substitute. In this new covenant, a loving God confessed the sins of the world over Jesus. Yet, unlike any other sacrifice, the sins of the world actually came upon Jesus. He became sin.

At this, we begin to understand why Jesus had to become a man. A man brought sin into the world; only a man could bring righteousness into the world. A man brought death; only a man could establish freedom from death. Man sinned, so man had to die. In Jesus the sins of all men were met, and in Him they all were judged.

Prior to the cross, Jesus declared, *"Now is the judgment of this world"* (John 12:31). The judgment of the world for sins took place two thousand years ago. In the King James Version, verse 32 continues to say, *"If I be lifted up...[I] will draw all men unto me."* The word *men* is in italics, which means it is not in the original language. The context of the verse is judgment. Jesus is speaking of the judgment for all men's sin.

When the translators inserted the word *"men"* into this verse, it made it sound like He was saying that all men would be drawn unto Him. This misunderstanding has been a source of many erroneous doctrines. There are people who believe that in the end all men will be saved. It is called the doctrine of ultimate reconciliation. Sadly, not all men will believe and receive Jesus as Lord.

When you remove the word *"men"* from this passage, it reads like this: "Now is the judgment of this world; now the ruler of this world will be cast out. And I, if I am lifted up from the earth, will draw all to Myself." The unanswered question is what will He draw to Himself? The context is judgment. When Jesus died on the cross, He drew the judgment that all men would deserve to Himself. He paid the price that we could not pay.

Until this time, the world (mankind) was an enemy of God. Our sinful nature kept us bound to sin, and then our conscience made us run from God. Similarly, God was obligated to judge sin in man. However, that situation was changed in Jesus.

First John 2:2 says of Jesus, *"And he is the propitiation for our sins."* The word *"propitiation"* has several meanings, but it is best understood as appeasement. Jesus is the appeasement for our sins. To appease something means to satisfy. What was it that Jesus appeased? He appeased the wrath of God, which is the righteous penalty of the law. God's wrath has been satisfied in Jesus. *"Being now justified by his blood , we shall be saved from wrath through Him"* (Romans 5:9). In Jesus, we are made righteous (justified). In Him, the wrath of God is satisfied. How did He do that? He suffered the wrath that we deserve.

"But God commendeth his love toward us, in that, while we were yet sinners, Christ died for us" (v. 8). The death of Christ shows God's love for man only when we truly understand the price He paid. Envision this: You have two children. One is always obedient. He always does what you ask and more. The other one is always in trouble. The good child represents Jesus, who is completely obedient and completely satisfying to the Father. The other child represents mankind, who has strayed for 6,000 years.

Imagine these are your children. You leave them at home with specific responsibilities. The dependable one does everything that you asked. The undependable child fails to complete his chores. What's worse is that he breaks one of your most prized possessions.

When you arrive home, you are immediately faced with the uncompleted chores. Then you find your valuable vase broken beyond repair. Your disappointment and anger boils to overflowing. You call both children into the room and begin to question them both very carefully. You discover which child has failed to do his work, and to your amazement, even carelessly broke your valuable vase.

It seems that the issue of punishment would be simple. However, there is a problem. The one you do not want to punish is the one who deserves it. You know he is too frail. He has problems in his life that make him unable to bear the pain of his consequences. Your incredible passion and mercy for this child prevents you from giving him what he deserves. Yet there is still an issue of punishment. At this point the faithful, innocent child says, "Let me pay for the vase." So you lay all the responsibility on him.

This is exactly what God did in Jesus. He knew that mankind, the guilty party, could not pay the price. He created man to be loved, not to be punished. So He allowed Jesus, the innocent Son to pay the full price for our transgressions.

Once the price is paid, wrath and anger are appeased. First John 2:2 says, *"And He Himself is the propitiation for our sins, and not for ours only but also for the whole world"* (NKJV). The word *"propitiation"* means "the satisfying of wrath." Just as the parent's wrath was satisfied when the innocent child paid for the vase, God's wrath was satisfied when Jesus paid the price for our sin. The guilty one doesn't pay, yet the judgment is satisfied.

This is an extreme simplification of the price Jesus paid for man. However, the difference is this: Jesus did not just take the punishment; He literally became the sin. If He had not become sin, man would not be free from the power of sin. Jesus *became* every kind of sin known to man. It was not just the becoming of sin in general; it was the becoming of *our* sins. He took on every sin man would ever commit so that we might be redeemed. He took on the sin of homosexuality. He took on the sin of alcoholism. He was punished as a thief. He was punished a liar. He took on all the sin that the world has. Had He not specifically become our sins, He would not have received our punishment. Remember, even in the Old Testament type, there had to be a specific confession of sins committed. Jesus became your specific sin, and He took your specific penalty. That is why He is worthy to be your Lord.

Because the price has been paid for your specific sins, you have no reason to fear the judgment of God. You have no reason to fear rejection. The chastisement for you to have peace with God was fulfilled in the Lord Jesus. Faith believes this and enters into fellowship with the Father.

We need have no fear of the wrathful chastening of the Lord. Remember, 1 John 4:18 says,

> *His perfect love for us eliminates all dread of what he might do to us. If we are afraid, it is for fear of what he might do to us, and shows that we are not fully convinced that he really loves us.* (TLB)

If we are expecting God to chasten us when we fail, it means that we do not believe in His quality of love and that we reject the sacrifice of Jesus on the cross.

Immediately one looks to Hebrews 12:6: *"For whom the Lord loveth he chasteneth."* There it is: If God loves us, He will chasten us. This is true, but there is a difference in the word *chasten* used in Isaiah and the word used in Hebrews.

The word used in Hebrews is not a word that means to beat or whip. It is a word that is used of training, teaching, and compelling a child to go in the right direction. Yet, if you look up this word *chasten* in many word study books, you will find it as a strong, negative word.

When Catholicism led the church into the Dark Ages, there was much perversion of truth. As a matter of fact, it was the perversion of truth that brought about the Dark Ages, just as it is our perversion of truth that leads us into darkness. During this time, the "church fathers" redefined the meaning of words. They twisted Scripture to provide a means for manipulating and controlling the people.

Archbishop Trench, in his book *Synonyms of the Greek New Testament,* explains how Augustine and other church fathers redefined the meanings of certain words, such as *chastisement* and *discipline,* to have negative connotations.

In their original use, these words were actually very positive. In order to protect their corrupt theology, Augustine acknowledged that these words originally meant to train a child; but in a religious context, he said, they had to give them a stronger meaning. From then until now, we have falsely translated the New Testament word for chastisement.

We have continued to see God as angry. We have refused to go to the cross to interpret our theology. Consequently, we have totally rejected the reality that at the cross Jesus was chastened to deliver us from chastisement.

Let's accept the reality, and with no longer any fear of an angry God chastening us in wrath, we can have peace in our hearts. We can accept peace between us and God.

Seven

&

Free from the Penalty

Seven

ಹಿ

Free from the Penalty

Everyone knows that God judges sin. Everyone knows that God hates sin. But few realize how God is able to judge sin without destroying man.

You see, while on the cross, Jesus became our sin. At that point, God judged that sin and gave it all the curse it rightfully deserved. Isaiah 53:5 says, *"He was wounded* [tormented] *for our transgressions, he was bruised for our iniquities: the chastisement of our peace was upon him."* When Jesus became sin, God judged sin in Him to deliver us from that judgment.

This is more than deliverance from a future hell. This is deliverance from the curse or the penalty of our sins in this present life. The Jews had a hope of the resurrection, but they did not have any good news about the here and now. They saw God as judgmental and angry until Jesus came and told them the good news about the curse of the law, the good news about God's dealings with sin, the good news that they were free from that penalty *now!*

Galatians 3:13 says it this way: *"Christ hath redeemed us from the curse of the law, being made a curse for us."* Jesus was made a curse for us. In other words, He suffered the curse so that we would not be required to. He redeemed us from the curse of our sin. While Jesus was on that cross, the wrath of God was poured on Him in the form of the curse of the law. All the punishment that we deserve for our sin was suffered by the Lord Jesus. What appreciation we should have! What an awesome price He paid! What a liberty we have! What perfect love God has shown for men!

Unfortunately, most men will never know this wonderful love of God. They will never know to what extremes God went to secure their freedom because the church is preaching an angry God. However, God is no longer angry. His anger has been appeased.

Psalm 22 is one of many psalms that vividly describe the punishment of Jesus while on the cross. It does not take much to grasp that this was more than a sacrifice for sin. This was a sacrifice that became sin and reaped the judgment. The psalm reads,

> *I am poured out like water, and all my bones are out of joint: my heart is like wax; it is melted in the midst of my bowels. My strength is dried up like a potsherd; and my tongue cleaveth to my jaws; and thou hast brought me into the dust of death.* (Psalm 22:14–15)

Why were Jesus' bones out of joint? Why was His torment so much more than the two thieves crucified with Him? Why did His death come so rapidly? According to the Scriptures, Jesus died of something other than mere crucifixion.

Death by crucifixion was slow and painful. It often took days. This is why the soldiers were going to break the legs of the two men who were crucified with Him. The length of time it took to die was a great part of the bitterness of this type of death. Yet, to their amazement, Jesus was already dead at the end of the first day.

Jesus died from the wrath of God as the curse of the law was poured upon Him. Isaiah 53:3 says, *"He is…a man of sorrows, and acquainted with grief."* The words *"sorrows"* and *"grief"* mean sickness and infirmity. Verse 4 goes on to say, *"Surely he hath borne our* [sickness], *and carried our* [infirmities]." This is the way Jesus quoted this verse in Matthew 8:17. Jesus carried our sicknesses and infirmities because they were the results of our sin. They were the curse we deserved.

Under the law, God was obligated to smite the violator with the curse as described in Deuteronomy 28. A major part of that curse was sickness. However, much of it was poverty, torments, and trials. The only way Jesus could set us free from the results of sin was to suffer those results in our place. Otherwise, the righteous requirements of the law would not be satisfied.

After God placed our sin on Jesus, He smote Jesus with the curse. Isaiah 53:5 says, *"And with his stripes we are healed."* For years I was taught that this meant the stripes of the Roman soldiers. For many reasons I could never reconcile that in my heart. Upon closer examination, I found that the word for *"stripes,"* here and in the New Testament, is actually the word *bruised.* Strong's says that the word *chabbuwrah* means "blueness, bruise, hurt, stripe, wound." In other words, "by His bruising we are healed." This is more than just the marks from the soldier's lashings. Verse 5 says, *"He was bruised for our iniquities."* Verse 10 says it pleased God to bruise Him and bring Him to sickness. God bruised Jesus with my sickness. If this is the case, and it is, then I need never fear God bruising me with sickness because Jesus already took it for me.

This is the same thing spoken of in 2 Corinthian 8:9: *"For ye know the grace of our Lord Jesus Christ, that, though he was rich, yet for your sakes he became poor, that ye through his poverty might be rich."* Although Jesus was rich, He had to suffer poverty as a part of the curse of the law. The poverty He suffered was the poverty we were supposed to suffer. Likewise, He was rejected by God so that we would not be rejected. More than that, because of His rejection we always have a guarantee of acceptance.

Jesus suffered every penalty sin would ever deserve. When these things come on us, they are not from God. For God to pour any part of the curse of the law on us would be a denial of the cross of Christ.

The book of Isaiah says that troubles and afflictions will come, but they will not be from God (Isaiah 54:15). You must remember, the devil is a lawbreaker. He does not obey the law of God. He will bring these things on you if you let him.

God has already done His part by setting you free from the curse. You must do your part in resisting the devil. He flees only if you resist him (James 4:7). The resisting is up to you.

First Peter 5:9 says, *"Whom resist stedfast in the faith."* The way to resist the devil is by believing the truth. When we exercise faith—trust in God—we are resisting the devil. He tries to lead us into deceit. If I believe a lie, I cannot benefit from the provisions of God.

I must resist fear; I must resist sickness; I must resist any part of the curse by believing the truth. I am delivered from the penalties that I deserve. I am given the blessings that I do not deserve because of Jesus and His work on the cross.

The devil's main tools against humanity are deceit and ignorance. If we are ignorant of the things of the cross, we will

.think God is tormenting us for our failure. Although we may deserve it, it is never God who torments.

In this life, man often finds himself yielding to sin. Nevertheless, because we have been freed from the penalty of sin, we do not lose our relationship with God when we sin. Because we are free from the penalty, we are free from the fear that could separate us from the only source of help.

When there is a penalty, man is compelled to defend himself. This leads to lying, deceit, and all manner of sin. When there is no penalty, the pure of heart are free to receive help from a loving God.

Eight

৪৩

The Exchange

Eight

ಐ

The Exchange

*For when we were yet without strength, in due time Christ
died for the ungodly....But God commendeth his love toward
us, in that, while we were yet sinners, Christ died for us. Much
more then, being now justified by his blood, we shall be saved
from wrath through him. For if, when* **we were enemies,** *we
were reconciled to God by the death of his Son, much more,
being reconciled, we shall be saved by his life. And not only so,
but we also joy [boast] in God through our Lord Jesus Christ,
by whom we have now received the atonement.*
—Romans 5:6, 8–11, emphasis added

*T*he Bible is clear about the fact that we were once
enemies of God. Colossians 1:21 explains this very
clearly: *"And you, that were sometime alienated and
enemies in your mind by wicked works, yet now hath he reconciled."* God has never been our enemy, but we have been
enemies of God.

Colossians says we were enemies in our minds by wicked
works. In other words, that status existed only in our minds.
It was not real. It was all in our heads, so to speak. God has

never been the enemy of mankind. God has always worked to restore and deliver mankind from sin and its effects.

Yet, when we sin, our hearts condemn us. We become afraid of God. We actually judge Him and determine that He must hate us for our wickedness. We assume how He must feel about the situation, and we act accordingly.

God solved this problem by making peace with us through the cross. Colossians 1:20 says, *"And, having made peace through the blood of his cross, by him to reconcile all things unto himself; by him, I say, whether they be things in earth, or things in heaven."*

When God solved this problem, He poured the curse of the law upon Jesus, delivering us from the penalty of our sin. God did not, however, stop at merely delivering us from wrath. His ultimate goal was to cause us to experience His love, life, and acceptance whereby we would enter into a meaningful relationship with Him.

Galatians clearly points out that God not only freed us from the curse, but He also put us in a position to receive all the promises and blessings that He made in times past. *"Christ hath redeemed us from the curse of the law...that the blessing of Abraham might come...that we might receive the promise of the Spirit"* (Galatians 3:13–14).

Freedom from wrath is only half the work of the cross. The word *reconciled* has several very strong and positive meanings. One is exchange. When we were enemies of God, we were exchanged to God. Beyond dying for our sins, Jesus took our place in order that we might take His place. In other words, He received what we were and what our lives deserved, while we receive what He is and what His life deserves.

In John 10:10 Jesus said it this way: *"I am come that they might have life, and that they might have it more abundantly."* He did not come just to set us free from the results of our sin. He also came to put us in the center of God's will so that we might receive God's blessings and promises.

God has always desired that man have His best. That was clearly demonstrated in the Garden of Eden. Adam was placed there in abundance and provision. There was no lack, suffering, or sickness, and there was no pain in the Garden of Eden. God proved His desire for man with the utopian setting He created for man. It was man, not God, who surrendered Paradise to make it the world it is today. Destruction, pain, suffering, sickness, and poverty all came in with sin. Sin was introduced by the devil and brought into Paradise by man. This was not God's desire or His judgment. It was the law of sowing and reaping.

Throughout Bible history, you see God's desire to pour His blessings on men. When God found men and women who believed Him and obeyed Him, He showered them with His goodness. Many of the patriarchs were very wealthy men. Some of them would even be multimillionaires by today's standards. Even the law gave provision for God's blessings. He has always wanted us to live in His provision and power. The stipulations of the law gave opportunity for curses, but it also gave the same opportunity for the blessings or promises. The law was filled with wonderful promises from God. These promises included health, healing, prosperity, success, peace, and joy. But you had to live a holy life before God to qualify for those blessings.

The weakness of the law was the flesh (Romans 8:3). Because the flesh was weak, man continually found himself in a position worthy of the curses. And because the flesh was weak, man seldom found himself in a position to receive the blessings. The entire law was based on the performance of man. The new covenant, on the other hand, is based on the performance of one Man, Christ Jesus.

Jesus was the One who lived the sinless life. He also was the One who became sin, suffered the penalty for sin, and then conquered sin by the Resurrection. The entire new covenant depends on the completed work of the Lord Jesus. We participate in that accomplished work by faith.

Romans 5:11 in the King James Version says that in Jesus we have *now* received atonement. The word *atonement* is almost the same as the word *reconciled* in the previous verses, and it means the same thing. In other words, in Jesus we have the exchange, and it is effective now. The exchange will not go into effect in some future time or dispensation; it went into effect when Jesus sat down at the right hand of the Father. We begin to participate in it the moment we believe it.

The word *atonement* as used in the old covenant is not found anywhere in the new covenant. Atonement means "covering" in the Hebrew language. The only thing the Old Testament believers received from the blood of the animals was a covering.

You do not have a covering in Jesus; you have an exchange—an exchange that took your sin away from you and gave you His righteousness. Your sins are not covered; they no longer exist. God is not pretending that they do not exist. *They do not exist.* When He looks at you, He does not pretend that you are righteous. You are righteous by the Lord Jesus.

When Jesus was raised from the dead, He conquered sin and death. He did not conquer sin in general; He conquered your specific sin, thereby guaranteeing you a specific victory over your specific sin. He was raised up in newness of life. The quality of life that Jesus now has is the quality of life the Father has. In Him, you receive that quality of life as well.

The Greek word used to describe the quality of life we have in Jesus is *zoe*. This is a quality of life that is possessed by the one who gives it. Because Jesus received this quality of life from the Father, I receive it, too. Remember, the inheritance He earned is the one I receive. I have the quality of life God has. I received it in the Lord Jesus.

In the exchange, we receive His righteousness. That righteousness qualifies us to receive all the promises of God. Colossians 1:12 says, *"Giving thanks unto the Father, which hath made us meet to be partakers of the inheritance of the saints in light." The New International Version* translates the word *"meet"* as *"qualified."* In other words, God has qualified us to receive the inheritance. How did He qualify us? In Jesus.

I receive nothing from God on my own merit. Instead, I receive every promise based on the finished work of Jesus. Thus the Scripture is fulfilled that says, *"No flesh should glory* [boast] *in his presence"* (1 Corinthians 1:29). My confidence is not in my accomplishments but in Jesus' accomplishments. I am qualified by Him, and I receive that inheritance by faith— not faith that says I am able, not faith that says I am worthy, not even faith that says I have enough faith, but faith that says Jesus did it all.

Because I am in Jesus and have His righteousness, every promise God ever made to anyone in the Bible is mine. *"For all the promises of God in him are yea, and in him Amen, unto the glory of God"* (2 Corinthians 1:20). Because I am free from works-righteousness, I can rest in Jesus with no fear or dread. Furthermore, I am compelled to a life of worship and praise.

I cannot help but continually give thanks to the One who has done so much for me. Because I know I am righteous, my heart desires righteousness; because I know I am free from sin, I am confidently compelled to stay free from sin. Why should I sin? I am righteous in Jesus.

On this issue, we are very prone to mix the old covenant with the new one. We are very quick to return to works as our basis of receiving from God. But if we are in works, then it is no more a promise. *"Now to him that worketh is the reward not reckoned of grace, but of debt"* (Romans 4:4). Works say that God owes. Grace and faith say that God promised.

Works say that I can get God to respond to me. Faith (trust) is my response to what God has done in Jesus. Works place the emphasis on what I have done. Faith places the emphasis on what Jesus has done. Works look to my righteousness for qualification. Faith looks to Jesus' righteousness for qualification.

The life I now live is the exchanged life. Jesus received what I deserve; I receive what He deserves. He was made to be my sin; I was made to be His righteousness. He received the penalties that my sin deserved; I am receiving the blessings that His righteousness deserves. Because He was rejected, I am accepted. Because He was chastened, I have peace before God. By Him I have been exchanged to God.

Nine

&

Faith-Righteousness

Nine

❧

Faith-Righteousness

*P*aul, as an apostle to the Gentiles, was given special insight into our identity in Jesus. Why? He was dealing with people who had no knowledge of the law, and God did not want them under law. He did not want them to try to mix law and grace. Therefore, He sent them a man who had lived by the letter of the law, yet still needed Jesus.

Paul, more than anyone, knew the futility of works-righteousness. Repeatedly, he spoke of who we are in Christ. All we have and all we do would be the result of the finished work of the Lord Jesus. Remember, he was sent to people who had no hope in the law. When the Judaizers came and tried to mix law with faith, he continually confirmed that Christ in us was the *"hope of glory"* (Colossians 1:27). We need not hope in the law.

We need not trust in any of our good works. But we must find our assurance in Christ Jesus, our one and only hope of glory. Paul knew that the secret of God's power was faith-righteousness, a message that still confuses the carnally minded.

Faith-righteousness is a message that is understood only by revelation, yet it is a message that is essential to every believer's victory. Without the absolute confidence of right standing before God, there cannot be an absolute assurance of the promises. And it is by these promises that we escape the corruption that is in the world through lust (2 Peter 1:4).

Paul knew that works-righteousness did not bring freedom, but bondage. It actually produced bondage! He also knew that faith-righteousness was the only way to know Jesus. It is the only way to fellowship or share in what was accomplished in His sufferings. And it is the only way to know the power of His resurrection (Philippians 3:10). People who never enter into faith-righteousness never get real freedom from the flesh and the various sins that work in the flesh.

Paul discounted all his works, all his qualifications, and all his personal accomplishments so that he might *"be found in him, not having mine own righteousness, which is of the law, but that which is through the faith of Christ, the righteousness which is of God by faith"* (Philippians 3:9). Faith-righteousness places Jesus at the very center of all we are, all we have, and all we can do in God. It acknowledges the vanity of our own attempts at righteousness and depends on Jesus' righteousness to be manifest in every area of life.

Faith-righteousness is the heart of the message of the cross, because on that cross an exchange took place. In that exchange, God *"made him to be sin for us, who knew no sin; that we might be made the righteousness of God in him"* (2 Corinthians 5:21). It is this message of the cross that will liberate us from sin and deliver us from the works of the flesh.

If we do not believe in righteousness by exchange, there is nothing left but works-righteousness. By the works of the law or flesh, no man has ever been justified (Galatians 2:16). Works-righteousness is a life of legalism that leaves out the grace of God, which works in us to deliver us from sin. It places man and his performance at the center.

In Richard Lenski's commentary on Romans, he talks about the realm of law and the realm of works. The Bible often speaks of law and works. When speaking of law, it is not limited to the old covenant law. It could be any realm of law. Anything we do to earn something from God, anything we do apart from faith, anything we do to make us righteous, is in the realm of law, works, and flesh. It is also sin (Romans 14:23). It is sin because it rejects the work of Jesus.

The term *flesh* is much like the term *law*. When the Bible speaks of the flesh, it is not talking about this body. It is talking about a realm where we are trying to be made righteous by our own abilities. It is the performance-oriented life. People who try to relate to God on the basis of works of law are in the flesh.

It was essential that we be delivered from law in order to be delivered from the flesh. Romans 7:5 says, *"For when we were in the flesh, the motions* [passions] *of sins, which were by the law, did work in our members."* Law or works causes passion to arise in our bodies. Until we are free from works, we cannot conquer sin.

In the exchange, we died to the law by the body of Christ (v. 4). Remember, when Christ died, we died. Now that we are delivered from the law (the realm of law), we are able to serve God in newness of spirit and not in the oldness of the letter.

In other words, we are no longer doing the best we can and hoping that it will be acceptable to God. We are believing that we are righteous because of Jesus and trusting the Spirit of God to change us and empower us to live in righteousness. Being in the Spirit is not when we are in a trancelike, mystical state of mind. It is when we are dependent on the Spirit to empower us for righteousness, thereby delivering us from the realm of the flesh.

When we try to serve God in the oldness of the letter, whether it is the old covenant or the new covenant turned to law, sin will revive. *"For I was alive without the law once: but when the commandment came, sin revived"* (Romans 7:9). Sin comes back to life in a heart that has no room for faith-righteousness. Sin thrives where man tries to operate in his own ability. Even if we are able to conquer a problem by the sheer power of our will, we become self-righteous. One way or another, sin revives.

Romans 6:14 states that the very reason we are free from sin is that we are no longer under law, but under grace. Grace is God's ability working in us. Works and law frustrate the grace of God (Galatians 2:21). The word *frustrate* means "to set aside or nullify, make void, disesteem, and neutralize." When we enter the realm of works, God's power to free us from sin is nullified. Therefore, sin will always dominate the man who lives in the realm of works.

Many people have debated exactly what Romans 7 refers to. Is it Paul before he got saved, or after he got saved? Personally, I believe it describes the plight of any person who departs from faith and grace and enters the realm of works. Likewise, when Paul talked about falling from grace in Galatians 5:4, he was not discussing whether the person would go to heaven. He was discussing leaving the realm of grace (God's ability) and entering back into our own ability.

Christ is of no effect in the life of the person bound to works. We must accept our righteousness in Jesus. This is totally contrary to all the natural aspects of man. We all look at our own failures and shortcomings and say, "How can I call myself righteous? I have all kinds of problems and sins!" Yet we will never be really free from those sins until we receive His righteousness.

Receiving that righteousness starts with believing. If Jesus' mission was accomplished, and it was, then *you are righteous in Christ.* If you believe that, you will not be able to live any kind of life you choose. If you believe it, you will confess it, thank God for it, and live in step with the Spirit of Christ.

The power of righteousness comes alive in the person who believes he is righteous in Jesus. That person has a "righteousness conscience." On the other hand, the person who is operating in law has a consciousness of sin. What we have awareness of grows in our life. Accordingly, the person aware of sin falls into more sin, and the person aware of righteousness grows in a life of righteousness.

After explaining the exchange, Romans 5:12 gives this example: Sin entered the world through one man. Few people have trouble with this. We all know that we are sinners because of Adam. In him, we all became sinners. We were born with a sin nature. Now, before you got saved, I am sure you did some good things, but those good things did not make you righteous. You were still a sinner. It was your nature to sin. Despite your efforts, you always went back to sin—*sin was your nature.* Keep in mind, doing good occasionally did not cause you to have a righteous nature.

Because of the sin of Adam, the sentence of death was passed upon all men. You did nothing to receive the ability to die; you were born with that ability. However, likewise, in Jesus, by His life we receive the gift of righteousness (Romans

5:17). Natural birth guarantees us a sin nature, but a spiritual birth guarantees us a righteous nature by the gift of righteousness. Just as sin passed the judgment of death on all men, righteousness passes the life of God unto all men. You will recall from our discussion in chapter eight that the word for *life* in the original language is the word *zoe*. According to the *Biblio-Theological Lexicon of New Testament Greek*, *zoe* is the quality of life of the one who gives it. Because we have Jesus' righteousness, we get to participate in the *zoe* life of God. This life makes available to us everything that God has and is. And more importantly, it is a product of Jesus' righteousness.

Romans 5:10 says it this way: *"Being reconciled* [exchanged], *we shall be saved by his life* [*zoe*]." The word *"saved"* means more than born again. It means healed, delivered, protected, made whole, made well, and so on. The reason we have this complete salvation is that we receive His *zoe*. We receive His *zoe* because we receive His righteousness. We receive His righteousness because of the exchange. Accordingly, it is all ours by faith.

You are righteous because you were born of God. Being righteous does not mean you never sin. It means you have a righteous nature. It is now natural for you to live a righteous life. Even though you may fall, you are not a sinner. As the psalmist said, *"Though he fall, he shall not be utterly cast down: for the* LORD *upholdeth him with his hand"* (Psalm 37:24). Proverbs says it like this: *"For a just man falleth seven times, and riseth up again: but the wicked shall fall into mischief"* (Proverbs 24:16).

When you had a sin nature, you did some good works occasionally. However, those good works could not change your unrighteous nature to become righteous. Likewise, now that you have a righteous nature, when you fall, that cannot change your righteous nature to make you unrighteous. We were born into unrighteousness. Our works did not bring about that state of being. Likewise, we are born into righteousness; our works will not bring about that state of being.

This is not a permit to sin. On the contrary, a righteous heart hates sin. A righteous heart wants to please God. A righteous heart loves righteousness. And the heart is made righteous only by faith (Romans 5:1; 10:10).

There is a fear in us that this belief will somehow make it possible for men to get away with things. And some could try to use it as a license to sin. But Paul, Peter, and John warned against and dealt with these same fears. There were groups in the early church that tried to abuse freedom. The apostles, though, dealt with the issue without abandoning this truth.

To abandon faith-righteousness is to abandon the finished work of Jesus. Regardless of how sincere the motive, a departure from faith-righteousness is a departure from truth.

Ten

&

Faith to Faith

Ten

Faith to Faith

The weakness of modern Christianity traces back to the foundation of our belief system. Everything we believe is slanted in the direction of and interpreted by our foundational beliefs. Our one and only foundation should be the death, burial, and resurrection of the Lord Jesus.

The slight deviations from what happened at the cross are what create confusion and destruction in the major areas of our lives. It's like firing a weapon. When a bullet is fired from a gun, the barrel must be exact. A deviation of only a fraction of an inch could result in a miss of many feet. And the farther the bullet travels from the barrel of the gun, the greater the degree of error.

Likewise, there are many things we believe about the cross that may not really seem significant until we weave them into our daily lives. Then, in that setting, we end up miles away from our desired destination in Christ.

Paul said in Romans 1:16, *"For I am not ashamed of the gospel of Christ: for it is the power of God unto salvation to every one that believeth; to the Jew first, and also to the Greek."*

The Gospel is the *"power of God unto salvation."* It should produce the salvation of God. We know that salvation is more than being born again. It is the full benefit of God's provision. So if what we believe is not producing salvation, then we must face the truth: Either we do not believe the truth, or maybe what we do believe is not true.

When Paul said he was not ashamed of the Gospel, he was not speaking of Jesus personally. The Jews did not have that great of a problem with Jesus. They had a problem with what Jesus had accomplished for man. The Judaizers who followed Paul around the world and caused so much of his persecution did not tell people to reject Jesus. They simply told people that Jesus could not make you righteous.

The good news of Jesus is that righteousness is now a free gift. Any deviation from this is not good news. The Jews had righteousness by works. In Christianity, we have so compromised the Gospel that today we have no more than the Jews had.

In verse 17 Paul continued, *"For therein is the righteousness of God revealed from faith to faith: as it is written, The just shall live by faith."* Paul said that in the Gospel, the righteousness of God is *"revealed from faith to faith."* He did not say that it was revealed from faith to works.

Most Christians actually believe that Jesus saves you, but that your works make you righteous. Jesus gets you saved; you keep yourself saved. Jesus purchased your healing; you qualify yourself to receive healing. Jesus conquered the devil; your works deliver you from his attacks. We do not really believe that righteousness begins with faith and ends with faith.

Faith-righteousness should be woven through every thread of our belief system. The moment we depart from faith-righteousness, we have departed from the Gospel. It must be the basis for all we are, all we hope to be, and all we will receive from God.

The Galatians had this same problem. Paul preached Jesus to them. They received a wonderful salvation. When Paul left, the Judaizers came in and said, "Believe on Jesus for salvation, but you must obey all the law to be righteous enough to receive the promises. If you don't live holy enough, God will smite you with the curses."

This is why Paul said, *"Are ye so foolish? having begun in the Spirit, are ye now made perfect by the flesh?"* (Galatians 3:3). In other words, this work was begun in you by the Spirit of God, and it can be completed only by the Spirit of God.

In Galatians 3:2, 5, Paul asked,

> *This only would I learn of you, Received ye the Spirit by the works of the law, or by the hearing of faith?...He therefore that ministereth to you the Spirit, and worketh miracles among you, doeth he it by the works of the law, or by the hearing of faith?*

In other words, when you first received the Spirit, was it because you believed what you heard or because you earned it by keeping enough of the law? When people worked miracles among you, was it because people believed the truth or because they earned it by keeping the law?

Nothing changes in this regard after we are saved. This relationship with God was the product of a free gift. Our ability to maintain a relationship with God is the product of that free gift. Paul told the Colossian believers to continue in Christ the same way they began in Christ—rooted and grounded in faith. Don't try to change the rules.

Nearly every book of the New Testament was written because the churches were being deceived in the area of righteousness. While believing on the person of Jesus, they rejected His finished work of the cross. They believed they were saved by grace and made righteous by works. They didn't believe righteousness was from faith to faith.

This issue of righteousness is the stumbling block of the Gospel. People do not struggle with most of the major aspects of Jesus' life and ministry. They struggle with this issue of righteousness.

In Romans, Paul described the dilemma:

What shall we say then? That the Gentiles, which followed not after righteousness, have attained to righteousness, even the righteousness which is of faith. But Israel, which followed after the law of righteousness, hath not attained to the law of righteousness.

(Romans 9:30–31)

Israel really wanted to find righteousness, but they could not find it. The Gentiles were not really looking for righteousness, but they found it.

Verse 32 explains why the Jews were unable to attain righteousness: *"Wherefore? Because they sought it not by faith, but as it were by the works of the law."* The Gentiles were willing to accept righteousness as a gift. That response is faith. The Jews, on the other hand, were not willing to accept that it was a gift. They sought to earn righteousness by their performance.

The last phrase of verse 32 is of the utmost importance: *"For they stumbled at that stumblingstone."* Faith-righteousness is the stumbling block of the Gospel. This is the rock of offense.

Jesus Himself is not the rock of offense. Jesus, as our righteousness, is what offends and causes those who will not believe to stumble. They stumble because of their unbelief concerning righteousness.

Romans 9:33 says, *"As it is written, Behold, I lay in Sion a stumblingstone and rock of offence: and whosoever believeth on him shall not be ashamed."* If a person believes on Jesus as his righteousness, he will not stumble; he will not be ashamed; he will not be confounded. But those who do not believe will stumble.

They rejected the cornerstone. Jesus, as our righteousness, is the Cornerstone of Christianity. Anything else will produce a faulty foundation. When we try to build on another foundation, the entire building will collapse. This is why Paul warned in 1 Corinthians 3:10–11 about the need to take heed when building our lives:

> *According to the grace of God which is given unto me, as a wise masterbuilder, I have laid the foundation, and another buildeth thereon. But let every man take heed how he buildeth thereupon. For other foundation can no man lay than that is laid, which is Jesus Christ.*

We should continue in our Christian life. We should grow in our understanding of God. We should grow in good works. But all these things should be built upon the foundation of faith-righteousness. They should never be the foundation of our righteousness. Every Christian should live a godly life. Every Christian should bear fruit. However, the moment these things become our hope and confidence for being accepted by God, they are no longer gold, silver, and precious stones. Because they are not built on the foundation, they are wood, hay, and stubble.

Healing is true, but if it is not built on the foundation of faith-righteousness, it will collapse. All the promises of God are true, but they will not stand when built on a faulty foundation. We are like people who have tried to build skyscrapers on mud puddles. When the building falls, we question the validity of the promise. The promises are good, but they must be built upon the sure foundation of Jesus as our righteousness. Our every belief must be built upon faith-righteousness. The only righteousness that qualifies us for all the promises is His righteousness.

Eleven

&

Being Righteous We "Have Peace"

Eleven

✿

Being Righteous We "Have Peace"

*F*rom the giving of the law at Mount Sinai, the Jews had to earn the blessings of God. As we stated earlier, if they were good (righteous), they received the blessings. If they were unrighteous, they received the curses. Keep in mind that it is God who established His standard of righteousness. God is the only One who can define and determine the standards of right and wrong. Any attempt on our part to define righteousness apart from the Word of God is actually humanism. That is exactly what Adam did in the Garden of Eden.

From the time that Adam partook of the fruit of the Tree of Knowledge of Good and Evil, man has been a god unto himself. He has decided right and wrong by his own definition. He even has attempted to make God accept his standards. The ability to determine right and wrong, however, belongs only to God. Keep in mind, that was satan's basic temptation: "You can be gods and determine right and wrong for yourselves." This is where we have the birth of humanism, which is the basis for all false religion.

Humanism places man at the center of the universe. His personal opinions are the determining factors for right and wrong. Man is a god to himself. He makes his own standards and his own rules. But worst of all, he fabricates his own definition of righteousness. This is a right that belongs only to God.

The word *her esy* is used very loosely in Christian circles. Usually, we define a heretic to be anyone who disagrees with our beliefs. The word *her esy,* however, has its roots in a word that means "to choose." So a heretic is one who chooses what he believes. The Word of God is not the absolute authority for a heretic. He views truth as optional; therefore, he lives life by preference instead of conviction.

One becomes a Christian by making Jesus Lord of his life. As Lord, His Word is the final authority about what we should believe. It should form all our views and opinions. Regardless of how we may feel about a particular thing, we surrender the right of choice to His lordship. When one enters the realm of choice about his beliefs, he is functioning outside the realm of Christ's lordship. This option of choice has been a detrimental factor for the church down through the ages. We have chosen to believe many wrong things about God, about the cross of Christ, and about how to have a relationship with God.

Church history reveals that man has continually opted for beliefs that are more convenient or less threatening. For example, baptism by immersion was the standard for hundreds of years. Later, when it was not convenient, the church modified it to sprinkling. This was more socially acceptable.

Some people have a false concept of God as an angry taskmaster. However, we see God's character revealed in Jesus. He said, "If you've seen Me, you've seen the Father." (See John 14:9.) He was the exact representation of God. God would not relate to man in any fashion contrary with Jesus' life and ministry. When Jesus was confronted with the adulteress, He didn't judge her. Yet we insist that God is angry and faultfinding. Why? It is a convenient way to control others.

Christianity is not a religion of choice and convenience. Rather, we come to God hurting and faced with all sorts of problems that are the product of decisions based on our personal beliefs. Our lives cannot change if our beliefs do not change. One cannot come to Jesus and experience any change apart from surrendering his beliefs.

One who does not surrender his views and opinions to God will continue to be a god unto himself. He also will continue to experience the same hurts and difficulties as before. God works in our lives as a product of believing the truth.

The greatest devastation in the Christian's life comes about by the refusal to accept God's standard and definition of righteousness. Because we do not understand faith-righteousness, we cling to works-righteousness. After all, it makes sense; we can understand it. It does not require us to believe something that is beyond our present scope of understanding.

We all understand works-righteousness. It works like this: If I do only good things, I am acceptable to God and I get the blessings. If I do anything wrong, I am unacceptable to God, and I get chastened.

We saw it under the law. It was revived in the early church and ushered into the Dark Ages. Much of the theology that was developed by the early Catholic Church, particularly in this area, still influences our concept of God. Works-righteousness, though, always brings fear and rejection. One never knows if what he has done is good enough. One doesn't have the confidence of God's forgiveness. This fear is torment. The only deliverance from that torment is believing and experiencing the love of God (1 John 4:8).

In Romans 1:16 Paul said, *"I am not ashamed of the gospel* [the Good News] *of Christ: for it* [this Good News] *is the power of God unto salvation* [new birth, healing, deliverance, protection, and so on]." When one does not believe the Good News, he is void of the power of God. He is unable to live the salvation Jesus purchased for us. Whatever part of the Good News you believe, you can receive the power to live.

Paul went on to say in verse 17, *"For therein* [in this Good News] *is the righteousness of God revealed from faith to faith."* Faith-righteousness is the Good News. Faith-righteousness is the beginning and the end of the Christian life. It does not go from faith to works; it is faith to faith. This is why the people of the early church were called believers. Everything they experienced with God was a product of what they believed, not a product of what they did. The old covenant was the product of works. Righteous works qualified you to receive the provision of God. But we have a new and different covenant. It is a better covenant, with better promises.

God has established a new covenant. He intended that we would be free from the old one. He set us free from works-righteousness to qualify us to receive the life (*zoe*) that is earned by Jesus. Yet we stay bound to the old. We cling to works-righteousness simply because we do not believe and understand faith-righteousness. We enter into the realm of choice and justify it by our own reasoning. Sadly, we are the ones who suffer for it. We make the sacrifice of Jesus void of power through our traditional beliefs (Mark 7:13).

Works-righteousness appeals to the carnal mind. The carnal mind, according to Romans 8:5, is a mind set on the flesh. Remember, we live in the flesh when we attempt to be made righteous by the works of the flesh. To the carnal mind, works-righteousness makes sense. It is rational. It fits our preferential beliefs.

Romans 8:5 says, *"For they that are after the flesh do mind the things of the flesh; but they that are after the Spirit the things of the Spirit."* The person whose mind is set on what the flesh does is a person who has man and his works at the center of his religion. He erroneously places God on the outside. This mind is not set on the work of the Spirit of Christ. It has no awareness or sensitivity to the reality that righteousness is a work of the Spirit of righteousness.

Thus, Romans 8:8 declares, *"So then they that are in the flesh cannot please God."* Why? you ask. Hebrews 11:6 says it this way: *"But without faith it is impossible to please him."* Galatians 2:16 says it another way:

> *Knowing that a man is not justified by the works of the law, but by the faith of Jesus Christ, even we have believed in Jesus Christ, that we might be justified by the faith of Christ, and not by the works of the law: for by the works of the law shall no flesh be justified.*

God has defined righteousness. We cannot reject His definition for our reasonable, rational preferences.

The great restraint concerning faith-righteousness is that we do not *understand* it. We have mistakenly thought that we could believe by understanding. There is some truth to that in the natural realm, but the Bible presents just the opposite. In the spiritual realm, we must believe in order to understand. Hebrews 11:3 explains, *"Through faith we understand."* As we choose to believe God, understanding is opened to us. Therefore, we will never understand what we do not believe.

Why is it so essential that we receive righteousness as a gift? All of this may seem trivial until we see the practical difference it will make. Romans 5:1 says, *"Therefore being justified* [made righteous] *by faith, we have peace with God through our Lord Jesus Christ."* God is at peace with man. We have established that. But why is it so important that we see that?

Although God is at peace with us, we might not be at peace with Him. If we are living in fear or insecurity about our relationship with God, we cannot break free from sin. We have already seen how a works mentality actually causes sin to resurrect in our members. Law causes us to hide our sin. Mercy and forgiveness, on the other hand, create an environment of peace and love that lets us deal with our sin.

Until we can deal openly with our sin before God, we cannot be set free from it. We cannot deal openly and honestly with it if we do not realize God's peace. An environment that says God will judge you for your sin is a negative, unproductive environment. It is one that promotes self-righteousness and deceit. We become defensive of our actions. Instead of being teachable, we are ready to defend our every position. After all, if we are wrong, we run the risk of judgment. Yet if God poured all His judgment out on Jesus, we need not fear that He will judge us.

Many ministers are afraid of this message. They fear it will promote a loose and casual lifestyle. They are afraid people will take advantage of God's goodness and get into sin. Actually, if people believe this, they will be less compelled to sin. When one believes in the *"zoe"* life of God, when he sees all the good things God has to offer, when he sees the goodness of God, he will also see that the world has nothing to offer.

Most people believe the world has good things to offer in comparison to the false "suffering message" of Christianity.

They think that being a Christian is a defeated lifestyle of eating crumbs and wearing worn-out clothes. That is simply not true. Try to explain that to Abraham, David, and the other patriarchs!

There is indeed a time of scriptural suffering, but we should not suffer because of unbelief or ignorance. If I must suffer for the Gospel, I will do it gladly. Even in that suffering, I am victorious. Or, if I must suffer, I will suffer as Jesus did. Hebrews 2:18 says He suffered when He was tempted. His suffering was in denying Himself, living for God, and saying no to sin. I will gladly say no to sin and self. This is what it means to take up my cross. I also will suffer by surrendering my will, my opinions, and my preferences to His will, His view, and His opinion.

The message of wrath, suffering, trials, and testing has turned the world away from the Gospel. As a matter of fact, this is not the Gospel (Good News) at all. The world will be won by the Good News. The news that God is not angry with you; the news that God loves you; the news that righteousness is a free gift; the news that your sins have been paid for; the news that Jesus provided all of this is the Good News the world needs to hear. The message of wrath does not keep people from sin; it makes them hypocrites and liars. They do not stay out of sin any better than anyone else; they just hide it better. A person who wants to sin will sin, regardless of what he believes. Whatever his theological position, he will find a way to justify his sin. Before a person can properly deal with sin, he must be free from the fear of judgment.

God said, *"Come...let us reason together"* (Isaiah 1:18). There is no reasoning with wrath. In fact, the book of Proverbs warns against dealing with angry, unreasonable people. Our reasoning with God is not trying to convince Him we are right or justified in our sin. Our reasoning with God is where we come face-to-face with a loving God in an environment of peace and confess our sins. It is here that mercy and truth meet together. It is here that the goodness of God draws us into repentance (Romans 2:4). It is here that a troubled and convicted heart finds mercy and grace to help in time of need (Hebrews 4:16).

If I am not fully convinced that I am righteous through the Lord Jesus, I will never have peace. I will never be sure. Recently I sat and talked with a person who had gone into error. This person believed that everyone would eventually go to heaven. As we discussed why she believed this she said, "I used to be so afraid that I might not be forgiven and that I might go to hell. When I heard this, it gave me peace." The absence of peace makes people susceptible to error that offers false peace.

Many people have given up on God and returned to sin. When I talked to one man he said, "I just could not go on not knowing if God had really forgiven me." Because he did not know he was righteous, he did not have peace. That lack of peace destroyed his walk with God.

Then there are those who are bitter. They have labored to do right. They attempted to earn the blessings. When they did not get peace or when they did not get the reward they expected, they became bitter and angry at God.

Our peace cannot be based on our performance; that is too unpredictable. It causes us to vacillate up and down. Neither can our peace be in a false doctrine. Then we would have to defend that doctrine to maintain our peace. Our peace must be rooted in the certainty of the finished work of Jesus.

If Jesus is my righteousness, He is the center of my life. For every promise in the Bible, I look to Him and His finished work and say, "Because of You, I am qualified." When trouble comes my way, I look to Jesus and say, "Because of You, I know this is not from God." When fear tries to enter my mind, I look to Jesus and say, "Because of You, I don't have to be afraid. *You* are my peace."

Twelve

&

The Covenant
of Peace

Twelve

❧

The Covenant of Peace

Isaiah 53 graphically describes the exchange that took place on the cross. It depicts the terrible suffering that Jesus endured for our sakes. Then, chapter 54 begins to explain the new covenant that will go into effect as a result of that exchange.

Isaiah 54:7–8 says,

> For a small moment have I forsaken thee; but with great mercies will I gather thee. In a little wrath I hid my face from thee for a moment; but with everlasting kindness will I have mercy on thee, saith the LORD thy Redeemer.

Before God could have fellowship with man, He had to settle the sin problem. Sin had to be judged. Righteousness demands the judgment of sin.

God, in His great love for man, judged the sin of the world in Jesus. Because His wrath and righteous judgment have already taken place, man is now free to enter into a peaceful relationship with a holy God. Before His wrath was appeased, the consequence of sin was the main thing that kept men walking upright.

The fear of penalty may change one's actions, but it will not change one's heart. The heart is changed by love. Since God is a heart God (1 Samuel 16:7), He desires a relationship. Now that judgment has been satisfied, God can love us into a heart relationship.

Romans 2:4 says it is *"the goodness of God* [that] *leadeth …to repentance."* The word *"repentance,"* contrary to popular teaching, is not a grieving or weeping. It may include those elements, but that is not repentance. In fact, the Bible talks about two kinds of repentance. One is an afterthought because of consequences. This is what the Bible speaks of when it says that Judas repented before committing suicide (Matthew 27:3).

The repentance that God requires is a change of mind. Judas did not change his mind about his sin; he simply was sorry for the results. The judgment message may make one dread the results, but it will not change the heart. If we have a loving relationship with a loving God, that relationship will draw us into a change of mind. It will bring us to the place where we do not desire to sin.

I so enjoy and depend on my loving, heavenly Father that I do not want to sin. His goodness is too precious to me to disrupt it with sin. This is not to say I never sin, but this is the motivation for staying out of sin. Likewise, this is the motivation for repentance.

Isaiah 54:9 goes on to say,

> *For this is as the waters of Noah unto me: for as I have sworn that the waters of Noah should no more go over the earth; so have I sworn that I would not be wroth with thee, nor rebuke thee.*

In His covenant with Noah, God swore that He would never judge the earth by water again. He then set the rainbow in the sky as a seal to that covenant. God has faithfully kept that promise.

Now He says, "This is just like My covenant with Noah." In other words, this covenant is just as sure as His covenant with Noah. This covenant says, "I will never be angry with you or rebuke you" (Isaiah 54:9). This is what God has sworn to us, and this covenant is as sure as any He has ever made.

This is a covenant of peace.

> *For the mountains shall depart, and the hills be removed; but my kindness shall not depart from thee, neither shall the covenant of my peace be removed, saith the* LORD *that hath mercy on thee.* (Isaiah 54:10)

The exchange made it possible for God to be at peace with man. Sin has been judged in Jesus. We have been made righteous in Him; now we have peaceful fellowship with God. He swore that His kindness and peace would not depart from us.

If someone came on the scene and proclaimed that God was going to judge the world by water, we all would quickly realize the error. God says, "As surely as I will never destroy the world with water, I will not be angry with you; I will not rebuke you; My kindness will not depart from you; the covenant of peace will not be removed from you, because *I am a merciful God.*"

The covenant with Noah was sealed with a rainbow. The covenant of peace was sealed in the blood of Jesus. If God violates this covenant, then He has denounced the blood of Jesus. A violation of this covenant would be total rejection of the blood, the death, and the resurrection of His Son. But this covenant is sure.

God will never destroy the world by water. So what would you do if your favorite preacher, the person you trust most, stands up and says, "I've heard from God. He's going to destroy the world by water." Regardless of how much you love and trust that person, you would not receive that message. You would confidently look back to the covenant God made with Noah. You would stand on God's Word. What if that same person stood up and said, "God's not going to judge the world with water, but He is going to destroy one nation by water"? Again, the error would be obvious. What if that person said, "Well, God's not going to destroy the world by water, but He's so mad He's going to drown one person"? Again, the error would be obvious.

The reason the error would be obvious is that we all know about the covenant with Noah. Unfortunately, we are more aware of the covenant with Noah than we are of the covenant with Jesus. Ignorance causes people to go into captivity and bondage. Our top priority as Christians should be to know the new covenant. We are to live, worship, and minister by this covenant.

God swore that He would be at peace with mankind. This means both believers and nonbelievers. Jesus did not appease the wrath of God for the sins of the church. He appeased the wrath of God for the world. So at the present time, God is judging no man for his sin.

There surely will be a time of judgment for those who are not found in Christ, but today, God is judging no man. This covenant of peace is sure.

Righteousness is what makes all of this possible. *"In righteousness shalt thou be established"* (Isaiah 54:14). Verse 17 is quick to point out, *"And their righteousness is of me, saith the LORD"*—not the righteousness of man that comes by works, but the righteousness of faith that comes by the Lord Jesus.

As God said in Isaiah 40:2, *"Speak ye comfortably to Jerusalem, and cry unto her, that her warfare is accomplished, that her iniquity is pardoned."* The war is over. God saw the problem, and He did all it would take to solve it through Jesus. Because this thing is of God, it is sure and consistent.

What about the message that says God is judging you? What about the message that makes one feel God is the source of all his pain and affliction? Isaiah 54:17 says, *"And every tongue that shall rise against thee in judgment thou shalt condemn."* The Emphasized Bible says it this way: *"And every tongue that riseth against thee in judgment, shalt thou prove to be lawless."* The tongue that pronounces the judgment of God on man is a lawless tongue. It does not speak in line with the new covenant. We can no more accept the message of God's wrath being poured out on man at this time than we could accept the prophecy of another worldwide flood. This is why the angels sang, *"Glory to God in the highest, and **on earth peace, good will toward men***" (Luke 2:14, emphasis added).

The message that says God is judging someone before the time of judgment is as absurd as someone saying God is going to judge the world by water. We have a sure word and a sure covenant sealed in the blood of Jesus.

There is a rationale, however, that says, "If I violate my covenant, then God is freed from His side of the covenant." We must understand that God did not establish His covenant with us; He established it with Jesus. In order for this covenant to be broken, Jesus must fail. He did not fail. He finished every aspect of the work. Thus this covenant is established, it is settled, it is sure, and it is unchangeable.

Galatians 3:16 explains, *"Now to Abraham and his seed were the promises made. He saith not, And to seeds, as of many; but as of one, And to thy seed, which is Christ."* The promises were made to Jesus. The covenant was with Jesus. Because I am in Him, I qualify to participate in the covenant.

We accept that God made a covenant with Noah that benefits all of us. We would never think that our actions could alter the covenant made with Noah. Likewise, our actions cannot alter the covenant made with Jesus.

We have a covenant of peace, and it is sure. It is sealed with the blood of Jesus.

Thirteen

&

The Love of God

Thirteen

&

The Love of God

And we have known and believed the love that God hath to
us. God is love; and he that dwelleth in love dwelleth in God,
and God in him.
—1 John 4:16

The apostle John not only believed in God's love, but he also had experienced it. He had tapped into the greatest power in existence—the love of God.

When I was first saved, I wanted desperately to know God's power. I wanted to see God's mighty acts. Like Elijah, I expected to know God in the earthquake, in the fire, and in the wind. I soon discovered that you could see all these things and still not know God. Knowing God's power soon became secondary to knowing God.

You will grasp the fullness of God's power only to the degree that you grasp the fullness of His love. Paul understood this when he prayed for the Ephesians to be

> *rooted and grounded in love,* [that they] *may be able*
> *to comprehend with all saints what is the breadth, and*
> *length, and depth, and height; and to know the love of*

Christ, which passeth knowledge, that ye might be filled
with all the fulness of God.   (Ephesians 3:17–19)

Paul knew that the key to being filled with God's power was knowing and believing His love.

Love is the motivating factor behind all that God does. More than anything else, God is love. Therefore, you know and understand God only by understanding the God-kind of love. This is the major key to miracles, healing, faith, and peace.

When I pray for the sick, cast out devils, or intercede, it is not a matter of my trying to work up a super faith. It is not a matter of trying to change God's mind. It is not a matter of the individual having a good enough life to receive. All I know is the great love of God that has already given the very best He has to offer—Jesus. I do not trust in my super faith; I trust in God's super love. My faith is simply a response to the love and integrity of God.

In Romans 8:32–34 Paul presented a series of questions that should cause us to realize that God is not the one causing our problems. *"He that spared not his own Son, but delivered him up for us all, how shall he not with him also freely give us all things?"* (v. 32). In Paul's first question he reminded us that God has already given the best. Why would God withhold anything from us after He has already given us the best He has?

He also pointed out that God freely gives all these things. We received Jesus freely. We were not worthy. Our lives were not good enough. So why would God require us to earn anything else? If anything should have been earned, surely it would have been the right to become sons of God. But that was given freely. When Jesus sent out His disciples, He said, *"Heal the sick, cleanse the lepers, raise the dead, cast out devils:* **freely ye have received, freely give**" (Matthew 10:8, emphasis added). Jesus placed no price on His goodness, then or now.

It seems we are afraid that if we preach a free Gospel, the undeserving will receive. That is exactly the point; the undeserving need to experience the love of God. When the undeserving experience the love of God, that kindness will bring them to a change of mind (repentance) about God. When they taste and see that the Lord is good, they may not want to go back to the pigpen to eat.

Paul continued to ask, *"Who shall lay any thing to the charge of God's elect? It is God that justifieth"* (Romans 8:33). The original language says, "Who shall bring an accusation against the chosen ones of God? Will God who acquits them?" God is not looking for fault in us, so the obvious answer is no. If God is the One who acquitted us, if God is the One who justifies, if God is the One who makes us righteous, why would He turn around and bring a charge or accusation against us? God is not the faultfinder.

Think of it! God gave me the righteousness that I have. I do not come before Him with my righteousness; I come before Him with the righteousness He gave Jesus. Therefore, if God finds fault with me, He has found fault with His own work. I am His workmanship, created in Christ Jesus. (See Ephesians 2:10.)

Why would God find fault with His own work? Obviously, He doesn't. That means the feelings of not measuring up and the sense of fear and uncertainty I feel about approaching God are the products of my own heart. God is not finding fault with me.

It is obvious that if I sin, my heart will condemn me. I need to listen to my heart. I need to change the behavior that is robbing me of my confidence before God. But God is greater than my heart. My heart tells me that I need to change my behavior to live in proper relationship with other people. The finished work of Jesus, though, tells me that God still loves and accepts me. It tells me I can come before Him with boldness and get help, even though I may have problems.

Paul continued, *"Who is he that condemneth? It is Christ that died, yea rather, that is risen again, who is even at the right hand of God, who also maketh intercession for us"* (Romans 8:34). Again, Paul pointed out the absurdity that condemnation, faultfinding, and judgment would come from the Lord Jesus. Why would He find fault if He is the one who died for us? Obviously, He would not.

If Jesus is for me, He cannot be against me. He would not be for me in the presence of God and against me in my presence. The feelings of condemnation, the expectations of judgment, are not from Him. Jesus is for me, not against me.

Although most Christians agree with that, they draw the line when a person sins. It is easy to believe God loves us when we do right, but few people believe that God loves us when we do wrong. First John 2:1 says, *"My little children, these things write I unto you, that ye sin not."* It is obvious that God does not want us to sin, but the verse does not stop there. *"And if any man sin, we have an advocate with the Father, Jesus Christ the righteous."* It does not say that God judges us when we sin. It does not say Jesus will accuse us. It says that when we sin, Jesus is still our Advocate. An advocate is one who is for you, not against you. Even when you sin, Jesus is still for you. He's not the one who condemns you. He's the One who helps you come out of sin.

The Bible says satan, not Jesus, is the accuser of the brethren. Condemnation does not help anyone come out of sin. Rather, it destroys confidence and self-worth. It paralyzes the confidence that God wants to help us. Condemnation is the strongest tool the devil has against the believer. If he can make you believe that God is against you, he can separate you from the only One who can help you.

We have been so conditioned to think God that is the source of our difficulties. When trouble comes, our first thought is very often, "Oh, no, what have I done now? Why is God doing this to me?" Isaiah 54:15 says, *"They shall surely gather together, but not by me."* Or as Jeremiah prophesied, *"And they shall fight against thee; but they shall not prevail against thee; for I am with thee, saith the LORD, to deliver thee"* (Jeremiah 1:19).

Now, if God is the Deliverer, He cannot be the destroyer. If God is for you, He cannot be against you. The New Testament says it this way: *"Let no man say when he is tempted, I am tempted of God: for God cannot be tempted with evil, neither tempteth he any man"* (James 1:13). The word *"tempted"* means "solicitated to evil, trial, or tribulation," or "scrutinized." Do not say that your trials are from God. When you feel you are being scrutinized, do not say it is God. God is not looking you over for fault. He has made you righteous in Jesus.

We have made God out to be the bad guy. The world does not want to come to the God we have presented to them. Most people (Christians) feel that it is easier to be a sinner than to be a Christian. But be assured, the God we have shown the world is not the God Jesus showed to the world. Either He was wrong about God, or we are.

I remember sharing about the love of God with an alcoholic. I assured him of God's love and mercy. As he sat weeping, he suddenly said, "Let me see your Bible." I handed it to him and asked, "What are you looking for?" He said, "I wanted to see if this was the same Bible the other preachers use." He continued, "I've never heard of the God you're talking about." Here was a man who lived in the Bible Belt of America. He grew up in church, yet he had never heard of God's love.

God does not have a double standard. He does not require us to love and yet exempt Himself from loving. He is the Author of love. All real love comes from God. His love was demonstrated in the fact that He sent Jesus to die for us. We did not deserve it and did not even want it, yet in His love, He sent His only Son.

When Jesus comes in us, He brings the *zo e* life of God. All the healing, power, prosperity, and fullness of God are in you in Christ. As you become persuaded in the love of God, you will allow His life (*zo e*) to flow into you with confidence, joy, and thanksgiving.

Fourteen

❧

Good News Faith

Fourteen

&

Good News Faith

The Gospel of peace is the only source for building real faith. For years we have taken Romans 10:17 to mean, "If you keep hearing the Word, faith will come." There was a time when I believed and taught it that way. That, however, is not what the Scripture says, and history certainly does not bear it out.

If just hearing the Word would build faith, why aren't all people working miracles, healing the sick, and raising the dead? Why don't all people who hear the Word trust God? If faith (trust) comes from just hearing the Word, it would be a simple thing to bring all people to a life-changing faith in God. But many people who read the Bible become fearful. They often pull away from God. The majority of people sitting in churches don't really trust God with every aspect of their lives. Yet they are hearing the Word.

Romans 10:17 says, *"So then faith cometh by hearing, and hearing by the word of God."* To understand this, or any Scripture, we must understand it in light of the context. The context for understanding this passage is the previous ten chapters of Romans, which are all about faith-righteousness.

In Romans 10:13, the Scripture begins to get specific: *"For whosoever shall call upon the name of the Lord shall be saved."* It then explains the progression whereby a person is compelled to call upon the name of the Lord. Verse 14 explains that he will not call on the name of the Lord if he does not believe.

The Bible goes on to say that people will not believe if they have not heard. What you hear about God will determine if you call on Him. If what you hear makes you believe that God loves and accepts you, you will confidently call upon Him. If what you hear makes you unsure of God's love for you, you will not call on Him with confident trust (faith).

Then the Scripture asks, *"How shall they hear without a preacher?"* (v. 14). Regardless of what the Bible says, the preacher you hear will affect the way you hear (understand) the Word. A man once came to Jesus and asked Him a question. Jesus' reply was not what one would expect. He asked the man, *"What is written in the law? how readest thou?"* (Luke 10:26). Jesus asked him two questions: first, What does the Word say? and second, How do you interpret that?

What the Word says and how we read or interpret it can be worlds apart. We have been tempered and molded to see God the way the preacher sees Him. This is why it is so essential to read the Bible for yourself and to develop your own concepts of God through the Word and personal involvement.

In Luke 8:18, Jesus warns, *"Take heed therefore **how** ye hear"* (emphasis added). How you hear is as important as what you hear. If you hear a promise of God, it is absolutely true. But if you place a wrong stipulation on receiving that promise, you have taken what could bring life and turned it to bring death.

I must allow the Word to speak for itself. I must not place what seems to be reasonable interpretation on the Word of God apart from it having a foundation in the new covenant. I can't look to the old covenant to understand how God will operate under the new covenant, although it may seem reasonable and logical. To do so is to reject the validity of the new covenant.

I must realize that the person who preaches the Word to me affects my hearing. I am partaking of his perceptions and preferences. Thus the Bible says, *"How shall they preach, except they be sent?"* (Romans 10:15). There are too many who are not sent forth with the message of the new covenant. They have run forth out of their own zeal. They are anxious to perpetuate their own perceptions, but they are not sent with the Gospel of peace.

The whole of Romans 10:15 says,

> *And how shall they preach, except they be sent? as it is written, How beautiful are the feet of them that preach the gospel of peace, and bring glad tidings of good things!*

Not every preacher has beautiful feet. Not every preacher walks in the pathway of peace. Scripture says those who *"preach the gospel of peace,"* those who *"bring glad tidings of good things,"* are the ones who are sent.

Unfortunately, not all the preachers who have gone forth believe the report. They do not believe there is a covenant of peace. Therefore, they preach a message of fear and condemnation. Thus we have the fulfillment of Romans 10:16: *"But they have not all obeyed the gospel. For Esaias saith, Lord, who hath believed our report?"*

Faith does not come from hearing the Word in general. Faith comes when we hear the Good News, the glad tidings of the Gospel of peace. Hearing the Gospel of peace will build faith (trust). Hearing bad news about works, law, and performance will destroy confident trust (faith). The message of peace makes one run to God; the message of judgment makes one run away from God.

Hebrews 11:1 says, *"Now faith is the substance of things hoped for, the evidence of things not seen."* Real faith is always the product of hope. The word *hope* in the original language means "a confident expectation of good things." A confident expectation of bad things produces fear. A confident expectation of good things always produces faith.

Expectation of good things should be the general view of all Christians. In every situation we should be expecting good things from God. We will never do that if we are hearing teaching that labels God as the source of all our hurts, trials, problems, and tribulations. That kind of teaching promotes the expectation of bad things from God. The Bible calls that *fear*. According to Hebrews 11:1, faith cannot exist where there is no hope (confident expectation of good).

Even faith itself is turned to law if you have a wrong concept of God. I have seen many Christians trying to change God's mind and earn His acceptance with their faith. That is nothing more than works. It is not faith at all. Faith functions on the basis of promises, not works. Faith trusts God because He is good. It does not try to get Him to do good. Faith knows God is good.

We have wrongly been taught that faith is what we do to get God to respond. If we must do anything to get God to respond, then we are in works. Faith is not what we do to get God to respond; faith is our response to what God has already done in Jesus. If we must provoke God to do something, then we do not believe it is already done in Jesus. If we know that

God has given all provision in Jesus, then we have a confident expectation in this life.

Either hope or fear will rule our lives in every situation. If we are not confidently expecting good, then we are in fear or worry. This basic concept we have of God affects our faith more than anything else. We can learn all the techniques or methods of working faith, but without the confident expectation of good, faith will not come.

The wrong concept of God generally comes from the inability to separate the old and new covenants. Most Christians have mixed the two together and are trying to relate to God on the basis of a perverted covenant. In Psalm 78:37 God explains that Israel's problem was a heart problem: *"For their heart was not right with him, neither were they stedfast in his covenant."* Likewise, we are not steadfast in this new covenant.

Because we are not steadfast in the new covenant, we are quick to pervert it by mixing it with the old. We are continually looking to the Old Testament to understand how God will relate to man. Since our beliefs are not based in the new covenant, we come to God with certain predetermined perspectives. These perspectives determine how we hear, read, interpret, and understand the Word of God.

I once heard a story about a young boy who sat on the seashore and watched the boats going by. As he watched, he realized that the wind blew only in one direction, but the boats went in every direction. He asked a wise elderly man, "How is it the wind blows only one direction, but the boats sail in every direction?" The wise old man answered, "It is not the direction of the wind that determines the direction of the boat; it is the setting of the sail."

Likewise, in our lives, it is not the direction of the Word we read as much as it is the direction of the beliefs of our hearts.

We have set our sails through our traditions. Those traditions can make the Word of God to be of no effect in our lives, just as it did for the Pharisees in the time of Jesus (Mark 7:13).

Apart from the Gospel of peace, we won't have the hope that brings faith. Jesus read the same Scripture as the Pharisees, yet He found God to be a healer and miracle worker. He found God to be a merciful Father, ready to forgive and restore men. The Pharisees read the Scripture and found an angry God who would weigh men down with heavy religious burdens. What was the difference? The setting of the sail.

You see, you find what you look for. If you believe God to be mean and judgmental, or just hard to please, you will find Scriptures to reinforce that. But if, like Jesus, you see God as a loving Father, you will find the promises that give hope.

Proverbs 10:29 says, *"The way of the* Lord *is strength to the upright: but destruction...to the workers of iniquity."* According to the condition of your heart, the word that sets one man free can make you bound. The word that shows one man the love of God can show you something different. Therefore, we should be careful who or what is forming our view of God.

Our view of God is continually being developed. We should guard our hearts against anything that would cause us to lose confidence and trust in God. The Bible says in Romans 1:17, *"For therein* [in the Gospel] *is the righteousness of God revealed from faith to faith: as it is written, The just shall live by faith."* Everything I hear and believe should support the view of faith-righteousness and thereby cause me to trust God.

Fifteen

Sowing and Reaping

Fifteen
৩০

Sowing and Reaping

*M*any people fear that the Gospel of peace will promote a liberal lifestyle. It seems that the negative mind sees retribution as the only way to curtail sin. Through this fear of people taking advantage of God, we have, with good intentions, withheld the truth. Paul, however, said that he was not ashamed of the Gospel (Good News). He realized it to be the power of God unto salvation (Romans 1:16). He knew that only the good news of faith-righteousness could bring about the kind of salvation God has provided and expects.

Paul faced persecution for his message. In the book of Romans, he pointed out that he had been accused of encouraging sin. In the book of First Corinthians, he had to defend his message and his apostleship. In the book of Galatians, he talked about how the Judaizers had criticized his message. They tried to bring the people out of peace and grace and into a mixture of the old and new covenants. But Paul still confidently proclaimed, "I am not ashamed of the good news of faith-righteousness."

You must realize that there will be those who feel they can take advantage of the goodness of God. Such people will be the way they are regardless of what you preach. A perverted heart will always pervert anything to self-gratification. But we cannot let the perversion of some people license us to lie. Instead of changing his message, Paul warned in Galatians 5:13, *"Only use not liberty for an occasion to the flesh."* He gave similar warnings in Corinthians. Peter warned against the same thing. We must warn, but we cannot change the truth.

Galatians 6:7 says, *"Be not deceived; God is not mocked: for whatsoever a man soweth, that shall he also reap."* The Phillips translation says it this way: *"Don't be under any illusion: you cannot make a fool of God! A man's harvest in life will depend entirely on what he sows."* AIDS is not the judgment of an angry God; neither is sickness, poverty, or all the other plagues of humanity. Some of our pains are obviously the work of the devil, but the majority of that which hurts us is the product of sinful sowing and consequent reaping.

We should warn people of the destruction of sin. We should make them realize how much pain sin can bring into a person's life. But we should never try to make them think that the pain is God's judgment against them for their sin. This life is a series of decisions. We must live with the consequences of the decisions we make. When we act independently of truth, we will reap a crop of destruction. When we make decisions based on truth, we will reap a good harvest.

The law of sowing and reaping is not a matter of God's blessings or punishment. It is just a natural law that God set in place. When you plant a crop, you can't plant just any kind of seed and get the desired results. You must plant the seed that will produce what you want.

When people realize that sin is the source of their pain, they will hate sin. Since people think God is the source of their pain, they hate God. God has not hurt anyone under the new covenant. He has set us free from the curse of the law, and He has given us the wisdom of His Word to know how to avoid painful decisions.

God has shown us how to live in victory. He has made the way possible through the Lord Jesus. If we choose to live in destruction, it is not God judging us; it is the product of our actions. Do not be deceived; the law of sowing and reaping is sure. But praise God, there is a higher law. It is the law of the Spirit of life (*zo e*) in Christ Jesus (Romans 8:2).

When we are tired of the destruction of our own way, we can turn to a loving, merciful God, receive forgiveness, and be delivered from the law of sowing and reaping. You might ask, Does this mean a person could sin, ask for forgiveness, and never suffer any penalty of his sin? Yes, if there is true repentance, confession, and turning back to the Lord. But there is an effect of sin that is more devastating than any of the afflictions that come on our flesh.

The Bible warns that we should guard our hearts with all diligence, because all the issues of life come from the heart (Proverbs 4:23). Everything your life is or will be is a product of your heart. You cannot rise above the condition of your heart. You will ultimately live out the abundance of your heart. Therefore, the most devastating effects of sin are seen in how it affects the heart.

Hebrews 3:13 says, *"But exhort one another daily, while it is called To day; lest any of you be hardened through the deceitfulness of sin."* Sin hardens the heart. It makes the heart insensitive to God. Paul warned Christians in the book of Ephesians not to live like the Gentiles do.

This I say therefore, and testify in the Lord, that ye henceforth walk not as other Gentiles walk, in the vanity of their mind, having the understanding darkened, being alienated from the life [zoe] of God through the ignorance that is in them, because of the blindness [hardness] of their heart: who being past feeling have given themselves over. (Ephesians 4:17–19)

Paul warned that living in sin will darken our understanding of God, which will result in our being alienated from the life, the abundance, the *zoe* of God.

Alienation happens through ignorance of godly things, which is a product of blindness, or hardness, of heart. Even after we have received forgiveness from our sin, there is still a problem with our hearts. This problem can be solved, but it is not easily detected.

Hardness of heart refers to a callus on the heart. When one works with a hoe or shovel without gloves, he usually gets blisters on his hands. These blisters are very painful and make it difficult to go back to the same kind of activity. Similarly, when we as Christians get involved in sin, it is very painful to our hearts. Since we have a righteous nature, we can no longer sin without feeling pain. But if the person doing that yard work goes back to the same type of work, those sensitive blisters will eventually become calluses that inhibit feeling pain. Likewise, one who continues in sin will callous his heart to the point of not being able to feel or detect the work, conviction, and direction of the Holy Spirit.

As Paul said in verse 19, he will be past feeling. Lenski says this is "to cease to feel the pain of conviction." Now the man continues in the sin, not realizing the destruction that is being created. Often, one even reaches a point of feeling that his sin is acceptable to God. After all, he does not feel any discomfort.

That lack of pain in the heart is not God's approval, however. It is the devastating, deceitful effect of sin.

Hebrews 3:12 warns, *"Take heed, brethren, lest there be in any of you an evil heart of unbelief, in departing from the living God."* The deceitfulness of sin is not obvious. The deceitfulness of sin is the inward effect on the heart. Be assured, though, a hardened heart will eventually choose to turn away from God—*and feel no pain.*

The book of Hebrews contains six strong warnings about sin. These warnings are stronger than most preachers and Christians like to admit. Basically, we are warned against apostasy. You will not find this word in the King James Version, but it is found in the original language. An apostate is one who turns away, never to return. An apostate is not one who loses his salvation; he is one who throws it away.

We have security in Christ, but we also have a freedom of choice. No one gets up in the morning and says, "Hey, I think I'll throw away my relationship with God today. I believe I'll turn from God so I can spend eternity in hell." No, it does not happen that way. Rather, through a long, deceitful process, sin can bring us to that point. And the reason it is so hard to turn around is that *we feel no pain!*

If you are backslidden, do not assume you have reached this point. As long as you are alive, you can turn around. But hear the strength of this warning: If you stay in sin, you may ultimately throw God away.

God never quits loving you when you are in sin. Jesus never turns against you. He will forever be for you (1 John 2:1). But you will turn against Him. So, along with the message of peace, we have to present the warnings. You cannot take advantage of God. He won't get you, but your sin will.

We also must understand the effects of sin in this life. Although God is merciful, people are not. Long after we have experienced God's forgiveness, we must still live with the way our sins have affected other people. There may be a lack of trust. There may be anger. There may be those who will never forgive what we have done to them. This is only one of the many painful aspects of sowing and reaping.

Sixteen

&

A Relationship of Love

Seventeen

&

Discerning the
Heart

Seventeen

ॐ

Discerning the Heart

S ince the heart is the most important aspect of our being, we should know more about the heart than anything else. However, we are a people void of understanding. That is why we reduce our relationship with God to rules and regulations.

Law does not allow a person to understand his own heart. A person can do all the right things for all the wrong reasons. For instance, two people can commit the same actions. One person can be sincere and honest; another can be manipulative and deceitful. On the outside they may look the same; however, on the inside were different motivations.

Nowhere does the Bible give us the right to judge the heart, or the motivation, of another. Many times I hear people say, "Oh, he has such a good heart." I often want to ask, "How do you know? And who gave you the right to pass that judgment?" Judgment belongs to the Lord. We cannot even properly judge our own hearts, much less the heart of another. The Bible says the Word of God will discern, or judge, or sift our hearts. The Word of God is the mirror that I use to understand my own heart. If I look into the Word and put it into practice with love as my motive, my deeds are revealed as light or darkness. By walking in the love described in God's Word, I put my heart to rest in God's presence and drive out all condemnation.

In recent years, I have had the opportunity to rescue many people who are coming out of a legalistic environment. When these people leave a church or pastor that kept them in line through judgment and condemnation, they fall apart. They get to the place where they do not want to go to a church, pray, tithe, or anything. Many onlookers would say, "See, this liberal message promotes sin." It is quite the opposite. The mercy, truth, and light of God do not promote sin; they expose it. What a shock it is to these people to find that when they had no one to "browbeat" them, they stopped serving God. When the element of fear was removed, they found that they were not really in love with God. Many people spend a lifetime going through the motions and never understanding why they have no real, inner victory in living for God.

You see, these are not people who are in a loving relationship with Jesus, a relationship in which He and the Father come to them and manifest themselves. They are living under law and know very little of the goodness of God. Many of these people have never experienced the real repentance that brings a change of mind and heart. There has been only the repentance that abstains for fear of the results. These people, though doing good works, are backslidden in their hearts. They serve God, but not from the heart. It is lip service. I am not challenging their salvation, but I do question the joy of their salvation.

Proverbs 14:14 says, *"The backslider in heart shall be filled with his own ways."* The condition of your heart is filling your life with good or bad things. All may look good on the outside, but what's on the inside? Every person I have known who grasps this message goes through a major upheaval in the inner man.

I sat one day talking with a man who had come from a very performance-oriented background. For a number of years he had been a "high achiever." He was one of the up-and-coming young men in a rather large congregation.

As he sat talking to me, he said, "This just isn't working. Since I've been hearing this message I haven't been as dedicated. I don't pray as much. I don't read my Bible as much. I don't witness as much." My simple response was, "It sounds like it's working to me." "How could that be?" he asked.

I said, "How many of those things that you did, for all those years, were done because you loved God and you loved people? Or how many of those things were done because you were trying to get on staff? Or were you possibly trying to gain the favor of the leaders?"

We sat staring at one another for a few long moments of silence. He dropped his head into his hands and began to cry. "Most of it was to get on staff," he responded. "I wanted the oversight to approve of me."

I believe in living a productive life; I just prefer that people do it out of love. I see people like this young man go through these difficult changes. I see them struggle to get back in touch with God. It is so hard to find reality and relationship after so many years of performance and hypocrisy. But then I see these people begin to bear fruit. I see them enter into a joy and peace that is beyond anything they have ever known.

Love demands proper attitudes and motives. Love does not work by law and obligation. The Gospel of peace requires a right heart. Be assured, this message will produce havoc in a person whose heart is not right before the Lord. If this message produces the attitude of loose or ungodly living, you have a heart problem. If you feel that you can take advantage of God's mercy and forgiveness, you have a heart problem. The problem is not the message. Remember, *"The way of the* LORD *is strength to the upright: but destruction...to the workers of iniquity"* (Proverbs 10:29).

The heart is the seat of our emotions and our will. Emotions can come from different sources. They can be stimulated from the spirit or from the flesh. Emotions can be very deceitful. Many people live for God, yet they are robbed of confidence because of condemnation. Others live for self and deceive themselves into believing they are right before God. So emotions are not a stable indicator of the condition of our heart. First John 3:18–21 tells us how to assure or persuade our hearts before God. Verses 18–19 say that the only way to know we are in truth is by loving in both word and deed. Walking in love can settle the issue when our hearts condemn us. Works do not earn me a position or favor with God. But the fruit that comes forth because of my relationship with God helps to assure my heart. It becomes a mirror to my inner man.

When my heart does not condemn me, I have confidence, and I receive whatsoever I ask. Confidence is an important part of faith. I must first have a confident expectation of God. I must have confidence of my own standing before God.

First John 3:22 says, *"And whatsoever we ask, we receive of him, because we keep his commandments, and do those things that are pleasing in his sight."* One would quickly say, "See, you must keep the commandments to get your prayers answered." Remember, the context is walking in love. Keeping the commandments does not earn answered prayer. Instead, keeping His commandments assures our hearts.

Verse 23 goes on to say, *"And this is his commandment, That we should believe on the name of his Son Jesus Christ, and love one another, as he gave us commandment."* Believing on Jesus and walking in love fulfills the commandments of the Lord. Therefore, the way I live, in regard to my belief on the Lord Jesus and walking in love, reveals the condition of my heart. I don't have to relate to the Lord and His people in the "right" way in order to avoid judgment. They are things I do because of the love of God in my heart.

When the threat of judgment is removed, we have the opportunity to see what is really in a person's heart. If you hear this message of love and peace and feel it gives you a license to sin, your heart has been revealed. Now you know why you have struggled in the past. Now you know what you have really been dealing with. Truth will reveal the condition of the heart. It will sort out the real motives and intentions. *"For the word of God...is a discerner of the thoughts and intents of the heart"* (Hebrews 4:12).

Eighteen

&

Bringing Forth the Heart

Eighteen

❧

Bringing Forth the Heart

*I*n our negative thinking, we have assumed that the Lord could change man only through harsh, painful deal-ings. But, praise God, that is not the case. Only a fool has to learn the hard way. God does not relate to us as fools, but as sons. Under the old covenant, He had to deal with man from the outside. He used negative circumstances to urge people in the right direction. He brought about pain and affliction to make one realize the error of his way. However, that is not needed for the pure of heart.

Even under the old covenant, God tried every way possible to help man avoid ultimate destruction. Because man was not regenerated, God could not speak to his heart. He always dealt with man from the outside. There were parents, elders, teach-ers, prophets, and others who would instruct a person in the way. There was the teaching of the Word of God. There were many avenues for man to hear instruction, learn, and change. A wise man would hear a rebuke and learn. A wise man could be taught. A wise man did not have to experience pain to heed his ways. This is why Proverbs 10:8 says, *"The wise in heart will receive commandments: but a prating fool shall fall."*

149

A foolish man is very different. Proverbs 19:29 tells us, *"Judgments are prepared for scorners, and stripes for the back of fools."* A fool is one who will not learn by instruction. He will learn only from the consequences. Pain is the only hope for the man who will not read the Word and believe. Consequences are the only deterrents to a person who will not be led by the Holy Spirit.

What God did on the outside under the law, He now does on the inside in the heart. I know by experience that there is nothing more painful than a healthy conscience that is pricked by sin. I know the severity of going in a direction that is not pleasing to the Lord. The pain I feel is not judgment, though; the pain is what a renewed nature feels when it violates that nature.

When Jesus came into our lives, He made us new creations. We no longer have a sin nature. We are no longer able to live in sin comfortably. We are now righteous. The Holy Spirit is continually convicting us that we are righteous. Consequently, we are not compatible with sin.

Besides the pain of our conscience, sin also brings pain into our lives from several sources. One of the main areas sin causes pain and difficulty is in our relationships. Its effects destroy meaningful relationships and separate us from those we love.

We must never falsely assume that all the pain we experience from our foolish or sinful ways is the wrath of God. God said sin would kill us. If we do not believe that and do not avoid sin, we will learn about the pain of sin as an unteachable fool does. God does not add pain to our sin, either. Rather, He draws us out of sin and gives us the strength to change.

How does the Lord change and chasten us? The word *chasten* means "to train a child." Until the time of Augustine, *chasten* was a positive word. It described a father developing and compelling his child in the right direction. Augustine redefined the word under the assumption that in Christianity it had to have a harsher meaning. Therefore, we still have a negative view of God's dealings with His children.

The book of Hebrews says,

> *My son, despise not thou the chastening of the Lord, nor faint when thou art rebuked of him: for whom the Lord loveth he chasteneth, and scourgeth every son whom he receiveth.* (Hebrews 12:5–6)

This passage is quoted from the book of Proverbs, which goes on to say, *"For whom the LORD loveth he correcteth; even as a father the son in whom he delighteth"* (Proverbs 3:12).

It does not say the Lord chastens as the father who hates his child. He chastens as a father who delights in his child. God delights in you because you are in Jesus, not because of your works. Because we are in Jesus, we have the high calling of being conformed to the likeness of Jesus (Romans 8:29). This is God's will for us; this is our high calling. God wants to make us just like Jesus. To accomplish this, God deals with our hearts. The change is a work of His grace in our hearts.

Proverbs 17:3 says, *"The fining pot is for silver, and the furnace for gold: but the LORD trieth the hearts."* In order to make gold and silver pure, it must be put in the furnace. The heat causes the precious metals to separate from the impurities and come forth as treasure. As the Scripture points out, the furnace does this, *"but...."* It does not say the furnace does this *and* the Lord tries the heart. If the conjunction were an *and,* the sentence would mean that the Lord does the same thing as the furnace. Instead, it says *"but."* Although it takes the furnace to make the metals pure, it takes the Lord to make the heart pure. The word *"trieth"* means "to bring forth." What

God does in you does not come by the furnace; it comes from the heart. The way God purifies us is to *bring forth* our hearts. If God can get our hearts pure, then our lives will be pure.

In Psalm 51:6, David acknowledged, *"Behold, thou desirest truth in the inward parts: and in the hidden part thou shalt make me to know wisdom."* After his experience with Bathsheba, David realized that God desired more than good works. He desired truth in the heart.

Change that comes from the heart abides. It governs our every action. It is second nature. It is effortless to walk in the beliefs of the heart. Change on the outside is nothing more than behavioral modification. That change will last only as long as we put forth effort. Its motive cannot be trusted. God wants a heart change in us.

Be assured, when we sin and suffer the consequences of sowing and reaping, we learn as fools do. I must say, although it is hard, it is better to learn as a fool than not to learn at all. Many times I have seen my children headed for difficulty. I usually warn them and suggest the steps to divert the problem. If they are wise, they heed my counsel. If they are foolish, they go ahead anyway. The Bible says, *"The simple pass on, and are punished* [destroyed]*"* (Proverbs 22:3). I am not going to let my children be destroyed, so I do not follow this same rule in extremely severe situations. But when at all possible, when they will not listen to counsel, I will let them make the wrong decision. When they begin to suffer the hardship of their decisions, they become very teachable. I could *make* them do the right thing, but then they would never grow up. I could get the desired results on the outside, but I want to see them change on the inside.

Similarly, when we stray, it can become a learning experience. God can work in us in any situation, and He will; but be assured, He did not bring the hardship. His desire is for us to be teachable and changeable through fellowship and communion with Him.

John 15:2 says, *"And every branch that beareth fruit, he purgeth it, that it may bring forth more fruit."* I have heard some "horror" sermons about God taking out His big clippers and cutting away at our lives. What is worse, I have preached some of those sermons. In verse 3 of that same chapter, Jesus continues, *"Now ye are clean through the word which I have spoken unto you."* The word *"purgeth"* in the Greek has the same root word as *clean.* Jesus did not purge His disciples by creating hardship and disaster; He did it through the Word that He spoke to them. Likewise, He cleanses, purges, chastises, and brings forth our hearts *by His Word.*

The parable of the sower in Mark 4 clearly states that the purpose of affliction and persecution is to steal the Word. Persecutions do not make us grow. Operating the Word, walking with God, and resisting temptation will make us grow up in the midst of affliction and persecution.

When my children spurn my advice, I do not reject them. I am sorry for them because I know the results of their actions will bring them only pain. If I reject them, they will have no place to go when they fail. If I love them, accept them, and try to help them, they will have the confidence and freedom to come back to me when they realize the error of their decision.

The Bible says we should come to the throne of grace in our time of need. My time of need is usually when I have failed or when I am in sin. If I believe I am rejected by God, I will not have the confidence to come to Him in my time of need. Even if I do come to Him, I will not feel free to receive His forgiveness and restoration.

Grace is a divine influence that works in one's heart to make him able to do the will of God. I do not come to the throne of grace and get a whipping. I come to the throne of grace and get mercy and find grace *to help*.

In that environment of peace, love, and acceptance, God works in my heart. In my heart, He changes me and makes me able to overcome the things that have placed me in need. Hebrews 4:16 says God wants to help in my time of need. Maybe it is time we reexamine our view and opinion of God. It is time we find the God whom Jesus showed and demonstrated. Maybe it is time we let His love, mercy, and grace help us out of our problems. We should put forth every effort to allow the Lord to work in our hearts to produce real change from within.

Nineteen

☙

The Heart of
the Father

Nineteen

❧

The Heart of the Father

One of the first parables I ever heard after salvation was the parable of the Prodigal Son. Although I was taught much valuable truth about the wayward son, I have since found the emphasis of this parable to be the forgiveness of the father.

In Luke 15, Jesus was surrounded by publicans and sinners. These people were unreachable by the Pharisees. Their message of judgment and legalism had no appeal to these people who were captives of their sinful lifestyles. Instead of rejoicing because someone was finally reaching these people, the religious leaders found this to be a reproach. *"This man receiveth sinners, and eateth with them"* (v. 2), they complained.

Jesus responded to their murmurings with a series of parables. The first parable—the one of the lost sheep—showed the Father's desire to reach those who had gone astray. He showed the Father's concern and ultimate joy over the repentance of one sinner. *"I say unto you, that likewise joy shall be in heaven over one sinner that repenteth, more than over ninety and nine just persons, which need no repentance"* (Luke 15:7).

In the third parable (Luke 15:11–32)—that of the Prodigal Son—Jesus clearly shows the heart of the forgiving Father, the fear of the one who fails, and the criticism of the self-righteous. The parable begins with the younger son taking his inheritance and going to the world. It is noteworthy that this is a son; this is not a foreigner. This is a child of God who has an inheritance. He totally abuses the good things of God.

While he is in the world, a famine strikes and leaves the backslider in want. Now, this famine is not the product of the Father. God does not create this situation. John 10:10 is clear that the thief comes to steal, kill, and destroy. After he lures us out into the world and destroys our confidence through sin, he then attacks. As the accuser of the brethren, he convinces us that God cannot love us or forgive us. He convinces us that it would be wrong to run back to the Father just because we are in trouble. In fact, if he can convince us that God is the one who is punishing us, he can get us to turn totally against God.

Like most of us who fall, this young man did not turn immediately to his father. He joined himself to a citizen of that country. He went to the world for help. He did not have the confidence to return to his father. What he thought he would receive and what he actually encountered when he eventually did return home were two different things.

Despite his credentials, he found himself feeding the swine of this citizen of the world. There was nothing more contemptible to a Jew than swine. That is the ultimate goal of the devil for you: shame, humiliation, and loss of identity. However, the prodigal was still the son of a wealthy man. He still had a home and identity. The only thing that stood in his way was his improper thinking about his father.

Luke 15:17 reads, *"When he came to himself."* This man had to begin to deal with the truth. Until this time, he was the product of wrong thinking about his father. He thought surely there could be no return for him. He thought his father would reject him. He thought many negative things that were not based on fact.

Most of our decisions are not based on fact. They are based on our perception of the facts. This is why the devil works so hard to establish religious perversion. If he can promote error, he can keep you from freedom. (See John 8:32.) The greatest error that permeates the church today is a carryover from the Dark Ages, when the Catholic Church used fear and judgment to control the masses. They held the people in darkness and deception by perverting the truth about God.

The judgment message is a product of that era. Until the church is free from that message, it cannot return to the Father. Since most people assume God to be the source of their problems, they never "come to themselves" as this young man did. Fortunately, although persecution and affliction are works of the devil designed to steal the Word from us, many of us do come to our senses (Mark 4:14–17).

One thing this young man had on his side was that he knew how good it was to be in his father's household. Unfortunately, many Christians have never fully realized or experienced the goodness of God. I have heard many Christians make this statement: "I had it better before I got saved. At least then I didn't have all these trials and testings." If you do not know the goodness of God, you cannot "come to yourself" as this man did. You have to know the truth before you can remember it. If your thoughts of God are negative, you will keep running away every time you fail.

Although this young man did not understand the complete truth, he did remember how good it was to live in his father's home. "Even the hired servants have it better than this," he reasoned. In Luke 15:17–19, he prepares his statement. What a contrast between what he says and what the father says! What a difference between what he expected and what he experienced!

When he returned to the father, he did not hear a list of his failures. The father had compassion, not judgment. The father did not hesitate for one moment. While the son returned with head hanging down, the father ran to meet him. Before a word of explanation was given, the father gave him a kiss of love and acceptance.

The son said, *"I have sinned…and am no more worthy"* (v. 21). The father said, *"Bring forth the best"* (v. 22). Although repentance is absolutely necessary, we must know beyond all doubt that the Father will meet us with a kiss and restore us to His best.

When the father clothed the son in a robe and placed a ring on his hand, the son was clearly restored to the position he had held before squandering it all. He did not return to a lower position. Though it took time for others to accept and recognize him, there was no waiting period for the father. The bringing forth of the calf and the feast shows a return to the father's provision. When we return to the Lord as our Shepherd, we leave the realm of lack (Psalm 23:1). His provision can supersede the law of sowing and reaping.

The elder son represents those people who have never fallen. They do not know what it means to be taken captive by sin. They do not know the shame and heartache of living with the past. Often they even despise God's goodness bestowed on the repentant sinner. It is easy for those who have never fallen to lose the whole point of the Gospel. Jesus came to seek and save that which was lost. This includes the backslidden Christian as well as the obstinate sinner.

Like this elder son, they are not receiving many of the blessings of the Father. Even though all He has is theirs, they do not experience it. They think the inheritance is a product of works. They serve God day and night, but not with joy. The idea of enjoying some of the blessings seems frivolous or beyond their reach. For this reason, they desire to see the repentant sinner suffer and live in a state of want. They want to see him suffer as his sins obviously deserve. They do not mind his being forgiven; they just do not want him restored.

If you have fallen, return to the Father. Let Him meet you with a kiss and restore you. If you are an elder brother, enter into the joy of the Lord. As you experience His goodness you may learn the power and peace of mercy. Let God make you a real peacemaker, as you proclaim the Gospel of peace to a world that believes He is an angry God.

Twenty

&

Angry Preachers

Twenty

೮

Angry Preachers

From the earliest of times, angry men have misrepresented God. As ministers, we must realize that our opinions and emotions are not necessarily God's. Angry, judgmental preachers usually feel that "strong messages" will bring the people in line. But the Bible warns, *"Be...slow to speak, slow to wrath: for the wrath of man worketh not the righteousness of God"* (James 1:19–20). Many an angry preacher thought he was helping God out.

Hard words do not bring about repentance. They actually create new problems. The Bible says, *"Grievous words stir up anger"* (Proverbs 15:1). *"A wrathful man stirreth up strife"* (v. 18). *"The north wind driveth away rain* ["bringeth forth rain" in the original Hebrew]: *so doth an angry countenance* [bring forth] *a backbiting tongue"* (Proverbs 25:23). *"An angry man stirreth up strife"* (Proverbs 29:22). Hard preaching does not bring repentance; it brings rebellion. This is not my opinion; this is the Bible. When we ignore biblical principles of communication and instruction, we create problems. Angry preachers are like parents who gossip in front of their children, and then chastise them for having bad attitudes. When we criticize and judge from the pulpit, our people criticize and judge.

The only sure way to properly represent God is to walk in love. First John 4:12–13 says that when we walk in love, we dwell in God. The pulpit is not exempt from 1 Corinthians 13. We must preach with the same standards of communication as those required in daily life.

It is so important to understand the power of the minister. The way we relate to people is the way they assume God relates to them. Therefore, we dictate how they deal with sin. If we reject, they assume God rejects. If we restore and forgive, they believe God restores and forgives.

Several years ago I received a late-night call. A desperate voice on the other end asked me to come immediately to his home. I walked in to find a tear-stained face, overcome with shame and grief. This man was a dear friend. I was helping him to find his place in the ministry. But that night there was nothing but shame and despair.

As I sat down, he began to share a tale of perversion and sin. That night, it all came to a head. He felt he was over the edge. His secret sin had finally carried him to a point of destruction. After honestly confessing his sin to me, I asked him if he had confessed to God and asked Him for forgiveness. I shared a few words of encouragement and got up to leave. In utter amazement he asked, "Aren't you going to cast something out of me or deal with me?" The words sprang out of my heart, "You didn't sin against me; you sinned against God. If you've settled it with Him, it's settled with me. I don't discern a need for deliverance, but if you feel tempted, you take authority over it."

As I drove home I asked the Lord, "Did I say enough? Did I say the right things?" The Lord replied, "Because you showed him mercy, he was able to receive My mercy. Because you showed him love and acceptance, he was able to receive My love and acceptance."

Some years later, after I had gone through some personal destruction, I saw this man in a minister's conference. I went to talk with him. We talked briefly about the problems I had experienced. He gave me nothing but mercy and forgiveness. Then he said, "That night you came to my house, you saved my life." The way I related to him had given him confidence about the mercy of God.

Whatever you show a person is what he believes he will receive from the Lord. Be sure that you do not let your anger and disgust drive him from the mercy and grace he needs. Preachers are often overwhelmed by the sins of people. At times it seems that everyone is in sin. This can often overwhelm us to the point that we begin to pronounce judgment instead of peace.

Remember, everyone who comes to the doctor is sick. He does not turn against his patients because they are sick; he exists for the purpose of getting them well. I fear that our real ministerial motives are clearly revealed when we are merciless. Am I in the ministry to serve and heal hurting people, or am I using these people to build a ministry? We are here to serve the ones who are lost and the ones who backslide, as well as the ones who live godly lives.

It would be easy to become pessimistic and fearful. It would be easy to lose sight of the cures and focus on the sickness. But the doctor never reaches a place where he tries to destroy the patient; he tries to destroy the sickness. Likewise, we cannot destroy the people who are in the sin. The wrath of man will do that.

Fellowship with God is the only way they will be changed. If we drive them from God with a judgment message, we drive them from the only help available. *"But if we walk in the light, as he is in the light, we have fellowship one with another, and the blood of Jesus Christ his Son cleanse th us from all sin"* (1 John 1:7). They need the fellowship with Jesus in order to be cleansed from the power of the sin that is working in them.

Even Moses had a problem with being too judgmental. In Numbers 20:7–13, God told Moses how to represent Him before the people. Instead of speaking faith to the rock to bring forth water, he smote the rock twice. He was acting out of his anger with the people, but God was not. It was this sin that kept Moses out of the Promised Land.

Psalm 106:32–33 gives us some further insight: *"They angered him also at the waters of strife, so that it went ill with Moses for their sakes: because they provoked his spirit, so that he spake unadvisedly with his lips."* Because Moses was angry, he let his mouth get out of control. He displayed wrath instead of mercy.

Wrath always says God will kill you for this; mercy always says God will deliver you from this. Wrath is the product of frustration and unbelief. Proverbs 19:11 says, *"The discretion of a man deferreth his anger."* And Proverbs 14:29 says, *"He that is slow to wrath is of great understanding."* Unbelief does not see or believe that God is able to work in the situation. Understanding is calm because it believes the promises of God.

Moses learned that anger promotes foolishness and folly. *"He that is soon angry dealeth foolishly"* (v. 17). *"He that is hasty of spirit exalteth folly"* (v. 29). Our anger will lead us into a perversion of truth. After all, one of the root causes of anger in ministers is unforgiveness. We do not forgive those who hurt us, and we do not really want God to do so until they suffer. Anger for those who have sinned is also a form of gross self-righteousness. We fail to see the log in our eye because we are looking for the speck in theirs. We forget about our short-comings by focusing on theirs.

The smiting of the rock was like crucifying Christ afresh. Moses had already smitten the rock in the book of Exodus. The smiting of the rock brought water to an undeserving group of people. This time Moses displayed his feelings of anger and smote the rock again. This crucifying Christ afresh is the equivalent to pronouncing the judgment of God on those for whom Christ has already received judgment.

Shortly after I finished Bible college, a flood of judgment prophecies and books came forth. As I read these books, I began to take on that same spirit of destruction. I became angry with the people I once loved. Before, I had seen their potential. Now I saw their faults. Before, I believed God would change them. Now I wanted God to give them what they deserved. These books and prophecies offered no hope. It was too late for America and too late for the church. I will never forget the negative changes that came into my life from listening to these prophecies and reading these books.

Negative prophecies are self-fulfilling. They promote the fear and unbelief that it takes for them to come to pass. Proverbs 11:11 says, *"By the blessing of the upright the city is exalted: but it is overthrown by the mouth of the wicked."* We bless others when we speak good things. We curse others when we speak negatives. Jesus cursed the fig tree and it died. We curse our nation, our church, and our congregations by speaking negatives. Then they are brought to pass, but not by God. The fear and unbelief created by those words fulfill them.

Church members are often like children. Parents who have children who are emotionally disturbed are usually themselves faultfinding and critical. Preachers who should be building up are tearing down and destroying with their words of judgment. Finding fault does not make anyone more effective; it makes him introspective. When most people are in the presence of a faultfinder, they make more mistakes.

I have often heard it said, "I'm a prophet; therefore, I have a strong word." It is all right for it to be strong if it builds up. The New Testament guidelines for prophecy are edification, exhortation, and comfort (1 Corinthians 14:3). Let the Bible be the judge of the prophets of doom. Do their prophecies build up or tear down? Do they build faith or fear? Do they comfort or torment?

Ezekiel 13 warns against prophecy that comes out of your own heart. Verse 3 says, *"Woe unto the foolish prophets, that follow their own spirit, and have seen nothing!"* Let the New Testament measure of prophecy be the standard by which we judge all prophecy, and let these prophets of doom and gloom judge their own motivation.

First Timothy 1:5 says, *"Now the end* [goal] *of the commandment* [instruction] *is charity out of a pure heart, and of a good conscience, and of faith unfeigned."* We should understand the biblical goals of instruction. I want my teaching, preaching, and prophesying to bring a person to the place where he walks in love from a pure heart. I want him to have a conscience free from the pollutants of sin and guilt. I also want him to have a pure faith. That does not happen by promoting fear and rejection. Remember, every seed reproduces after its own kind.

What I sow from the pulpit is what I and the people will reap in the church and in our lives. If I am angry, I will breed anger. The anger I breed will be turned on me. If I criticize, I will produce criticism of me and the church. If I reject those who have faults, they will reject me when they see my faults.

I must get my own hurts healed so I can heal the hurting around me. I must be the one to whom people can come to see and experience the mercy and goodness of God.

Twenty-one

&

The Error of Balaam

Twenty-one

☙

The Error of Balaam

*T*hroughout church history there have been those who desired to work their own agendas with God's people. Some of them desire to use people for their own personal gain. Many, on the other hand, desire to see the church established, but because of ignorance or unbelief, they do not trust the methods of God.

Do I believe God can change people by His Spirit when they hear the truth? Or do I feel I must resort to carnal means of fear and manipulation to accomplish the will of God? No matter how I justify my actions, if I depart from biblical truth to "help" someone, I am in sin.

When I received Jesus, the man who shared Scripture with me was cursing and criticizing someone who had witnessed to him. The Scripture he quoted was laced with profanity. It came out of the mouth of a lost person. Yet, when I heard the Word of God, the Holy Spirit had something to work with in me. The Holy Spirit works with and confirms God's Word.

I am fully convinced that God can work with truth. We need not resort to our frail and foolish attempts to bring men to repentance. It seems that the most popular method of bringing people to repentance is the fear of judgment. We think we can scare people into returning to God. Fear may change one's actions, but only love will change one's heart.

The Bible warns against the error of Balaam and the way of Balaam. Now, these are not the same. They were sins committed by the same person, but they are different. We should know and avoid both of these sins. *"Woe unto them! for they have gone in the way of Cain, and ran greedily after the error of Balaam for reward, and perished in the gainsaying of Core"* (Jude 11). Lenski says Jude's warning has a climax: "taking the bad way (the way of Cain) which is to devote oneself to error, contradicting God's Word." They were willing to depart from God's Word because of what they had to gain. Let us examine this to understand how and why Balaam contradicted the Word of God.

Second Peter talks about the way of Balaam. The way of Balaam was to do unrighteousness for gain. This is a sin that is easy to detect. We are quick to label and deal with the one who uses the ministry for unrighteous profit. Yet there is a more deadly error that works among us. It brings more destruction and pain than the former, but it is considered to be acceptable. It also is the standard operating procedure for most Christians.

While Peter talked about the way of Balaam, Jude talked about the error of Balaam and associated it with Cain and Core. Balaam's error was to believe that God would curse what He had already blessed. He reasoned that since he was a prophet, if he spoke it, it would come about in truth. He tried to speak curses on God's people. Because he was motivated by greed, his greed caused him to justify his error.

It is easy for us to justify our actions when we enter the error of Balaam. Unlike Balaam, we are not doing it for greed.

Rather, we really want our friends, our family, or our church members to repent. We have a good motive, so the end justifies the means. But we are in sin, regardless of our motive, when we try to pronounce a curse on those whom God has blessed. Even if we think it will bring about repentance, it is sin.

It is even easier to justify when we see people change their behavior as a result of the fear we heap upon them. That type of change never lasts, however. In Christianity, people seem to cycle through life. They do pretty good, they get weary, they begin to compromise, they get into sin, they get miserable, and then they start the cycle all over again. Because they never come to have a meaningful relationship with God, their change is always short-lived. The fear that brought about repentance (an afterthought because of consequences) did not bring about real repentance (a change of mind).

The devil is a discourager. He always wants God's people to be cursed. Sadly, he is always able to find a willing soul to do his bidding. It is never too hard to find an angry, judgmental Christian who is ready to speak for God. In Numbers 22:12, God said to Balaam, *"Thou shalt not curse the peo ple: for they are blessed ."* How much more are the people of God blessed under this new covenant!

We have been set free from the curse, and no man, speaking by the Spirit, can pronounce the curse of God upon the people of God. In 1 Corinthians 12:3 we read, *"No man speak ing by the Spirit of God calleth Jesus accursed ."* We are the body of Christ. We are bone of His bone and flesh of His flesh. To pronounce judgment on God's people is to pronounce judgment on Jesus. Remember, when Paul persecuted the church, Jesus appeared to him and said, *"Saul, Saul, why pe rse cutest thou **me**?"* (Acts 9:4, emphasis added). To persecute the church is to persecute Jesus. To pronounce judgment on the church is to pronounce judgment on Jesus.

In Christ, we have been delivered from condemnation. *"There is therefore now no condemnation to them which are in Christ Jesus, who walk not after the flesh, but after the Spirit"* (Romans 8:1). Condemnation is the expectation of judgment. Because we are free from the flesh (that is, righteousness by the works of the flesh), we don't have to live in fear of not "measuring up." We should not be living in the tormenting expectancy of judgment.

Because we have been reconciled (exchanged) and made righteous, we are delivered from wrath. *"Much more then, being now justified by his blood, we shall be saved from wrath through him"* (Romans 5:9).

Since judgment is totally contrary to the work of the cross, those who pronounce judgment are speaking contrary to the cross. The motive may be pure, but the belief is the error of Balaam. We should repent of our attempts to manipulate people into right behavior. Regardless of our motive, regardless of our logic, regardless of our theological preference, we must return to the truth. *"Or despisest thou the riches of his goodness and forbearance and longsuffering; not knowing that the goodness of God leadeth thee to repentance?"* (Romans 2:4).

Ironically, I have seen those who believe in grace and peace become as intolerant as anyone else. We must not attack, condemn, or judge those who preach a judgment message. At the same time, we must not entertain their words for a moment. As I stated earlier from Isaiah 54:17, *"Every tongue that riseth against thee in judgment, shalt thou prove to be lawless"* (RHM). We cannot accept the judgment message as valid or scriptural.

We must never see it as the attitude of God toward man. He has declared peace and goodwill toward men, through the Lord Jesus.

Twenty-two

&

The Judgment
of God

Twenty-two

❧

The Judgment of God

One of the foundations of faith for the New Testament church is the doctrine of eternal judgment. Now, apart from knowing the truth about judgment, we could find ourselves in any one of many different types of error. But make no mistake, there will be a Day of Judgment. And that judgment will be far worse than anything being pronounced by the prophets of doom. It will be fierce, and it will be eternal.

The book of Revelation describes with vivid detail that time when the wrath of God will be poured out on the world. Even then we, the church, will be delivered from His wrath. John wrote, *"I was in the Spirit on the Lord's day"* (Revelation 1:10). *"The Lord's day"* refers to that great and terrible Day (period of time) when the judgment of God will come upon the earth. All the events in the book of Revelation take place at that time.

It is worthy to note, however, that even this fierce judgment does not bring repentance. *"Neither repented they of their murders, nor of their sorceries, nor of their fornication, nor of their thefts"* (Revelation 9:21). Judgment, regardless of how severe, does not bring repentance.

When unredeemed man stands before God, it will be in the Great White Throne Judgment. Those who have not accepted Jesus as their righteousness will appear before God to be judged according to their works (Revelation 20:12). They will be judged according to their works because that is the only righteousness they will have. They will have rejected the free gift of righteousness in Jesus. But, unfortunately, *"by the deeds of the law there shall no flesh be justified in his sight: for by the law is the knowledge of sin"* (Romans 3:20). To stand before God, having rejected the righteousness of Jesus, will always mean an eternal hell.

The Bible says God will judge in righteousness. It is righteous to judge a world that has rejected the free gift of righteousness. Jesus suffered sin, the curse, hell, and torment for all the world. No man needs to suffer hell. It is total and absolute defiance for a man to reject such a great and merciful salvation. Righteousness demands the judgment of these people. These people will not be judged as to salvation; they already had that opportunity. They will be judged by their works in which they trusted.

With the absolute certainty of this future judgment, we should proclaim that God's mercy is available now. Pointing out a future judgment is not bad, if you give people the Good News as well. The Good News is this: You do not have to be judged. You do not have to go to hell. Jesus has paid the price. You can have the free gift of righteousness.

The believer will never come into the White Throne Judgment. The believer will appear before the judgment seat of Christ. Second Corinthians 5:10 says, *"For we must all appear before the judgment seat of Christ; that every one may receive the things done in his body, according to that he hath done, whether it be good or bad."*

Does this mean, as some say, that we will all stand before Jesus and have our every past sin exposed? I think not. Most of the Scriptures used to support that view are taken out of context.

I am not sure how this will happen, but all our works will pass through the fire before appearing before the Lord. *"Every man's work shall be made manifest: for the day shall declare it, because it shall be revealed by fire; and the fire shall try every man's works of what sort it is"* (1 Corinthians 3:13). The fire will test our works to determine if they are wood, hay, stubble, or precious metals.

Works that are based on the foundation of faith-righteousness are good works. We are called to good works in Christ Jesus. We have a purpose in this life: We should bear fruit. Dead works, on the other hand, are those things we do to make ourselves righteous and acceptable before God. Those dead works will be burned. They are a testimony to our unbelief in the finished work of Jesus. But even if all our works are burned, we will be saved. *"If any man's work shall be burned, he shall suffer loss: but he himself shall be saved; yet so as by fire"* (v. 15).

The real purpose for our standing before the Lord is to receive rewards. First Corinthians 3:14 says, *"If any man's work abide which he hath built thereupon, he shall receive a reward."* There will be wonderful rewards for what we have done in this life in response to the goodness of God. There is much I do not understand about this time of rewards. I dare not even speculate, but I know it will be glorious.

Although people should know about the eternal judgments of the Great White Throne Judgment, they also should know about the judgment seat of Christ, where our works will be judged and we will be given rewards. Since there will be these judgments, let us judge our own motives. Let us live, walk, and minister in the love of God so we will receive our reward. Let us minister in a way that glorifies Jesus instead of man.

Because there will be a Day of Judgment, let us preach, teach, and warn men everywhere to turn from wickedness. But let's do it in love and goodness, which bring men to repentance.

Let us not despise the lost and the backslidden, but let us, with mercy and kindness, restore them to the Lord. Let us have the same value for the human race as God did when He sacrificed His Son to reconcile the world to Himself. Let them taste and see that the Lord is good when they experience (taste) God through us. If God is at peace with the world through Jesus, then we, as His ambassadors, should be at peace.

Let us refrain from breeding fear and living in fear. Fear is not from God. Fear causes people to run from a loving Father into an eternal destruction. As Revelation 21:8 says, *"But the fearful, and unbelieving...shall have their part in the lake which burneth with fire and brimstone: which is the seco nd death."* Of all the sins that would enslave a man, fear and unbelief are at the top of the list.

Fear prevents you from believing and trusting the God who loves you and freely gives you the gift of righteousness in Jesus. We should understand the reality of the judgment that Jesus received in our place when He went to the cross. We should be confident that we do not have to fear judgment in this life.

Twenty-three

&

The Need for Peace

Twenty-three

꿍

The Need for Peace

*I*n my early days of ministry, I put a strong emphasis on meeting the physical needs of people. I have always had great compassion for people who are hurting. Because of my struggles with sickness, I understood the suffering of people in physical pain. Motivated by compassion, I saw many wonderful miracles. As I have traveled around the world, I have seen every miracle in the New Testament. I have seen many of them hundreds of times.

Although I still place a high value on the physical needs of man, I now see the emotional/spiritual needs to be far more essential than the physical. As a matter of fact, when the emotional needs are met, it is relatively easy to take care of the physical needs. But the emotional needs of a person are met only through personally experiencing the love of God through the Lord Jesus Christ.

People need to feel the love and peace of God. We all need to be permeated with the positive emotions that come from a meaningful relationship with God. We can endure sickness, poverty, and pain, but we cannot endure poverty of the inner man. Proverbs 18:14 says it this way: *"The spirit of a man will sustain his infirmity; but a wounded spirit who can bear ?"*

Physical healing is meaningless to the person who has a broken heart. Prosperity does not ease the pain of loneliness. Success is no substitute for a sense of dignity and worth that comes from the Lord Jesus. We do not want to deny God's desire and willingness to meet the physical needs, but we must bring it into perspective.

God created man. He placed him in a garden called Paradise. There was no pain, suffering, or sorrow. Man lived in a peaceful, loving relationship with God. That is the environment for which we were created. We were never designed to live apart from peace, love, and acceptance.

The day Adam ate the forbidden fruit, he acquired a new capacity for the human race: the knowledge of good and evil. With this knowledge, man now started making decisions about good and evil independently of God. Man began to determine righteousness apart from God. Subsequently, he rejected God's standards and developed his own. Hence, we have the birth of religion.

Religion has always been mean, and it is still mean. The first religion is the same as it has always been. It is man attempting to relate to God on his own terms. In order to do that we must, of course, reject God's terms. We also must reject anyone who does not comply to our terms.

The first religion caused Cain to kill Abel. He hated him because Abel's sacrifice was accepted and his wasn't. He had labored for his sacrifice. Logic would say that his was of more value, but Cain was operating in his own knowledge of righteousness and unrighteousness. *"Cain...slew his brother. And wherefore slew he him? Because his own works were evil, and his brother's righteous"* (1 John 3:12).

Thousands of years later, Paul said in the book of Galatians that the children of the flesh always persecute the children of the Spirit. In other words, the religious always persecute the righteous. Why? The religious despise the righteousness that God has chosen and given.

There is a logic to religion. Religion is man's attempt to be right with God and find peace in a way that makes sense to him. Religion sees the greatest need of man as being right. To the religious logic, being right is equivalent to being right with God. If someone doesn't agree with us, he is implying that we are wrong.

Since it is essential that we be right, we must prove him wrong. If we can't prove him wrong, then we kill him. That's exactly what Cain did. The need to be right has tormented men since the day Adam ate the fruit. Adam started making decisions apart from God right off the bat. "We had better make some clothes to cover ourselves, because I don't think it's right to be naked before God. We had better hide when God calls us. He's probably mad." Man began to scramble to be right. But every decision to be right, apart from God's perspective, drove him deeper into pain, suffering, and a self-imposed separation from God.

Regardless of how pure the motives, regardless of how sincere the intention, regardless of the dedication to God, regardless of how good we are, the attempt to establish right and wrong apart from God is a rejection of God and His truth. *"For they being ignorant of God's righteousness, and going about to establish their own righteousness, have not submitted themselves unto the righteousness of God"* (Romans 10:3).

Every attempt at being righteous with God apart from accepting His terms ultimately will have a negative effect. As long as we're doing everything right, we will have peace, but when we fail, we will lose peace. There will never be an abiding sense of confidence and peace—one that lasts despite our success or failure. The Bible says that law cannot make one righteous; it can only give him an awareness of sin. So when you fail you will no longer have peace.

Then there is the problem of those who disagree with us. They have a different definition of *righteous* than we have. We must prove them wrong in order to maintain our peace. The struggle is endless. You cannot live this way. You were not created to live this way.

God wants you to live in a harmonious relationship with Him and in harmonious relationships with people. This can happen only when you have peace. You can have peace only when you know you are righteous. You can know you are righteous only when you accept the gift of righteousness through the Lord Jesus Christ. Romans 5:1 says it best: *"Therefore being justified* [made righteous] *by faith, we have peace with God through our Lord Jesus Christ."*

Peace is far more essential to Christian living than we have ever realized. The gift of righteousness produces peace through Jesus. Peace gives boldness and confidence to pursue a relationship with God. Through Him we have access to grace (God's ability) in which we stand. When there is no peace, there will be no relationship, no confidence, and no grace to work in our lives. And apart from grace we are limited to our own ability to serve God and live a righteous life. We need peace!

Twenty-four

&

More than a State of Mind

Twenty-four

❧

More than a State of Mind

There are many things a person can do to have a tranquil state of mind. There is nothing wrong with many of those things. But tranquility apart from reality (truth) is a deception. If you convince yourself that there is no God, you can gain a certain degree of tranquility. It may work in this life, but it will fail the test of eternity.

There are many things of which an individual could convince himself. If you believe there is no hell, it could bring you peace while you reject God. But that is not a reality. If you convince yourself that God loves you because you live right, that will produce peace as long as you live right. Again, that is not a reality.

God's peace is based on a reality. It is based on the uncompromising, unfailing love of God that was demonstrated at the cross of Christ. Only by knowing and believing the message of the cross will you find a peace that abides. It does not fluctuate with circumstances. It is not based on a lie.

When one believes the truth, the Holy Spirit is able to perform that truth and shed the love of God abroad in his heart.

It is the reality or unreality you believe that becomes the reality you experience. The apostle John said it this way: *"And we have known and believed the love that God hath to us. God is love; and he that dwelleth in love dwelleth in God, and God in him"* (1 John 4:16).

The Greek word for *know* speaks of an experiential knowledge. To experience the love of God, you must first believe the love of God. The love of God can be realized only by what He did at the cross.

> *In this was manifested the love of God toward us, because that God sent his only begotten Son into the world, that we might live through him. Herein is love, not that we loved God, but that he loved us, and sent his Son to be the propitiation for our sins.* (1 John 4:9–10)

The reality that Jesus came into the world, took our sins, and appeased the wrath of God (as our propitiation) clearly demonstrates the love of God. The knowledge of being delivered from wrath causes us to realize His love. The knowledge of being made righteous causes us to experience His peace. No sedative, no sin, nothing can provide the tranquility and fulfillment that comes from experiencing and abiding in the love and peace of God.

God made peace with you through the cross. Will you accept that peace? It may be time for you to pray a prayer similar to the following:

> Father, today I choose to believe truth. You sent Jesus into this world; He became my sin; He took my punishment; He went to hell in my place. He came out of the grave and conquered my sin. In Him I have the gift of righteousness. I thank You that I am righteous apart from my performance. Today I acknowledge that You have never hurt me. You are not judging me. You are not

the source of pain in my life. My own sin and unbelief have brought me pain. I will never again believe that You are hurting me. I will abide in Your peace because I am righteous in Jesus! You love me; You accept me; You are with me. You have made me accepted in the Beloved!

Visit http://www.impactministries.com/gospel-of-peace

to view the complete video series

"The Way of Peace: The Place of Power"

℘

About the Author

About the Author

&

*I*n 1972, Dr. James B. Richards accepted Christ and answered the call to ministry. His dramatic conversion and passion to help hurting people launched him onto the streets of Huntsville, Alabama. Early on in his mission to reach teenagers and drug abusers, his ministry quickly grew into a home church that eventually led to the birth of Impact Ministries.

With doctorates in theology, human behavior, and alternative medicine, and an honorary doctorate in world evangelism, Jim has received certified training as a detox specialist and drug counselor.

His uncompromising yet positive approach to the Gospel strengthens, instructs and challenges people to new levels of victory, power and service. Jim's extensive experience in working with substance abuse, codependency, and other social/ emotional issues has led him to pioneer effective, creative, Bible-based approaches to ministry that meet the needs of today's world.

Most importantly, Jim believes that people need to be made whole by experiencing God's unconditional love. His messages are simple, practical, and powerful. His passion is to change the way the world sees God so that people can experience a relationship with Him through Jesus.

Bibliography

ʒ

Bromiley, Geoffrey. *The Theological Dictionary of the New Testament.* Edited by Gerhard Kittel and Gerhard Friedrich. Grand Rapids: Wm. B. Eerdmans, 1985.

Cremer, Hermann. *Biblico-Theological Lexicon of New Testament Greek.* Edinburgh: T&T Clark, 1895.

Lenski, Richard C. *The Interpretation of St. Paul's Epistle to the Romans.* Minneapolis, Minn.: Augsburg Fortress, 1936.

McIntosh and Twyman, trans. *The Archko Volume, or the Archeological Writings of the Sanhedrin and Talmuds of the Jews.* New York: McGraw Hill, 2000.

Richards, Dr. James B. *Grace: The Power to Change.* New Kensington, Pa.: Whitaker House, 2001.

———. *Taking the Limits Off God.* Huntsville, Ala.: Impact Ministries, 1989.

Strong, James, ed. *The New Strong's Exhaustive Concordance of the Bible.* Nashville: Thomas Nelson, 1997.

Thayer, Joseph H. *Thayer's Greek-English Lexicon of the New Testament.* Peabody, Mass.: Hendrickson Publishers, 1997.

Tregelles, Samuel Prideaux, LL.D. *Gesenius' Hebrew-Chaldee Lexicon to the Old Testament.* Grand Rapids: Baker Book House, 1979.

Trench, Richard Chenevix. *Trench's Synonyms of the New Testament.* Peabody, Mass.: Hendrickson Publishers, 2000.

Vaughan, Curtis, ed. *The Bible from 26 Translations.* Grand Rapids: Baker Book House, 1989.

ANOTHER POWERFUL BOOK

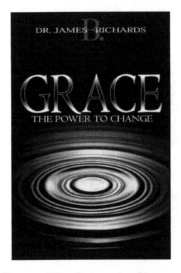

Grace: The Power to Change
Dr. James B. Richards

Christians everywhere have been missing the truth about grace—and living in defeat as a result. Grace is God's ability working in you to do what you cannot. It is the power to change. Take to heart the principles in this book, and discover the dimension of Christian living that Jesus called "easy and light." Jesus has finished the work, so relax and let His grace change your heart!

ISBN: 0-88368-730-5 • Trade • 192 pages

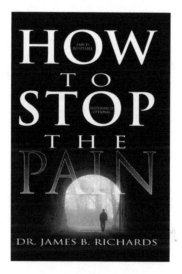

who has done so much for me. Because I love Him, I am going to walk in His Word. When I fail, I know I am not rejected. It is a wonderful thing to have a relationship with someone who has high standards, but who does not reject us when we fail to live up to those standards. The fact that someone believes in you will enable you to get up when you fall.

God does not have one standard of love for Himself and another standard for us. The love described in 1 Corinthians 13 is God's kind of love. We are required to walk in that kind of love because we are to be like God. God's love does not reject or condemn; neither does it allow us to do so. Although He is holy and perfect, He does not reject us in our imperfection. Instead, because we have an environment of peace and acceptance, we can continually draw from His strength until we do overcome.

In John 14:21, 23, Jesus said,

> He that hath my commandments, and keepeth them, he it is that loveth me: and he that loveth me shall be loved of my Father, and I will love him, and will manifest myself to him....If a man love me, he will keep my words: and my Father will love him, and we will come unto him, and make our abode with him.

Jesus wants to manifest Himself to you. He wants to have a personal relationship with you, one in which He and the Father come and fellowship with you, teach you, and love you. This is a relationship of the heart. It is like a marriage. In fact, the church is described as the bride of Christ. The Spirit of God led Paul to teach about husbands and wives so that we could understand the church's relationship to Jesus. I love my wife dearly, and I am not afraid of her hurting me or trying to bring me pain. She wants me to succeed and be happy. If I mistreat the person who desires so many good things for me, I am a fool.

I am not good to her out of fear of her. When my wife and I have a disagreement, she sometimes gives me the silent treatment. Although she can inflict pain by doing something like this to me, it doesn't necessarily make me stop relating properly to her. Rather, the loss of the joy, peace, and fulfillment of our relationship motivates me to make things right again. There are many good things in our relationship, and I have too much to lose by handling it improperly.

Likewise, Jesus loves me. He comforts me. When I am sick, He heals me. I never have to fear. I never have to lack because He is always there. Why should I withdraw from a relationship that means so much to me? The gratification of sin is not equal to the gratification of the relationship.

As you come to know and experience the goodness of the Lord, you will develop a loving relationship that is more precious than anything else in your life. The fulfillment of that relationship will keep you from sin. Love accomplishes far more than law. This happens only when we know and experience the love of God through an intimate, personal relationship with Him.

Sixteen

❧

A Relationship of Love

When I first began to attend church, I heard all the talk about making Jesus my personal Savior and having a personal relationship with the Lord. But as I began to fellowship with those who used this terminology, I found that they did not have a personal relationship with Jesus. They had a personal relationship with their ideas, doctrines, and beliefs.

They were good people, and they were no doubt saved. However, what I saw and was taught about God was anything but a relationship. Relationships require time and effort, two things most people are not willing and sometimes not able to give. I have actually had people say, "Just give me some rules, and I'll keep them." Rules require very little, but Jesus came to restore us to a relationship with the Father. This relationship is to be built on love and trust.

In the book of John, as Jesus was spending His last hours teaching His disciples, He explained that He would die, but that He would be raised from the dead. He promised that after His resurrection He would send the Holy Spirit, the Comforter, the Counselor, the Spirit of Grace and Truth. He explained that He would be to us all that Jesus had been while He was here on earth, with one exception: The Comforter would live inside us. He would draw us into a relationship with the Father from our hearts.

Jesus said, *"If you love Me, keep My commandments"* (John 14:15 NKJV). Fear will cause a person to obey someone he hates or despises. A slave has no choice but to obey his master for fear of reprisals. But Jesus said, *"If you love Me, keep My commandments."* Our obedience should be the product of love, not fear.

As a young boy in Tennessee, I had a world of problems. I was full of anger and bitterness. I would curse, steal, fight, and do all the things a mean little boy would do. I loved my mother, but my home environment was so bad I hated being there. I made bad grades in school, and I had no interest in improving myself.

The one redeeming relationship in my life was with my uncle. When he came home from the military, I was staying with my grandmother, and he took an interest in me. He was my hero. He was everything I wanted to be. He had extremely high standards, and he expected me to live up to his standards, but there was no negativism in it at all. He always conveyed trust in me. He always told me I was able to do what he expected. Because he believed in me, he could get me to do, through love, what a hundred spankings had never been able to do. I did not obey him for fear of what he would do. I obeyed him because I loved him, respected him, and valued our relationship. I could not bear the idea of disappointing him with my behavior.

Similarly, when we come to know the love of God and His great goodness, we realize the value of the relationship. I do not want to do anything to displease or disappoint the One